JUL   2000

JUN   2004

JUN 09

X X 2015

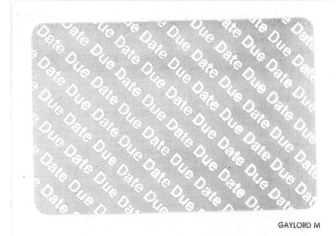

GAYLORD M

Wendell Berry

Twayne's United States Authors Series

Frank Day, Series Editor

Clemson University

TUSAS 654

WENDELL BERRY
©*Dan Carraco 1990*

Wendell Berry

Andrew J. Angyal

Elon College

Twayne Publishers
An Imprint of Simon & Schuster Macmillan
New York

Prentice Hall International
London   Mexico City   New Delhi   Singapore   Sydney   Toronto

95-122

Twayne's United States Authors Series No. 654

Wendell Berry
Andrew J. Angyal

Copyright © 1995 by Twayne Publishers

All rights reserved. No part of this book may be reproduced or transmitted in any form or by any means, electronic or mechanical, including photocopying, recording, or by any information storage and retrieval system, without permission in writing from the Publisher.

Library of Congress Cataloging-in-Publication Data

Angyal, Andrew J.
    Wendell Berry / by Andrew J. Angyal.
        p. cm. — (Twayne's United States authors series ; TUSAS 654)
    Includes bibliographical references (p. 163) and index.
    ISBN 0-8057-4628-5
    1. Berry, Wendell, 1934—Criticism and interpretation.
    I. Title.   II. Series.
    PS3552.E75Z58   1995
    818'.5409—dc20   95-2290
                                                                      CIP

The paper used in this publication meets the minimum requirements of American National Standard for Information Sciences—Permanence of Paper for Printed Library Materials. ANSI Z3948–1984. ⊚ ™

10 9 8 7 6 5 4 3 2 1 (hc)

Printed in the United States of America

For My Mother and Father

Contents

Preface

As poet, novelist, and essayist, Wendell Berry has created an enduring pastoral vision of rural America. His world is that of the hill farm, small landowner, and tobacco farmer of rural Kentucky. This world of small, self-sufficient rural farming communities survived more or less intact through the end of the Second World War, when the economic and social forces of the larger world began to draw away younger farmers and families, leaving elderly parents and the less ambitious to eke out a living in an economic order of rising costs, inadequate incomes, and a shortage of good farm labor. Tobacco had always been the major cash crop for southern farmers, but it was a labor-intensive crop that demanded extra hands for seeding beds, transplanting, pruning, harvesting, stripping, and storing. Around the seasonal labor of tobacco farming a rural culture evolved, with its own distinctive customs and traditions. It was a world largely of men and boys, who shared the work and passed on the skills and knowledge of tobacco farming and handling livestock from generation to generation through hands-on experience.

Berry grew up during the 1930s among the last generation of farmers who still used horses and mules and did most of their work by hand. He absorbed these skills and came to love them just as they were disappearing. To a large degree, his writings have been an attempt to articulate and preserve the best in this agricultural tradition before it is lost forever.

As an agrarian regionalist, Berry is an odd combination of conservative and radical. His cultural conservatism has led him to be politically radical in his attempt to resist the political and economic forces destroying traditional small-scale agricultural practices. He is a regionalist, one who cultivates the genius of place, but not a local colorist or a provincial, having made a conscious choice to return to his native region after studying in California and teaching in New York. He has struggled to be at home, to create a wholesome economic, ecological, and moral order within his family, his farm, and his community. At his home in Lane's Landing, he has practiced a disciplined life of farming, writing, and teaching at the University of Kentucky. The themes of home, work, husbandry, rootedness, stewardship, responsibility, thrift, order, memory, atonement, and harmony resonate throughout his work.

The place that Berry calls home rests in the fertile, rolling hills of Henry County, in north-central Kentucky at the conjunction of the Kentucky and Ohio rivers, sometimes called the "Cincinnati Arch." Perhaps better than any other American writer of his generation, Wendell Berry has expressed the role of love of place in shaping the literary imagination. He has explored every dimension of his land, through the farming saga of seven generations of the Coulter, Feltner, and Beechum families in his fictional Port William Membership. He has celebrated the natural history of his land and its settlement and farming history, marked its despoilment and ruin, and noted its potential for rejuvenation and recovery. He has marked its seasons and moods in his poetry, and he has also fought for its protection against the strip miners of eastern Kentucky and the Army Corps of Engineers project that would have dammed Kentucky's Red River Gorge. He has celebrated its artists and writers, such as Harlan Hubbard and Harry Caudill. He has, in short, worked to be at home in his particular place and to resist American restlessness and rootlessness, the desire always to be somewhere else, and the inability ever to feel at home anywhere. Berry has resisted the seductive promise of technology to make our lives better by relieving us of the work and skills that in fact give our lives meaning. He has insisted on our need to simplify our lives so as to live more fully and mindfully in the present moment.

As a farmer and writer, Berry takes his place in a distinguished tradition of southern authors who have written out of a deep love of land and place. Though not of the generation of the southern Agrarians, Berry echoes many of the major themes of the Jeffersonian agrarian tradition. His articulate defense of farming as a way of life and of its foundations, the family and the community, stands in the agrarian tradition. His analysis of the social, political, and economic forces that have eroded rural America since World War II is perceptive and compelling. Berry's agrarianism is no mere sentimental attachment to the past, but a compelling critique of progress and of the kind of society ours has become. Like the earlier generations of Agrarians, he opposes industrialism, urbanization, and technology, but he sharpens his advocacy of rural life with an informed ecological vision and an understanding of the complex relationships among the health of the individual, the family, the community, and the environment.

Berry's decision to leave the New York academic world in 1964 to return to his family farm in Kentucky was as deliberate a decision as Thoreau's retreat to his cabin on Walden Pond. It signaled a recognition that his roots as a writer and teacher could best be sustained in his native environment, in the community where his family had farmed for five generations. Apart from this community, he was rootless and adrift. Call it republican simplicity, pastoralism, or the simple life, Berry chose a way of life that implicitly questions the rootless, consumer society we have become. His literary vision echoes his reformist social and ecological vision, which combines respect for traditional rural values with an activist agenda for protecting those values against the encroachments of modern society.

Farming and writing are similar activities for Berry in that each, if practiced well, is a spiritual discipline that curbs the human impulse to work carelessly and to waste and destroy. Each demands the exercise of order and restraint to sustain the sources of fertility and creativity, and each is an art when practiced and valued within a sustaining culture. In his extended autobiographical essay "The Long-Legged House," Berry writes of the satisfactions of returning to his native Kentucky after studying and teaching in California and New York. He was drawn back to his native region by his affection for his birthplace and his sense that it would be the subject and focus of his work. Port Royal would become his Concord, his Lake District; the Port William Membership would become his Yoknapatawpha County. His abiding interest has always been in how people come to belong to a place, how they overcome the restlessness so prevalent in our culture and remain—or become—permanent members of a particular community. Few other modern American writers share so deep and intimate an identification with a particular location as Berry enjoys with the Kentucky River Valley. He knows his native region and people in all their various moods, seasons, and weather. Though his topics focus on farming, family, and nature, his true subject is how to live a good life. His passionate espousal of environmental responsibility is a "home defense" in the highest and best sense of the term. Berry's writing demonstrates the continued viability of Jefferson's agrarian dream of a democracy of independent yeoman farmers and small landholders.

Acknowledgments

This book would not have been possible without the cooperation of Wendell and Tanya Berry, who were kind enough to extend their hospitality during my two visits to their Lane's Landing Farm in Port Royal, Kentucky. Wendell Berry was also kind enough to take time for an interview on 9 May 1991 and to allow that interview to be published here. He has also granted me permission to quote from his essays, poems, and fiction.

Many friends and associates of Wendell Berry kindly responded to my requests for research information and assistance. My thanks to Russell Freedman, of Second Life Books in Lanesborough, Massachusetts, for sending me a copy of his unpublished Wendell Berry bibliography; Terry Birdwhistell, university archivist and director of the Oral History Program, Division of Special Collections and Archives, King Library, University of Kentucky; Linda J. Long, public service librarian in the Department of Special Collections, Stanford University Libraries; Prof. Joseph Burns, director of graduate studies at New York University; Prof. Bennett H. Hall, History Department, University of Georgia; Prof. Nancy Packer, director of the Creative Writing Program, Stanford University; Mrs. Tym Ricketts, librarian at the Henry County Public Library; Maurice Telleen, editor of the *Draft Horse Journal*; Dan Carraco of Carrollton, Kentucky; Amy Rankin of the Burley Tobacco Growers Cooperative Association; and Amelia Silvestri, coordinator of the Poetry Center, Trinity College, Hartford, Connecticut.

A faculty sabbatical from Elon College in the spring of 1991 allowed me to begin the research for this book, and a winter-term leave in 1993 gave me some uninterrupted writing time. The staff of McEwen Library offered their assistance on many occasions. My thanks to the English Department secretary, Linda Martindale, for computer and secretarial assistance. My special thanks to my colleague in the Economics Department, Jim Barbour, and his mother, Mrs. Bernice Barbour, who offered their hospitality during my stay in Lexington, Kentucky. I appreciate the generosity of my colleagues Russell Gill, John Herold, Tom Tiemann, and Anthony Weston, who read and commented on early drafts of these chapters. I especially appreciate the continual support and assistance of my wife Jennifer, my best editor and critic, to whom as always I owe a special debt of gratitude. And to my parents, who first introduced me to gardening and nature, I dedicate this book.

For permission to quote from copyrighted material, my thanks are extended to Wendell Berry and to his publishers, the University Press of Kentucky, Sierra Club Books, Harcourt Brace, North Point Press/Farrar, Straus & Giroux, and Pantheon Books. For permission to reprint parts of my articles on Wendell Berry's poetry and his poem "Where" I acknowledge the permission of Salem Press. And for permission to quote "Asphodel, That Greeny Flower," by William Carlos Williams, I am grateful to New Directions and Carcanet Press.

"Asphodel, That Greeny Flower" by William Carlos Williams: *Collected Poems 1939–1962,* Volume II. Copyright © 1962 by William Carlos Williams. Reprinted by permission of New Directions Publishing Corp. and Carcanet Press Ltd.

Excerpts from *Entries* by Wendell Berry. Copyright © 1994 by Wendell Berry. Reprinted by permission of Pantheon Books, a division of Random House, Inc.

Excerpts from *The Long-Legged House* by Wendell Berry. Copyright © 1969 by Wendell Berry. Excerpts from *The Broken Ground* by Wendell Berry. Copyright © 1964 by Wendell Berry. Reprinted by permission of Wendell Berry.

Excerpts from *Collected Poems* by Wendell Berry. Copyright © 1984 by Wendell Berry. Excerpts from *The Gift of Good Land* by Wendell Berry. Copyright © 1982 by Wendell Berry. Excerpts from *The Hidden Wound* by Wendell Berry. Copyright © 1989 by Wendell Berry. Excerpts from *A Place on Earth* by Wendell Berry. Copyright © 1983 by Wendell Berry. Excerpts from *A Part* by Wendell Berry. Copyright © 1980 by Wendell Berry. Excerpts from *Remembering* by Wendell Berry. Copyright © 1988 by Wendell Berry. Excerpts from *Standing by Words* by Wendell Berry. Copyright © 1983 by Wendell Berry. Excerpts from *What are People For?* by Wendell Berry. Copyright © 1990 by Wendell Berry. Excerpts from *The Wheel* by Wendell Berry. Copyright © 1982 by Wendell Berry. Reprinted by permission of North Point Press, a division of Farrar, Straus & Giroux, Inc.

Excerpts from "Zero and "The Silence" in *The Country of Marriage,* copyright © 1971 by Wendell Berry, reprinted by permission of Harcourt Brace & Company. Excerpts from "Where" and "The Clearing" in

Clearing, copyright © 1975 by Wendell Berry, reprinted by permission of Harcourt Brace & Company. Excerpt from "The Snake" in *Openings,* copyright © 1965 and renewed 1993 by Wendell Berry, reprinted by permission of Harcourt Brace & Company. Excerpts from "The Man Born to Farming" and "The Birth" in *Farming: A Hand Book,* copyright © 1970 by Wendell Berry, reprinted by permission of Harcourt Brace & Company. Excerpts from "The Silence" and "The Current" in *Farming: A Hand Book,* copyright © 1969 by Wendell Berry, reprinted by permission of Harcourt Brace & Company.

Excerpts from *The Unsettling of America: Culture and Agriculture* by Wendell Berry. Copyright © 1977 by Wendell Berry. Reprinted by permission of Sierra Club Books.

Reprinted from "Wendell Berry," in *Critical Survey of Poetry,* revised edition. By permission of the publisher, Salem Press, Inc. Copyright © 1992 by Salem Press, Inc. Reprinted from *Entries,* in *Magill's Literary Annual 1995.* By permission of the publisher, Salem Press, Inc. Copyright © 1995 by Salem Press, Inc.

Chronology

1934	Wendell Erdman Berry born 5 August in Henry County, Kentucky, the eldest of four children of John M. and Virginia Berry.
1948–1952	Attends Millersburg Military Institute (MMI) in Millersburg, Kentucky.
1952	Graduates from MMI.
1952–1956	Attends University of Kentucky at Lexington. Coedits *Stylus*, the university literary magazine, and in 1955 wins *Stylus*'s Dantzler Award for his short story "The Brothers."
1956	Graduates with a B.A. degree in English. Spends the summer after graduation at Indiana University School of Letters. "The Brothers" wins *Carolina Quarterly*'s fiction contest.
1956–1957	Completes master's degree in English at University of Kentucky.
1957	"Elegy" (poem) wins the Farquhar Award in Poetry. Two short stories, "Whippoorwills" and "Apples," are published in *Coraddi: Arts Forum 1957*. Marries Tanya Amyx on 29 May.
1957–1958	English instructor at Georgetown College, Georgetown, Kentucky.
1958	Daughter, Mary Dee, is born on 10 May.
1958–1959	Awarded a Wallace Stegner Fellowship, studies creative writing at Stanford University.
1959–1960	Appointed Edward H. Jones Lecturer in Creative Writing at Stanford University.
1960	*Nathan Coulter* (novel).
1960–1961	Spends a year farming in Kentucky.
1961–1962	Awarded a Guggenheim Foundation Fellowship, travels in France and Italy.

1962   Awarded Vachel Lindsay Prize by *Poetry* magazine. Son, Pryor Clifford, is born on 19 August.

1962–1964 Assistant professor of English and director of freshman English at New York University (University Heights campus in the Bronx).

1964–1977 Professor of English at the University of Kentucky, Lexington.

1964   *November Twenty Six Nineteen Hundred Sixty Three* (poetry). *The Broken Ground* (poetry).

1965   Awarded a Rockefeller Foundation Fellowship. Moves to Lane's Landing Farm, Port Royal, Kentucky, on 4 July.

1967   *A Place on Earth* (novel). Awarded Bess Hokin Prize by *Poetry*.

1968   *Openings* (poetry). *The Rise* (nonfiction).

1968–1969 Visiting professor of creative writing at Stanford.

1969   *The Long-Legged House* (essays). *Findings* (poetry). Receives National Endowment of the Arts grant.

1970   *Farming: A Hand Book* (poetry). *The Hidden Wound* (nonfiction).

1971   *The Unforeseen Wilderness: An Essay on Kentucky's Red River Gorge*. Named the University of Kentucky's Distinguished Professor of the Year. Receives National Institute of Arts and Letters Award for Writing.

1972   *A Continuous Harmony: Essays Cultural and Agricultural*.

1973   *The Country of Marriage* (poetry).

1974   Appointed Elliston Poet, University of Cincinnati. *The Memory of Old Jack* (novel). *The Eastward Look* (poetry).

1975   First-place award from Friends of American Writers for *The Memory of Old Jack*. *Sayings and Doings* (poetry). *To What Listens* (poetry). *Horses* (poetry).

1976   *The Kentucky River: Two Poems. There Is Singing around Me* (poetry).

1977   Leaves University of Kentucky. Appointed writer-in-residence, Centre College, Danville, Kentucky. *The*

Unsettling of America: Culture and Agriculture (nonfiction). *Clearing* (poetry). *Three Memorial Poems.*

1977–1979   Contributing editor, Rodale Press, Pennsylvania.

1978   Receives first honorary doctorate, from Centre College.

1979   *The Gift of Gravity* (poetry).

1980   *A Part* (poetry). *The Salad* (poetry).

1981   *Recollected Essays: 1965–1980. The Gift of Good Land: Further Essays Cultural and Agricultural. The Nativity* (poetry). Honorary doctorate from Transylvania College.

1982   *The Wheel* (poetry).

1983   *Standing by Words* (nonfiction). Honorary doctorate from Berea College. *A Place on Earth* (1967), revised edition.

1985   *Collected Poems: 1957–1982.*

1986   *The Wild Birds: Six Stories of the Port William Membership.* Honorary doctorate from the University of Kentucky.

1987   Returns to teaching in the English Department of the University of Kentucky. Writer-in-residence at Bucknell University. Receives the Jean Stein Award from the American Academy and Institute of Arts and Letters, and the Milner Award (the Kentucky Governor's Award). Awarded an honorary doctorate by Santa Clara University. *Sabbaths* (poetry). *Home Economics* (essays). *Some Differences* (poetry). *The Landscape of Harmony: Two Essays in Wilderness and Community.*

1988   *Remembering* (fiction).

1989   Receives the Lannan Foundation Award for Nonfiction. *Traveling at Home* (fiction and poetry). *The Hidden Wound,* paperback edition.

1990   *What Are People For?* (essays). *Harland Hubbard: Life and Work* (biography).

1991   *The Discovery of Kentucky* (fiction). *The Unforeseen Wilderness,* revised edition.

1992   *Fidelity: Five Stories* (fiction). Receives the Victory of

Spirit Ethics Award from the Louisville Community
Foundation.

1993   *Sex, Economy, Freedom, and Community: Eight Essays.*
Receives the Orion Society's John Hay Award.

1994   *Entries* (poetry). *Watch with Me: And Six Other Stories of
the Yet-Remembered Ptolemy Proudfoot and His Wife, Miss
Minnie, Née Quinch* (fiction). Receives the T. S. Eliot
Award for Creative Writing from the Ingersoll
Foundation.

Chapter One
A Kentucky Childhood

Wendell Erdman Berry was born in Henry County, Kentucky, on 5 August 1934. His father, John M. Berry, Sr., was a respected attorney and one of the founders of the Kentucky Burley Tobacco Growers Cooperative Association. His mother, Virginia, was of the Perry family, who farmed in Port Royal. John and Virginia Berry were married in 1933 and had four children: Wendell (1934), John Marshall, Jr. (1936), Mary Jo (1939), and Martha Francis (1940). The Berrys were strong-willed, independent-minded readers and thinkers. As a family, they were active members of the New Castle Baptist Church.

Both sides of Wendell Berry's family claim deep roots in Henry County reaching back to the earliest settlement. One of his ancestors, James Mathews, left the town of Cashel in County Tipperary, Ireland, after the Civil War to settle in Kentucky.[1] Mathews settled in Port Royal and worked as a shoemaker. Another ancestor, Berry's great-grandfather, John Johnson Berry, fought in the War of 1812 and later purchased 560 acres of a "survey of land" along Drennon Creek, about a mile from what later became the Berry homestead.[2] John J. Berry was a slaveholder, as apparently were members of both sides of his family.[3] Wendell Berry's grandfather, Pryor Thomas Berry, was born in 1864 and farmed 400 acres outside of Port Royal until his death in 1946. Wendell Berry represents the fourth generation of his father's family and the fifth of his mother's to farm in Henry County. Berry speaks of his family heritage as "a complex inheritance" (*Long-Legged House*, 172).

Berry's father, John Marshall Berry, Sr., was born near Port Royal on 7 November 1900 on the old Berry homestead, a farm now owned by Wendell's brother, John M. Berry, Jr. After graduating from Georgetown College in 1922, John M. Berry, Sr., returned to work on the family farm. In the summer of 1924, at a political meeting in Port Royal, he was persuaded to speak in favor of the newly formed Burley Tobacco Growers Cooperative. He urged farmers to join the effort and pool their tobacco rather than selling it individually. The Democratic candidate for Congress at that meeting, Virgil Chapman, later invited Berry to work for him in Washington, D.C. Berry spent the next three years in

1

Washington working for Chapman and at the same time attended
George Washington Law School, earning his L.L.B. degree in 1927. John
Berry developed strong Democratic political ties in Washington, but he
returned to practice law in Henry County, establishing a successful practice in New Castle, the county seat.

In 1931 his father faced a $10,000 debt from livestock losses in a
barn fire; John Berry helped to pay off the debt from his law practice.
Otherwise, the family farm would have been sold to pay the taxes, since
the income from the tobacco crop was insufficient to pay them.[4]

Henry County lies in northern Kentucky, about halfway between
Cincinnati and Louisville, on what is called the "Cincinnati Arch," where
the sharp bend of the Ohio River forms the boundary between
Kentucky, Ohio, and Indiana. The county, named for Patrick Henry, was
founded in 1798 as the 36th of Kentucky's 120 counties.[5] Port Royal
was located near a steamboat landing at the junction of the Ohio and
Kentucky rivers, known as Lane's Landing, on the land now owned by
Wendell Berry. The town of Port Royal was built on the plateau above
the river, with a narrow winding road running down to the landing. The
land is hilly and fertile, with rich soil and abundant hardwoods. The area
was known for its burley tobacco crop; nearby Carrollton on the Ohio
River provided tobacco warehousing for buyers in Louisville.

"This county is very vulnerable to erosion," he has observed; indeed,
the contour of the land in Henry County has shaped Berry's awareness of
good farming practices. "His father and grandfather Berry tried to keep
their hilly ground from eroding and were grieved when they allowed it
to happen. 'One of the strongest impressions I have is the impression of
living in a place that has been damaged.'"[6]

Farm Life in Henry County

During Berry's childhood, Henry County comprised many small self-
supporting farms. The agricultural economy was highly diversified, with
burley tobacco as the main cash crop; farm families also produced their
own feed grains, meat, milk, eggs, fruits, and vegetables. The economy
was geared to many small local producers, and farm families could market their surplus food. Farms were not mechanized, and farmers were
not burdened with heavy debt for tractors and chemical fertilizers.

This local, self-supporting system of agriculture survived until the
end of World War II, when it was gradually replaced by large, mechanized farms. The small family farms were consolidated into larger units

as young people left farming to seek industrial jobs in the cities. Fewer farmers were left to farm larger holdings, and they adopted the modern methods of intensive, mechanized, monocrop tillage. The plight of Henry County mirrored the larger changes taking place throughout rural America after World War II. With the decline of small family farms came the loss of rural communities and the rural culture they had nurtured. Much of Berry's fiction and poetry is set in rural Kentucky between the wars, and in his essays Berry reflects upon the larger implications of the decline of American farming as a way of life.[7]

Berry claims that, for as far back as he can remember, he always wanted to be a farmer. He had the good fortune to grow up during the Depression years among the last generation of farmers who used draft animals, and he learned early from his paternal grandfather how to handle a team of mules. He took great pride in learning the work of men and was grateful to be taught these skills before they disappeared, even though they were somewhat anachronistic. "I seem to have been born with an aptitude for a way of life that was doomed," he comments, "although I did not understand that at the time" (*Long-Legged House*, 172–73). Both Wendell and his younger brother John farmed small tobacco patches with horses and mules, and John remembers his brother gazing off into the woods, thinking deep thoughts, as the mule waited patiently at the end of a row.[8]

Burley tobacco (a light-colored leaf with low sugar content grown west of the Appalachians) was the major cash crop in Henry County. Berry's father, one of the founders of the Burley Tobacco Growers Cooperative Association, the largest growers' association in the South, grew up during the hard times at the beginning of the century when the large buyers established a cartel to hold prices down. The growers often earned barely enough to pay their warehouse commissions. Berry's father remembers a particularly hard year, 1907, when his father returned from Louisville with nothing to show for his year's work.[9] These were the years of the infamous "night riders" in western Kentucky's Black Belt, tobacco growers who became so frustrated by the price manipulations of James B. Duke's American Tobacco Company and the other large buyers that they attempted to organize themselves to hold their crops off the market in hopes of forcing a price increase. Night riders burned barns and warehouses holding tobacco earmarked for sale at the unacceptable low price. These tactics were partially successful, but bitterness and violence escalated on both sides until the governor was forced to call out the state militia to keep the peace.[10] Even with the tobacco allotment program begun during the Franklin Roosevelt administration, burley tobacco prices remained unstable. After helping to found the Burley Tobacco Growers Cooperative Association, John M. Berry, Sr., served as its vice president from 1941 through 1957, when he became president. In 1947 he also founded the Burley and Dark Leaf Tobacco Export Association. His son, John M. Berry, Jr., now serves as the president and general counsel of the Burley Coop.[11]

From an early age, Wendell Berry felt drawn to the black tenant farmers who helped his grandfather raise tobacco. Berry particularly recalls the influence of Nick Watkins, who came to work for his grandfather when Berry was about three. For the next eight years, Wendell and his brother tagged along after Nick, who tolerated the boys' presence as he worked. Nick Watkins was in his fifties when he came to work for Berry's grandfather on his farm outside of Lacy. Nick worked for a dollar a day, plus a meat hog, chickens, feed for his animals, and a garden spot. Berry remembers him as a quiet, dignified man, a hard worker and a skilled teamster. He served as a mentor for the boys, teaching them by his quiet example and tolerant good humor. Berry recalls inviting Nick to his birthday party when he was nine or ten and the family embarrassment caused by this innocent breach of the social code. Though Nick could not come in to join the festivities, he waited outside until Wendell excused himself to join him. Nick lived with Aunt Georgie, an elderly black woman skilled in herbal remedies and other folk arts. Wendell and his brother often visited her cottage to sit and listen to her stories. From Nick and Aunt Georgie, Wendell learned at an early age about the legacy of racism in the South, and from family stories he learned about his family's burden of responsibility as former slaveholders. As Berry remarks in *The Hidden Wound* (1970), he grew up in a world that was only one or two generations removed from slavery, in which local memories of that way of life still ran deep (67–68, 25).

A Close-knit Family

Berry came from a time and place rich in adult companionship. He learned much about farming simply by listening to the conversations of his elders and by working with and learning from older people who cared about the land. He recalls that his grandfather and father loved every aspect of farming: good land, good crops, good livestock, good pasture, and well-maintained farms. Wendell's grandfather, Pryor Thomas Berry, was an excellent judge of livestock and an excellent teacher, as Wendell's father recalls, because he could explain in the simplest and most direct terms the difference between a good calf or mule and a poor one. Farming and trading were his entire life. He loved the land, and any injury to it through erosion or poor farming practices was grievous to him.[12]

When he was a boy, Wendell liked to tag along with his father and another Henry County farmer, Owen Flood, and open farm gates for them. He and his brother John often worked for Flood, who was a man "of exceptional intelligence and abilities." Flood operated a farm near the Berry home place and often conversed with Berry's father about farming practices. On Sunday afternoons, Berry recalls, the two men would drive around from one farm to another, comparing farming methods. It was "a kind of traveling seminar" for the boys, who would listen to their elders talk about the local farms.[13] Much of what he heard in those days later worked its way into Berry's essays, in which he speaks of the inherited culture and practical local knowledge that can be lost if not valued and preserved.

Berry also learned the domestic arts from his Grandmother Berry, with whom he lived for a while after his grandfather's death to keep her company. From Martha Jo Carpenter Berry he learned how to milk a cow and take care of chickens, as well as how to can and preserve fruits and vegetables. It was his responsibility to milk his grandmother's cow, and he remembers her disappointment when he forgot to come home from playing one afternoon and she had to milk for him. For the most part, however, Berry's childhood play was purposeful play, as is still the case with Amish children, who learn adult responsibilities through their play. The value of his grandmother's lessons was later reflected in the essays in *Home Economics* (1987) and *What Are People For?* (1990).

The Long-Legged House

Another important influence in Berry's childhood was the Kentucky River, which flowed nearby. Sometime during the 1920s Berry's maternal great-uncle, Curran Matthews (the surname was now spelled with two *t*s), built a two-room fishing cabin on some family property adjacent to the river, below Port Royal. This cabin, called "Curran's Camp," or simply "the Camp," became a place for family picnics and gatherings during the summers. In his long autobiographical essay "The Long-Legged House," Berry speaks of the formative influence of this place on his imagination, both for its proximity to the river and for the rich

memories of family get-togethers. The Camp was his family's "wilderness place," and from early in his life Berry associated it with artistic and
imaginative freedom. Later in life, after he had inherited the land, Berry
moved the cabin up from the shore of the Kentucky River, where it had
been flooded, and rebuilt it on pylons as his writer's study.

The Camp was a place for boyhood adventures, such as the time during the flood of March 1945 when Wendell, his brother, and a friend
hitchhiked down to the camp one bright Saturday morning and took a
boat out on the river to explore the flooded backwaters. The three boys
felt like explorers, Berry recalls, paddling in their boat among the large
trees and mossy banks in the flooded hollows. Their grandparents spotted the boys in the boat and, fearing that they would be swept away and
drowned, waited anxiously for them to return to the cabin.

Two years later, after his Uncle Curran's death, Berry returned to the
Camp and, with his friend Pete, cleaned it up to use as a retreat from the
turmoil of adolescence—as a place to be alone, to think, to sort things out,
to get away from parents, to be independent, to be with nature. The boys
would often go to the Camp on weekends to fish or camp or simply get
away from the adult world. Berry also began to read at the Camp—
Thoreau's *Walden*, appropriately, and poems such as Gray's "Elegy Written
in a Country Churchyard" from a paperback anthology of English and
American poetry. For Berry, the Camp became an important retreat from
the pressures of boarding school after he was sent away at 14 to
Millersburg Military Institute (MMI) (*Long-Legged House*, 110–27).

Berry speaks of being impressed with the "charming strangeness" of
his Uncle Curran's carefree, unhurried bachelor life. Though never regu-
larly employed, Matthews appears to have been an inspired putterer and
tinkerer, a handyman good with tools and repairs, a thorough workman
who loved to use his hands. He had a small shop in the back of a store in
Port Royal where Berry loved to visit and watch his uncle as he worked.
Uncle Curran was a great bedtime storyteller, and Wendell and his
brother looked forward to the nightly yarns, adapted from *Tarzan* and
from Zane Grey novels, with their episodic adventures (*Long-Legged
House*, 119). He built the cabin on the Kentucky River sometime during
the 1920s, ostensibly to improve his health but more likely simply
because he enjoyed being out in nature. Matthews built the cabin with
lumber he scavenged from a nearby abandoned log house originally built
by Berry's great-grandfather, Ben Perry, on the "Old House Lot." The
cabin's two rooms, a bedroom and kitchen, were flanked by a small
screened porch. Berry imagines his Uncle Curran building it as a sort of

Thoreauvian task—an assertion of his freedom and independence from ordinary social conventions and of his allegiance to the woods.

Books and Schooling

Wendell Berry's earliest introduction to books and poetry came from his mother Virginia, who read to him as a child. His father recalls that Wendell was only about three or four weeks old when she sat him in her lap and began to read poetry to him. His mother thought that she detected a rhythmic response in him, and she kept it up for several years until he was three or four years old.[14] Later she would read to him when he was ill, and Berry recalls how he loved to be sick and stay home from school and be read to. His mother gave him the gift of books, and Berry emphasizes the formative influence of his childhood reading, which included the Billy Greenhill and Miss Minerva books, Sidney Lanier, and *Swiss Family Robinson*. He especially enjoyed reading *Huckleberry Finn*, which he discovered in the bookcase of his grandparents' living room. It was the Webster edition, with E. W. Kemble's illustrations, and had belonged to his great-grandmother. Berry recalls becoming so familiar with Huck's adventures that they literally became a part of his life and helped him to imagine the world of his parents and grandparents.[15]

Berry started school at the New Castle Elementary School, in the county seat. Though he enjoyed reading, he was an indifferent student and did not apply himself to his studies, being more interested in hunting, trapping, and fishing. In an attempt to teach his sons self-discipline, Berry's father decided to send Wendell and his brother John, Jr., to Millersburg Military Institute, a private military academy in the bluegrass region near Paris, Kentucky, about an hour east of Lexington.

Founded in 1893, MMI is a small, independent, all-male college preparatory school with an enrollment of about 100 students. It offers a traditional academic curriculum for grades 9 through 12, with 20 credits required for graduation. The students' daily schedule is strictly regulated, beginning with 6:00 A.M. reveille, and includes mandatory drill and study hall. The daily dress is army-issued fatigues, with dress uniforms worn on ceremonial occasions. The student body is organized into a corps of cadets composed of a battalion staff and individual cadet companies, all under cadet leadership. The student corps is self-governing; cadet leaders are responsible for each company. Athletics constitute a major part of student life, and each student is expected to take part in team sports.

Berry attended MMI from 1948 through 1952, when he graduated and entered the University of Kentucky in Lexington. For the most part, he has been circumspect about his MMI experience, although he did make some harsh comments about the school in his essay "A Long-Legged House." The strict military discipline did not agree with him, and he often longed to be home at the Camp. Being naturally sensitive and independent-minded, he chafed under the demands of military discipline and the regimen of sports and obedience to student officers. Berry rebelled against the military correctness, regularity, conformity, and mediocrity of the institution. He recalls being reprimanded for using a dictionary in study hall, and another time for reading Balzac's story "A Passion in the Desert" without permission (*Long-Legged House*, 126). He also recalls having a great craving for personal dignity as an adolescent—and having that desire squelched, since he was neither athletic nor passively obedient. But Berry concedes that Millersburg Military Institute taught him beneficial lessons as well. He made some good friends there, and he found that being away from home made him more attached to it. During his junior year he had some good teachers, including James Lafayette Joiner, who taught English. Berry read his first Shakespeare there, *The Merchant of Venice*, and from geometry he learned the value of logical thinking. Having to produce a theme each week in study hall taught him to write, and he polished his writing skills by working on the monthly campus newspaper, the *Communicadette*, which he edited during his senior year. Berry wrote editorials, reportage, and features and sharpened his essay style. It was a beautiful campus, Berry recalls, but being required to attend made his brother and him keenly aware of their lost freedom. His brother John, who ultimately rose in the ranks at MMI, was so unhappy there at first that he once ran away for a few days.[16]

The University of Kentucky

Berry entered the University of Kentucky at Lexington as a freshman in the fall of 1952, relieved to be at a civilian institution. By then he had decided to become a writer, and his obvious choice of major was English. (Berry also studied French for three years, reading Gide and Camus.)

At that time the University of Kentucky English Department was strongly grounded in New Critical theory and practice. In the spring of his freshman year, Berry took an introductory literature course with Prof. Thomas B. Stroup, whom Berry later credited as a demanding teacher who awakened his respect for literature. Berry recalled Stroup as a dapper man of precise speech and intonation who wore elegant neckties. Stroup taught from the classic Cleanth Brooks and Robert Penn Warren text, *Understanding Poetry* (1938), and like those authors, he emphasized close reading skills and precise interpretation. Student papers were often returned with the terse comment, "'Not good enough. Do it over.'"[17]

Though he wanted to become a writer, Berry could not decide whether to write poetry or prose. He had discovered the persuasive power of his verse on "a somewhat merciless young lady," and he sought further encouragement and confirmation of his budding talent from his instructors. He would bring some of his earliest verses to Dr. Stroup's office in the Fine Arts Building and show them to his teacher, waiting apprehensively for a verdict. As Berry recalls:

> His verdict, when it finally came, astounded me. He did not praise my poems, as I had hoped; he did not laugh at them, as I had feared, and as I know now they deserved; he condemned them cordially, with reference to the company, mainly unknown to me, that they aspired to keep; he not only told me that they had fallen short, but he told me what they had fallen short of.[18]

What Berry learned from Stroup was the necessity of revising, often many times, an essay or poem to clarify its style or meaning. Berry confesses that as an undergraduate he was sometimes guilty of intellectual impudence, which received a swift check in Stroup's classes. One morning, in exasperation, Stroup interrupted his class to observe to Berry, "Your audacity is exceeded only by your ignorance."[19] Berry's "audacity" was most likely an expression of his lack of polish and eagerness to learn. In his later tribute to Stroup, Berry recalled this occasion with some amusement, praising his teacher's generosity and wisdom and noting that he subsequently took every course that Stroup offered. Stroup taught him both critical judgment and appreciation of works of literature. One afternoon he read aloud to Berry from Eliot's "The Journey of the Magi," demonstrating through his oral interpretation the unity of the poem.

Other Kentucky faculty whose courses Berry took included the medievalist Arthur K. Moore, with whom Berry hunted quail and roamed the woods, and Holman Hamilton, a journalist of distinction who, in his forties, left that profession to follow his inclinations and become a historian. Berry became friends with some of the most distinguished faculty members at the University of Kentucky. These principled men were serious scholars and interesting teachers who were not swayed by the popular pressures that afflict so many college faculty members. Berry later acknowledged the influence of his undergraduate professors when he returned to the University of Kentucky as a member of the English Department.

Creative Writing and Kentucky Folklore

From Hollis B. Summers, the novelist and poet, Berry took two creative writing courses, a fiction-writing course and a creative writing workshop. In his freshman year, he published the essay "The Wings of the Future" in the *Green Pen*, an annual anthology of freshman writing at the University of Kentucky.[20] Drawing upon his experience as a high school newspaper editor, Berry chaired the editorial committee of the *Green Pen*, work that prepared him for a position later on the *Stylus*, the university literary magazine. From 1954 through 1957 Berry published six poems and six short stories in the *Stylus*.[21] His early poems included four lyrics, a long narrative poem, and an elegy. By 1955 he was serving as coeditor of *Stylus*, and he continued his association with the literary magazine through his first year of graduate study.

For Berry, there was never any question of having to find a subject or a place to write about: he had always been drawn to his native region, and as he observes, learning to be a writer entailed "learning what to do with the subject I had from the beginning and could not escape" (*Long-Legged House*, 141–42). As an undergraduate, Berry wrote a number of stories and sketches dealing with rural farming life. Perhaps the most notable of these early pieces is the story "The Brothers," which was published in two parts in *Stylus* and won the magazine's Dantzler Award in Prose in 1955.[22] A year later Berry won the same award a second time for his short story "The Chestnut Stud." With this encouragement, Berry decided in 1956 to enter both stories in the *Carolina Quarterly*'s fiction contest; "The Brothers" won the $100 first prize and was published in the quarterly that summer.[23]

By the time he began his graduate study at the University of Kentucky, Berry had sent out manuscripts that were accepted by *Prairie Schooner* and *Poetry* magazine. His poem "Elegy" won the Farquhar Award in Poetry in 1957 and was published in *Stylus* that year. He also published two other short stories, "Whippoorwills" and "Apples," in *Coraddi: Arts Forum 1957*, a literary annual published by the University of North Carolina at

Greensboro.[24] An economical writer, Berry did not waste his material: these two stories, together with "The Brothers," eventually found their way into his first novel, *Nathan Coulter* (1960).

Bennett H. Wall's U.S. history course heightened Berry's interest in his native region and eventually led to a close friendship with his professor. Berry sat in the front row of a large lecture class and offered sharp questions and comments that enlivened the course. He also appreciated any touch of irony or dry humor in Professor Wall's remarks. Berry lived for a while in the men's quadrangle that Dr. Wall supervised, and Wall remembers him as a "clear-eyed, very keen-minded student of Kentucky."[25]

Berry took a second, more advanced course with Wall and was invited to accompany his professor on his travels throughout Kentucky collecting manuscripts for the University of Kentucky library. They thoroughly covered the Knobs region and the eastern mountain area of the state. On one return trip along back roads, they came across an old log cabin, still occupied, set alongside a creek at the foot of a sharp bluff. Dried "shucky beans" were hung on the outside wall, and a log corn crib occupied a small knob. They stopped the car and watched a wisp of smoke trail out of the chimney. Fascinated by the scene, Berry observed that it was Kentucky as it had looked 200 years earlier, when the first pioneers crossed the Appalachians.

During one of their field trips, Berry invited his professor home to meet his family. Through Berry's father they contacted a wealthy widow in Cincinnati who gave them permission to search for manuscripts in her ancestral home in New Castle, Kentucky, on the bluffs of the Kentucky River. There they found fascinating letters from the antebellum period that revealed some dramatic incidents in the lives of slave owners and shed light on the history of slavery in Kentucky.

Berry very much enjoyed accompanying Professor Wall on these manuscript-hunting excursions into rural Kentucky. Wall was interested in every aspect of the land, including farming, fishing, hunting, shooting, hiking, and canoeing. He enjoyed talking with ordinary folk who pursued these activities, regardless of their position in society. There was no academic snobbery in him, nor any feeling of caste or class. He loved listening to rural storytellers, even if they did not use perfect English. Thus, by inclination, he gradually became a folklorist. He was highly sensitive to ironic and humorous situations and discovered great stories in ordinary situations ranging from birth to death. From these excursions Berry eagerly absorbed the atmosphere and flavor of rural Kentucky life and found material that would later shape his interests as a writer.[26]

Graduate Study and Marriage

Berry graduated from the University of Kentucky in May 1956 with a bachelor of arts degree in English; he spent that summer studying at the Indiana University School of Letters. He was pleased enough with Kentucky's English program, however, to apply to enter the master's program that fall. He spent the next year completing his master's degree, taking extra coursework rather than writing a master's thesis.

Berry met his future wife, Tanya Amyx, while he was a student at the University of Kentucky. Her father, Clifford Amyx, was a studio artist and professor of art at the university. Tanya grew up in suburban Lexington and had had little experience of farm life before she met Wendell, but she recognized his talent as a writer and found herself attracted to the rural life in Henry County. They were married on 29 May 1957.

They had decided to spend the first summer of their marriage at the Camp, so Berry worked frantically for weeks before the ceremony to transform his bachelor retreat into a habitat fit for a wife. He replaced broken window panes, repaired screens, whitewashed the walls, and, as a final touch, built a new privy. The ritual of preparing his house, he remarked, helped him prepare himself for marriage. The Camp had no electricity, plumbing, or new furniture, and the roof leaked when it rained hard, but these inconveniences taught them what the real essentials are by freeing their marriage from things. They had surrounding them the elemental world of the river, the trees, the wild creatures, the sun, and the stars. Their first summer was rich in memories of shared experiences—making strawberry preserves, catching huge catfish on trotlines, and staying up through an apocalyptic summer storm. Berry soon established a comfortable writing routine, working each morning at his desk on the screened porch overlooking the Kentucky River. There he composed his first serious poem, the river poem "Diagon," and completed some of his most important reading (*Long-Legged House*, 129–36).

He recalls reading with pleasure that spring and summer the poetry of Andrew Marvell, especially the long occasional poem "Upon Appleton House, to my Lord *Fairfax*." He studied the poetry of William Carlos Williams, in the volumes *Collected Earlier Poems* and *Journey to Love*, as well as Kenneth Rexroth's *100 Poems from the Chinese* (*Long-Legged House*, 137–43). The summer of 1957 served as the culmination of Berry's literary apprenticeship period. He was determined to become a Kentucky writer, but he wanted to avoid the facile clichés and stereotypes of southern literary regionalism. Rather than perpetuate the popular, sentimental picture of the Kentucky bluegrass region, Berry wanted to write the hard, unvarnished truth.

Wendell and Tanya Berry left the Camp late in the summer of 1957, piling their household items in an old Jeep station wagon and driving up the river road to Route 421, which took them back through Frankfort to Lexington. Berry had accepted a position as an English instructor at Georgetown College. His father's alma mater, Georgetown is a small, Baptist liberal arts college near Lexington. Berry stayed there one year, teaching primarily freshman English. A former Georgetown colleague remembers Berry as a demanding instructor who was impatient with religious cant. The college attracted many young men who wanted to enter the ministry and whose freshman papers were often preachy. One day when Berry had received a particularly muddled sermon, he said to the writer, "When it says, 'Thou shalt not take the name of the Lord thy God in vain,' it means: don't talk off the top of your head about God."[27]

As Berry continued to work intermittently on his first novel, he realized that he wanted to pursue his study in creative writing rather than grade freshman papers. He and his wife also wanted to strike out on their own and live for a while in a different part of the country. So he applied to study in the creative writing program at Stanford University and was awarded a Wallace Stegner Fellowship. When Berry received notice of the fellowship in the spring of 1958, he decided to read more of Stegner's work, since he had read only the novella *Field Guide to the Western Birds* (1956) in *New Short Novels 2* (1956). That summer he read Stegner's first novel, *Remembering Laughter* (1937), and his two short story collections, *The Women on the Wall* (1952) and *The City of the Living* (1957). Berry admired Stegner's mastery of the short story form, and thus his future teacher began to influence him even before they met.[28]

During the summer of 1958, Holman Hamilton, one of Berry's history professors at the University of Kentucky, was contacted by Craig Wylie, a publisher's representative and later senior trade editor from Houghton Mifflin who was scouting for manuscripts. Professor Hamilton asked Wylie whether he would be interested in looking over the manuscript of a novel written by one of his students. Wylie agreed, and Berry was invited to join them for lunch. He was offered an advance of $250 for the novel with a commitment to publish it when it was completed.[29]

In his free time that summer, Berry and his friend Ed McClanahan made a canoe trip down the river and spent one last night at the Camp, sleeping on the floor, before it was closed and shuttered. At the end of the summer, Berry and his wife and daughter, Mary Dee, born in the spring of 1958, left Kentucky for the West Coast. He would not return to the Camp until 1960.

Berry took with him to Stanford the first 110 pages of the manuscript of his first novel, *Nathan Coulter*, which he would finish during the next two years. His Stegner fellowship paid a modest annual stipend of $2,500, which barely covered essentials. As Berry recalls, they ate a lot of tuna fish while they were in California.[30] They found lodgings in Mill Valley, within commuting distance of Stanford, and Berry prepared to begin his program in creative writing.

Chapter Two

The Making of a Writer

The Stanford creative writing program did not confer a degree, but it did offer Berry a chance to study in Wallace Stegner's graduate seminar with a promising group of future writers that included Ken Kesey, Ernest J. Gaines, and Larry McMurtry. Stegner took over the writing seminar during the winter quarter of Berry's first year at Stanford. Berry remembers being somewhat in awe of his teacher beforehand, but Stegner turned out to be different from what Berry had expected. He was a handsome, neatly dressed man with an air of modesty, discretion, and reticence. Stegner was not magisterial or dogmatic, but he showed the indisputable authority of a master teacher and writer.

As the writing seminar met with Stegner for the first time in the Jones Room of Stanford Library, the 20 students felt that they were being led into "the Great Community" of past writers.[1] The seminar group sat around a long table while Stegner read aloud from a student's work, then sat back and asked for comments, listening attentively and sometimes smoking a cigar. One afternoon, as Berry recalls, Stegner read aloud to the class from a portion of his own novel in progress, *All the Live Little Things* (1967), then invited responses from the group. Students were also encouraged to read from their own works in progress. Stegner later recalled that Berry read aloud the last few chapters of *Nathan Coulter* in the seminar.[2] Berry also took a writing course during his first year with Prof. Richard Scowcroft.

In his second year Berry was appointed Edward H. Jones Lecturer in Creative Writing. A fellow Kentuckian, Gurney Norman from Hazard, succeeded him in the first-year Wallace Stegner Fellowship. Along with Ed McClanahan and James Baker Hall, Berry and Norman gravitated together as a small group of Kentuckians at Stanford.

While at Stanford, Berry published in various West Coast literary magazines four poems and a short story excerpted from *Nathan Coulter*.[3] He completed the manuscript of this novel with the help of a Stanford creative writing program fellowship, which allowed him a year of free time to write.

Farming, a Guggenheim, and Europe

After Berry completed his teaching responsibilities at Stanford, he and his wife decided to return to Kentucky. By June 1960 they had moved to a 250-acre farm in New Castle, in Henry County, on land belonging to Berry's father. The rambling white farmhouse, built in 1870, had been the home of his grandfather and father, and Wendell himself had lived there for a while as a boy. During the next year he helped to operate the sheep farm, rising about 5:30 A.M. each day to feed the animals, assist with the lambing, and take care of other farm chores before getting to his writing.

Berry did find time to apply for a Guggenheim Foundation Fellowship, which he was awarded in May 1961, along with 265 other recipients. The $4,000 grant came with no stipulations, so Berry decided to take his family to Europe that fall to travel in France and Italy. They were accompanied by Tanya's parents, Prof. and Mrs. Clifford Amyx. While they were in Europe, Berry began a second novel (*A Place on Earth* [1967]).

The Berrys arrived in New York on 3 September, visited some friends in Boston, then returned to New York so that Berry could meet with New York University faculty on 12 September to interview for a faculty position as an associate professor of English and director of freshman English at the NYU uptown campus in University Heights in the Bronx. On the strength of recommendations from Wallace Stegner and Craig Wylie, and the good personal impression he made during the interview, Berry was offered the position a month later, to begin the following September after he had returned from Europe.

In the fall of 1961, the Berrys settled in a small apartment in the Piazza San Francisco di Paola in Florence, where Berry could write. During his free time, he took excursions into the countryside to admire the steep, carefully cultivated hillside farms of Tuscany, which greatly impressed him. In January they decided to travel to the resort town of La Napoule, on the French Riviera, where they were offered an apartment and a place to write in a pension run by the La Napoule Art Foundation. There the Berrys befriended Wallace Fowlie, a Duke University professor of French literature who was also in Europe on a Guggenheim. The La Napoule Art Foundation had been established only recently, and Berry and Fowlie were the first two to be accepted as fellows.

Fowlie was assigned a small, unheated apartment that he found so unpleasant during the cold, damp winter that he often stopped in to visit Wendell and Tanya Berry and to warm up in front of their stove. There were few restaurants open off-season, so the pension residents had to provide for their own food. They subsisted on continental breakfasts of rolls and coffee until they discovered a small restaurant that offered a few entrées. During the day Berry and Fowlie would take long walks outside of town, and Berry would practice his French by asking Fowlie the names of the plants and trees.

The Berrys remained in La Napoule only until February, when they returned to Florence; Fowlie was so miserable that he finally left for Nice. During their brief stay together, the two men struck up a warm acquaintance, and Berry later dedicated the poem "Ripe" (1978) to Fowlie in a festschrift published in honor of the professor of French.[4]

In the spring of 1962, before their return home, the Berrys traveled to Ireland to visit the village of Cashel, in County Tipperary, where Berry's ancestors had lived. During their stay, Berry walked up to the Rock of Cashel of St. Patrick's Rock to view the ruins of the thirteenth-century cathedral and choir and the even more ancient Cormic's Chapel, which was begun in 1127. As he wandered about the stone slabs and crosses in the graveyard, he tried to find the gravestones of his great-great-grandparents, Edward and Mary Cooney Mathews, but their graves were apparently unmarked. His visit to Cashel—to which he would return 20 years later—left Berry with a sense of loss about his inaccessible personal history.[5]

Nathan Coulter

Berry's first novel, *Nathan Coulter*, was published by Houghton Mifflin in April 1960. The novel's sales were small, even for a first novel. It received some favorable reviews, however, and Craig Wylie, the senior trade editor at Houghton Mifflin, expressed confidence in the firm's young author.[6] The Kentucky reviewers were especially enthusiastic, praising the novel's graceful style and placing it in a tradition of "tobacco novels," such as W. W. Chamberlain's *Leaf Gold* (1941), Sarah Bell Hackley's *The Tobacco Tiller* (1909), Francis Ogilvie's *Green Bondage* (1931), Robert Penn Warren's *Night Riders* (1939), and Harry H. Kroll's narrative history *Riders in the Night* (1965).[7] The first edition of the novel was 204 pages long; when Berry revised the novel in 1985 for reissue by North Point Press, he shortened it to 180 pages, dropping the last three chapters. Berry's revision gives the novel better focus and unity by ending with Grandpa's stroke in the field and not tracing the consequences of his death for Nathan, his father, or Uncle Burley.

Nathan Coulter is a short, spare, straightforward story of a young boy's coming of age in Kentucky's burley tobacco country. A pastoral novel narrated in the first person by young Nathan, the book is not a disguised autobiography, though it clearly reflects the rural tobacco-growing culture of Berry's Henry County childhood. Nathan's great-grandmother, Parthenia Coulter, buried in the town cemetery under the family monument with an angel on top, shares her first name with Berry's own great-grandmother, Parthenia Antle.[8]

The germ of the novel was the early sketch "The Brothers," which Berry first published as an undergraduate in the *Stylus* and later in the *Carolina Quarterly*.[9] The original sketch had three sections: "The Crow," "Birth" (later dropped from the novel), and "Death," which describes the death of the mother of the two brothers, Tom and Nathan Coulter. The revised version of *Nathan Coulter* is loosely organized into five sections that follow the lives of the two brothers, from childhood through adolescence to early manhood. Each section is built around one or two major episodes in the lives of the boys and their family. Nathan's childhood is touched by grief and loss: his mother dies; his father's barn burns after lightning strikes it; his older brother leaves home after a fight with his father; and his grandfather dies. In this first novel, Berry introduces three generations of Coulters and other townsfolk from his fictional Port William. The novel is starkly patriarchal; a strong, competitive work ethic separates Grandpa Dave Coulter, his son Jarrat (the boys' father), and Tom and Nathan. Grandpa Coulter and Jarrat farm adjoining tracts of land because they cannot bear to be dependent upon each other. Nathan witnesses the fierce male rivalry between his older brother Tom and his father, which leads to a fight between the two during tobacco harvest one year. Beaten and humiliated by his father, Tom leaves home to seek a life elsewhere.

Nathan Coulter is an understated, starkly realistic novel that consciously tries to avoid the clichés and sentimentality of regional fiction. Nathan's first-person narration provides an honest and intimate account of the tensions in his family and of the seasonal rhythms of rural Kentucky farm life in the years before World War II. The novel's action is built around the hard work of tobacco planting, cultivation, and harvest. Its tone combines earthy folk humor with episodes of harshness and cruelty. Already present in this early novel is an implicit division between those who neglect or abuse the land and those who respect it and live on its bounty. Grandpa Coulter and Jarrat are linked by their fierce, stubborn pride and the obsessive work ethic that drives them to exhaustion and makes life unpleasant for those around them. Their unrelenting competition is mirrored in Nathan's recurrent dream of a lion, whose blue eyes remind him of his grandfather's. Though they are hardworking farmers, the husbandry Grandpa and Jarrat practice is ultimately sterile and unproductive; they are bound up in impatience, anger, and grief, which they are unable to express in any way but to lash out at their wives and children. Uncle Burley, on the other hand, Jarrat's brother and the boys' uncle, is a kind and relaxed but unambitious bachelor who refuses to be bound by land ownership or other responsibilities. He works enough to support his simple needs but prefers to fish or hunt or go on periodic drinking binges, from which he is rescued by his father and brother to be nursed back to sobriety.

In this first novel, Berry presents a portrait of an intact rural culture, one bound by the uncertain economics of burley tobacco and the common work and fellowship of shared, neighborly farm labor, but limited by ignorance, cruelty, and hardship. Berry presents a male culture in which women are strangely absent or subordinate. Without a female presence, the boys are neglected and the men grow hard and bitter from unrelenting work. Weakened by the birth of her second child, Mrs. Coulter remains sick and struggles with her household chores, often needing to rest in the afternoon. Her condition steadily declines, and the boys' grandmother comes to cook and do the housework after she becomes bedridden. Mr. Coulter takes out his grief and worry on the boys, who are too young to realize the seriousness of their mother's condition. After her death, they are sent to live with their grandparents while their father broods alone in his grief. Never a kind or affectionate father, he grows more harsh and distant with his sons after his wife's death, almost as if he blames them for her death. Nathan remembers his father's large, active, work-scarred hands, hands that could just as easily split a log or lift the boys bodily off the floor to shake them in grief and rage after their mother's death. Later Daddy drives Tom away by taunting, beating, and insulting him after challenging him to keep up with his father in the grueling work of stripping the rows of tobacco leaves during the harvest.

There is much cruelty in this portrait of rural life—the unconscious cruelty of people who live in close proximity with birth and death and do not spare themselves hard work or grief. Early in the novel the boys blow apart a friend's crow with a dynamite cap; at the Fourth of July fair,

Uncle Burley wrings the necks of his mother's ducks when they become
too tired to avoid the rings thrown at them as they swim around in a
tub; several sticks of dynamite are thrown into the local river to blow the
fish out of the water; and a Roman candle is tied to the tail of a stray dog
in Port William. Some of these incidents may be influenced by the tall-
tale exaggeration and hyperbole of southern humor and the humor of
Mark Twain, but to a certain extent the violence is part of the legacy of
the frontier and is endemic to American life.

The violence in *Nathan Coulter* is tempered somewhat by Berry's colorful and affectionate portraits of the minor characters, some of whom
appear in later Port William novels and stories. These include one-eyed
Gander Loyd; the Montgomery twins, Mushmouth and Chicken Little;
Big Ellis; and Jig Pendleton, the crazy religious fanatic who lives alone in
his fishing shack, strung inside with spools, strings, and pulleys hooked
to the treadwheel of an old Singer sewing machine, which he pedals furi-
ously when drunk, singing and shouting for the Lord to purify him.
Many of the episodes in the novel have the colorful and authentic flavor
of country anecdotes, particularly those involving Uncle Burley, such as
his "dunking ducks" scheme at the Fourth of July fair. In another incident, Uncle Burley drops a stick of dynamite at the feet of the game
warden who comes to arrest him for illegal fishing. When the warden
throws it in the river, Uncle Burley charges him for the fish that float to
the surface.

New York University

Thanks to a generous recommendation from Wallace Stegner, Berry
secured a position as assistant professor of English and director of freshman English at the uptown University Heights campus of New York
University in the Bronx, when he and his family returned in 1962 from
their year in Italy on a Guggenheim Fellowship. The University Heights
campus had been an all-male liberal arts and preprofessional branch of
NYU and was trying to find a new identity as a coed institution. The
chairman of the English Department, Oscar Cargill, made it clear in hir-
ing Berry that NYU was looking for someone who had both teaching
and administrative ability and who could also be expected to continue
writing creatively. In his letter to Berry in Florence offering him the
three-year appointment, Oscar Cargill expressed his complete faith in
Berry as a writer and in his ability to administer the freshman English
program at University Heights.[10]

Berry and his family returned to the States in June 1962 and spent the summer in Kentucky, visiting with his family, before he reported for work at the annual department meeting on 22 September. Tanya Berry was expecting their second child, and they needed to find an apartment before the fall term began. With the help of Prof. William Gibson, who arranged to show them homes in Westchester County and in New Jersey, within a short commuting distance of University Heights, they found an apartment on Davenport Avenue in New Rochelle. Berry and his family spent one year in New Rochelle, then moved to a downtown Manhattan apartment on Greenwich Street, near City Hall.

Berry worked for two years at the NYU–University Heights campus, but he found the literary and intellectual life in New York uncongenial and disliked being away from Kentucky. He placed five poems in *Poetry* magazine, for which he won the Vachel Lindsay Prize in 1962, but the work on his second novel progressed slowly.[11]

"November Twenty Six Nineteen Hundred Sixty Three"

A notable success for Berry was the reception of his elegy written after John F. Kennedy's assassination in Dallas on 22 November 1963. Entitled "November Twenty Six Nineteen Hundred Sixty Three," the 11-stanza elegy first appeared in *The Nation* on 21 December 1963.[12] The simple eloquence of Berry's text so moved the noted American artist Ben Shahn that he was inspired to illustrate Berry's words. Shahn, renowned for his calligraphy, lettered each of Berry's stanzas opposite the simple, black-and-white line drawings he had done. Then he bound the book and showed it to his friends, including the publisher George Braziller, who offered to publish it. In his introduction to the book, Shahn wrote that he found Berry's poem "extraordinarily moving. It was right in every way; it was modest and unrhetorical."[13] Berry's elegy was republished in a hardcover edition with Ben Shahn's drawings and received much critical acclaim.

Each stanza of Berry's simple free-verse tribute begins with the refrain, "We know." He uses the traditional elegiac conventions of the winter season, the slain youthful leader, the mourners, the funeral procession, the shared feelings of grief and bereavement, the finality of death and the grave, the loss of hope, the slow cycle of healing through time, leading to an acceptance of the loss and a gradual apotheosis of Kennedy's spirit among the American people.

A Return to Kentucky

After his first year at NYU, Berry and his family spent the summer of
1963 back at the Camp on the Kentucky River. In the winter of 1963 he
accepted a position at the University of Kentucky in Lexington, to begin
in the fall of 1964. Oscar Cargill tried to persuade Berry not to leave New
York by alluding to another southern writer, Thomas Wolfe, who had also
taught at NYU, but Berry was determined to return to Kentucky.[14]

Berry and his family left New York in June 1964 and rented a fur-
nished house in Lexington for the school year while Berry winterized the
Camp so that it could continue to serve as a weekend writing retreat.
Back at the University of Kentucky, Berry taught an introductory fiction-writing course and several other introductory literature courses.
That year he arranged his schedule so that he could teach Tuesday
through Thursday and spend the other four days of the week working on
his novel. Throughout 1964–65 he would leave Lexington on Thursday
evening, drive the 60 miles to Port Royal, write at the Camp, and return
to Lexington by Monday evening.

In November 1964 the Lane's Landing property came on the market,
across the road from the Camp. He bought the land and was able to
consider moving permanently back to Port Royal.

A Place on Earth

Wendell Berry started his second novel, *A Place on Earth*, on 1 January
1960, while he was still at Stanford. According to his editor Craig Wylie,
he had about 100 pages of the manuscript completed by the time he
interviewed for the position at New York University.[15] A Rockefeller
Foundation Fellowship in 1965 provided Berry with the time and means
to concentrate on finishing the novel.

Progress was slow, however; Berry would work on it intermittently
for over seven years until its publication by Harcourt, Brace & World in
1967. His editor at that time, Dan Wickenden, helped him cut many
pages from the typescript and edit the manuscript, but the first edition
of the novel was still, in Berry's words, "clumsy, overwritten, wasteful."[16]
Berry was fond of the book, however, and when North Point Press
offered to reissue it in 1983, after it had been out of print for more than
10 years, he took the opportunity to revise and cut about one-third of
the original text. He also added chapter titles to the revised edition and
divided it into five parts.

A *Place on Earth* is a portrait of a small Kentucky town, Port William, from the late winter through the fall of 1945. The name Port William first appears in this novel; according to Berry, it was the original name of Carrollton, Kentucky.[17] The novel depicts in sympathetic terms the disruptive impact of World War II on the close-knit families and agricultural customs of the small tobacco farmers in the Kentucky River Valley. A novel of loss and atonement, through war, flood, and suicide, it records the decline of traditional farming practices and the disruptive impact of the airplane and the automobile. The novel contrasts the natural rhythms of the seasons, of winter flood and spring renewal, with the gradual disintegration of the local community. It is a gray and somber novel, set in the muted tones and moods of late winter, with bare, sodden fields and heavy, leaden skies.

The novel focuses on the family of Mat Feltner, a 61-year-old tobacco farmer whose son Virgil has been listed as missing in action in Europe. Mat, his wife Margaret, and their daughter-in-law Hannah, who is expecting her first child, all gradually learn to measure their loss against the permanent cycle of the returning seasons, the fertile lands of their valley farm, and the memories they share of Virgil as a boy and a young man, first helping his father farm and later, before being called away to war, planning to establish a farm and home of his own. Berry writes in a movingly laconic and understated style of these good and decent people and of how they learn to bear their loss. His narrative is deliberately slow and measured as he enters into the cycle of their lives and re-creates the casual and unhurried pace of premechanized rural American life. Berry shows the same affectionate regard for his region and its people as we find in some other contemporary southern writers—Reynolds Price, Fred Chappell, Peter Taylor, Doris Betts.

Berry is an agrarian (though not a dogmatic one) who has learned his lessons well from the earlier generation of the southern Agrarians, who valued place, history, family ties, and religion as the conditions that would create a distinctive southern literature. His characters are drawn from the same sturdy yeoman stock that Jefferson hoped would be the foundation of American democracy. The best of his characters take pride in their farms and land and a quiet pleasure in work well done. The images of family, land, and region become the measure of life, just as the habitual acts of good husbandry, of cherishing and nurturing crops and livestock, mark good farming practices and help to sustain a sense of place. The measure of a man's character is in his use or abuse of the land. Berry contrasts the heedless waste of the early settlers and their heirs, the wastrels such as Roger Merchant, with the good husbandry and wise farming practices of men such as Mat Feltner and Jack Beechum, who try to sustain and renew what they have inherited. As Mat Feltner comments, "The earth is the genius of our life," and it is through his renewed contact with the land and his efforts to help his neighbors after a disastrous late winter flood that Mat discovers the conditions through which he can learn to accept the loss of his son.[18] That loss is even more difficult to bear for Virgil's wife, Hannah, but through the birth of her daughter and the loving support of her husband's parents, she too finds the strength to carry on her life. A number of other vivid and engaging townspeople are introduced, including 85-year-old Jack Beechum, whose story is told more fully in Berry's third novel, *The Memory of Old Jack* (1974).

The sense of loss in *A Place on Earth* is not merely for young men lost in the war, but for a threatened way of life. The migration of young men from the farms to the city had already begun, and the war merely hastened that movement, leaving the older men and the unfit behind. Tobacco, the staple crop, was labor-intensive and required much cooperative effort. Throughout the novel, Mat Feltner muses over how he will be able to continue to farm without his son. And who will inherit his land and his skills? Good farming demands that sons serve a long and careful apprenticeship program learning the necessary skills from their fathers. The land is a strict taskmaster, and the margin for error is small. Mat's worst fear is that without a new generation of young farmers to take over after the war, tobacco farming will disappear and the community will decline into absentee ownership and neglect of the land.

The novel opens with four older men playing cards in Frank Lathrop's empty store on a rainy afternoon. Mat Feltner, Frank Lathrop, Old Jack Beechum, and Jayber Crow are the village elders, pondering the future of Port William. World War II has clearly been a watershed. All the young men are away at war—Frank Lathrop's son Jasper, Tom and Nathan Coulter, Virgil Feltner, and Grover Gibbs's son Billy, the bomber pilot. The older men have struggled to maintain their farms without the help of their sons, and now the heavy rains have delayed their spring preparation of the tobacco seed beds. With the enforced idleness of bad weather, the men are reduced to card playing. Mat worries about his son, who has not been heard from in some time. Burley Coulter, Nathan's uncle, writes long letters to his nephew recounting the local news, which is dominated by the flood and the army's notification that Virgil is missing in action. Aside from radio news broadcasts, the Port William community is isolated, with limited awareness of the outside world. The inhabitants are still tied to the seasonal rhythms of planting and harvest. The flooding on the creeks and tributaries of the Kentucky River further isolates the families of Port William, but their strong fellowship unites them in the face of common danger. The flood washes out a footbridge on Gideon and Ida Crop's farm and sweeps away their daughter Annie. When Gideon disappears after searching for the girl, Mat Feltner and Burley Coulter put aside time from their own work to care for the Crops' farm. The death of Annie Crop serves as a counterpoint to the loss of Virgil Feltner, and Mat and Ida console each other. But they are both also consoled by their sense of duty and obligation to their farms, to the daily routine of work that gives their lives meaning and helps to heal their losses.

Another subplot involves Mat's cousin, Ernest Finley, a bachelor carpenter and handyman crippled in World War I. Mat hires Ernest to rebuild the Crops' footbridge and barn. During the weeks Ernest works alone to repair the flood damage, he slowly becomes infatuated with Ida, left alone after her husband's disappearance. Ernest dreams of a married life with Ida, but when his work is completed and Gideon suddenly reappears in late August, he is emotionally devastated and commits suicide in his woodshop.

The moral order of Berry's world demands that work and love be united to create a full and meaningful life. Mat Feltner is clearly the moral exemplar of a man happily married to his farm and family. He and his wife Margaret have created a good life for themselves and their two children, Virgil and Bess, though the order of their lives has been disrupted by the war. Mat inherited his farm from his father Ben, owns it free of debt, and has farmed it wisely and well. Others are not so fortunate.

Old Jack Beechum owns his well-kept farm outright but can no longer farm it for himself, so his lawyer, Wheeler Catlett, has arranged for a young couple, Elton and Mary Penn, to farm it as tenants. Jack is pleased with the hardworking young couple, who seem to be the spiritual heirs to his rectitude, and he spends a pleasant day visiting with them. But he is afraid that his daughter and her rich banker husband will sell his farm once he is dead. The question for both Mat and Old Jack is: who will inherit the land? Without the proper heirs, their work and love will be for naught.

The lives of a number of characters in *A Place on Earth* are deficient in either work or love. Some, like Jack Beechum, have been good farmers

but failed in their marriages; others, like Jarrat Coulter, have outlived
their wives and become bitter and self-isolated widowers. The widowed
Mrs. Hendrick, forced to run a hotel, is angry at her husband for leaving
her impoverished. And the garrulous, deaf, old gravedigger, "Uncle"
Stanley Gibbs, and his prim Christian wife, Miss Pauline, live in mutual
estrangement. Others, like Gideon and Ida Crop, are tenant farmers
whose good works and love profit others.

The town's bachelors pursue works without love. Burley Coulter is a
hard worker who has never married or owned land. The orphaned Jayber
Crow, the town barber, has failed to use his college education and
retreats into his wide but unfocused learning. The crippled Ernest Finley
is a skilled carpenter, but his good works are also unredeemed by love or
marriage. And then there are the complete wastrels, like Mat's cousin
Roger Merchant, a middle-aged bachelor and habitual drunkard, the
owner of 500 neglected acres, who enjoys neither good works nor love.
Whacker Spradlin, the hugely obese town bootlegger, pulling his milk
can full of corn liquor in a child's red wagon, is another drunkard and
wastrel. Jayber Crow imagines Port William as a "heavenly city," but it
is more like purgatory for many.

Throughout the summer, Mat Feltner grieves silently for his son, his
pain deepened by his inability to share it with his wife. While Margaret
and Hannah are sustained by the birth of Hannah's daughter, Mat continues to experience all the stages of bereavement—denial, anger,
depression, withdrawal, resignation, and a final, belated acceptance.
While waiting in the hospital for Hannah's baby to be born, Mat has a
premonition of Virgil's death in a dream that enables him to speak of his
loss and insist to Margaret and Hannah that Virgil is dead. The suicide
of his cousin Ernest intensifies his sense of loss. Mat is consoled, finally,
by his attachment to his land and the sense of permanence he feels in his
relationship to the cycles of nature.

World War II remains the subtext throughout the novel. Word that
the atomic bomb was dropped on Hiroshima comes on 6 August, as
Mat is preparing the barns for the tobacco harvest. The news seems to
bear him along, like a man in a boat, toward the culmination of the terrible logic of violence. Ernest Finley takes his life on the evening of the
13th, and Japan surrenders on the 15th. While the Feltners are holding
a wake for Ernest, the townspeople of Port William celebrate the end of
the war with a bonfire and an impromptu outdoor dance to fiddle
music. Burley, attracted by the noise and festivity, gets drunk and,
along with Big Ellis and Jayber Crow, holds a mock funeral and inter-

ment for Whacker Spradlin, who has passed out. They carry his huge, inert body to the graveyard and lower him into the grave prepared for Ernest Finley's funeral the next day. Gideon Crop returns home to Ida, and Mat walks his far pastures in search of a cow that has calved late in the season. Life and death, comedy and grief intermingle in the aftermath of war.

The one-act verse-play "The Bringer of Water," included in *Farming: A Hand Book* (1970), serves as an epilogue to *A Place on Earth*.[19] A short closet drama arranged in four scenes, the play, set in early July 1948, describes the courtship of the recently widowed Hannah Feltner by Nathan Coulter, a neighboring farmer. The men of the Port William Membership—a small Kentucky farming community similar to Berry's native Port Royal—are out in the fields hoeing tobacco, and Hannah brings them water in the midafternoon. While the men are resting from their labor, Nathan proposes to meet Hannah at dusk at the ridge of a sloping field on the nearby farm he has just bought. Their courtship seems somewhat awkward and tentative, but after Nathan proposes to Hannah, they reach an implicit understanding that they will share a common future.

The Memory of Old Jack

The Memory of Old Jack (1974) is Berry's third and perhaps most successful novel. It is shorter than *A Place on Earth*, with better narrative focus and unity. Using a series of flashbacks, the novel recounts the life of Old Jack Beechum, a retired 92-year-old farmer living in Mrs. Hendrick's dilapidated hotel. On a pleasant day in September 1952, Jack relives his past and knits together the lives of his friends and family. The 12 chapters and epilogue pick up the unfinished stories of Old Jack, Nathan and Hannah Coulter, Elton and Mary Penn, and other characters in the Port William Membership.

Like Mat Feltner and Dave Coulter, Old Jack is a strong patriarchal figure, but his is the unhappy story of work without love, of an unhappy relationship between two strong-willed people utterly unsuited for each other. Jack's marriage to Ruth Lightwood has been the great regret of his life. Jack, born in 1860, was raised by his elder sister, Nancy, who later married Ben Feltner. Ben became a surrogate father for Jack, who in turn befriended Ben's son, Mat, after Ben's death in 1912.

In 1885, Jack bought his family's 150-acre farm from the other heirs and set the neglected land in order. A fun-loving bachelor, he would ride for miles on weekends after a hard week's farm work to attend a country dance. At a church service on a Sunday in May 1889, he met Ruth Lightwood, who was visiting her kin, Percy Clemmons's family. Jack and Ruth, strongly attracted to each other, were tragically mismatched in values. While Jack was satisfied with farming his 150 acres as well as he could, the ambitious Ruth wished to advance herself and marry well. She accepted Jack's marriage proposal but was repelled by his coarseness and lack of ambition. Jack, in turn, was put off by her coldness and disapproval of him. The failure of their marriage was "the failure of each of them to be what the other desired."[20]

After their first child, a boy, was stillborn, Ruth turned her silent disapproval on her husband. Jack was driven to mortgage his land and buy an adjoining farm, the old Farrier place, in order to make more money. He failed in this venture because, paradoxically, he lost his independence and became a slave to mortgage payments on the extra land, which he could not farm without additional help. Driven by his wife's greed and discontent, he overreached himself, losing the Farrier place, nearly losing his own farm, and becoming burdened by debt for years afterward.

In Berry's world, there are two kinds of people—those who are contented with their lot and those who are not. Jack creates order and peacefulness in his later life through his "marriage" to his land and his willingness to live within the limits of what the land can reasonably produce without being ruined. He deprives himself in order to provide a good life for his wife Ruth and their daughter Clara, who is sent to an exclusive finishing school and groomed by her mother for an advantageous marriage. Clara's society marriage to Gladston Pettit, a wealthy Louisville banker, takes her away from the farm to the town, away from her father's simple, self-sufficient values to an ostentatious life of luxury and extravagance.

With the death of Old Jack at the end of the novel comes the end of an era and way of life for the Port William Membership. Jack is a symbol of that passing way of life, of good husbandry, careful farming, thrift, probity, hard work, simplicity, and an abiding love of the land. It will be up to his spiritual heirs, Mat Feltner, Wheeler Catlett, Burley Coulter, and Elton Penn, to pass on these values to a younger generation and to try to preserve farming as a way of life. It is significant that Old Jack wills money enough to buy his farm to Elton Penn, his spiritual son and heir, who will farm it well and prevent it from being sold by Clara and her husband.

Berry and Faulkner

Berry's first three novels of the Port William Membership bear inevitable parallels with Faulkner's Yoknapatawpha County, although Berry's fictional world is on a smaller scale. Both southern novelists are regionalists depicting the decline of an old, stable agricultural order and its replacement by the culture of the city and the machine. Each returned home to write about what Faulkner called his "own little postage stamp of native soil,"[21] but their sensibilities and views of history are quite different. Faulkner was romantic and mythic, obsessed with southern history (particularly the Civil War and its aftermath), the decline of the great plantation families and their aristocratic way of life, and their replacement by a new commercial order. Berry, on the other hand, is an ecologically oriented realist and moralist primarily concerned with the protection of the land and of farming as a way of life. His view of southern history is less romantic than Faulkner's, and his attachment to the land is perhaps more intense. For both writers, slavery, violence, and land greed are the besetting sins of the South, but Berry is much less concerned than Faulkner with the myth of the Old South and its demise. His leading families—the Coulters, Feltners, and Beechums—can barely trace their lineage back to the Civil War. In Port William, the great watershed is World War II, not the Civil War.

Both Berry and Faulkner value the rootedness of southern life, with its emphasis on family, traditional values, and place. They have populated their fictional towns, Port William and Jefferson, with a full and representative range of small-town humanity—farmers, sharecroppers, storekeepers, ministers, Negroes, women, children. Neither cares much for organized religion, and ministers are often depicted in disparaging terms. Marriage is seen as a trap, at least for some, while women are the keepers of a domestic order violated by the carelessness of men. Wisdom often resides in the disenfranchised—Negroes and children—and in their intuitive relationship with nature.

These two writers share an extravagant comic sensibility. Faulkner created in the Snopes trilogy a brilliant expression of southern humor, with its grotesques, extravagance, caricatures, violence, and exuberance. For Berry, the drunken follies and escapades of Burley Coulter and his buddies provide much amusement. In an early uncollected comic sketch, "Uncle Trav Wilson and the Dog" (1969), Berry describes the heedless, destructive consequences of Uncle Trav's drink-matching spree: he inadvertently squashes the puppy he has brought home with him on horseback from the town saloon.[22] The male impulse unchecked by work, love, discipline, and responsibility wreaks havoc on the land, on life, and on human relationships.

Finally, in both Faulkner and Berry, one finds expression of the original richness, abundance, and natural bounty of the land, whose settlement by whites has been a history of defilement and destruction. Clear-cutting of forests and strip-mining left the land ravaged and prone to flooding and erosion. Slavery and the unjust expropriation of Native American lands compounded the careless farming practices and land use that depleted the original fertility of the land. For both writers, the struggle for personal and social atonement and redemption is a struggle to become worthy of the land one has inherited. These moral and ethical issues involving agriculture, the environment, racism, and violence would become the focus of Wendell Berry's essays and nonfiction in the coming years.

Chapter Three
A Return to Kentucky

Wendell Berry has written about farming from the lyrical, narrative, and expository perspectives. Much of his tone is elegiac, expressing his regret for the passing of a rural culture and way of life. His arguments are comprehensive and deeply felt, extending from personal experience to encompass social, historical, environmental, and philosophical issues. His deep love of farming is apparent in his protest against the loss of the economic viability of small family farms in his part of Kentucky and in the rest of rural America.

The problem quite simply is that family farming is disappearing as a way of life. The small, diversified, self-sufficient farms that were common throughout rural America before World War II have given way to large-scale industrial agriculture, which allows fewer farmers to manage larger land holdings but demands large inputs of energy, machinery, and chemicals. The drive to produce cash crops for export markets has changed the scale of farming. Farmers are under pressure to borrow to expand production, but unless they can minimize production costs, the cost of raising cash crops can often exceed their market price; many farmers can no longer make an adequate living. The small family farmer cannot afford to emulate the methods of large-scale, corporate farming, given the small profit margins and the huge capital investments needed. Given the high cost of farmland and farm machinery, few young people can put together the kind of money needed to buy a farm, so the average age of American farmers keeps increasing. As a result, rural communities have declined as corporate farmers, speculators, and developers consolidate their holdings, driving small farmers from the land.

Wendell Berry's concerns are both economic and moral at heart. He presents a comprehensive criticism of the methods, assumptions, and effects of industrial agriculture and proposes that American farmers adopt instead methods of sustainable agriculture based on the use of solar energy, diversified crops, organic fertilizers, crop rotation, and draft animals. Using these methods would reduce farmers' production costs and allow small farmers to compete successfully with agribusiness interests. Adapting methods of sustainable agriculture would also benefit the environment by reducing soil erosion and soil and water pollution from agricultural chemicals and fertilizers.

Berry has called himself an "agrarian traditionalist," and his thinking reflects both Jeffersonian agrarianism and the more recent southern Agrarian tradition.[1] In opposition to Alexander Hamilton's commercialism, Thomas Jefferson promoted the ideal of an agrarian republic. Farmers and small landowners, Jefferson believed, were the "natural aristocracy" who would create an agrarian republic. "Those who labor in the earth," he wrote, "are the chosen people of God."[2] Jefferson praised the independence and lack of corruption of those who cultivate the soil and live by their own industry. In a 23 August 1785 letter to John Jay, he wrote that the "cultivators of the earth are the most valuable citizens. They are the most vigorous, the most independent, and the most virtuous, and they are tied to their country, and wedded to its liberty and interests, by the most lasting bonds."[3] Jefferson's goal was to create an agrarian republic whose citizens would promote the republican virtues of self-reliance, simplicity, modesty, thrift, probity, and integrity. Some of the virtues associated with the ownership and cultivation of land—equality, industry, opportunity—would, in Jefferson's opinion, help America to avoid the corruption of Europe. The problem with the Jeffersonian ideal, however, was that America lacked the settled agricultural customs, traditions, and communities in which to realize his dream; moreover, agrarian simplicity did not sit well with the American ambition to make money and get ahead. Americans were too restless to continue farming in settled communities on the eastern seaboard when free land and better opportunities lay west of the Appalachians. The Louisiana Purchase in 1803, ironically, ensured the ultimate failure of Jefferson's agrarian dream and, with the extension of slavery to the new states that entered the Union, created the conditions for the conflict that would eventually pit the agrarian South against the industrial North.

There is a strong agrarian tradition in American letters that dates from St. John de Crèvecoeur's *Letters from an American Farmer* (1782); this tradition is reflected throughout Berry's writings. Agrarian writers have generally opposed industrialism, urbanization, and "progress" in favor of the simplicity of rural life.[4] Berry is not an economist, and he rejects the specialist mentality. In his defense of farming as a way of life, he is concerned about restoring the proper balance between means and ends, as well as the ecological health of his community in its broadest sense.

He values farming as a way of life, not as part of an extractive economy that has led to the ruin of the land and the destruction of rural communities. In his essays, he traces the history of the agrarian ideal from the earliest settlement of Kentucky through his family history and examines the social, political, and economic forces that have led to the decline of family farming and rural communities since World War II. In his defense of traditional farming practices, he offers not an economic treatise or a sociological blueprint, but a vision of the good life.

The Long-Legged House

The essays in *The Long-Legged House* (1969), Berry's first collection, reflect his intense pleasure in returning to Kentucky and his intention to live a simple, self-sufficient life on his Lane's Landing farm. The title essay is a long autobiographical piece tracing the history of the fishing cabin on stilts that Berry inherited from his Uncle Curran Matthews and eventually converted into a writer's study. The 12 essays in the book, written during the 1960s, deal with environmental, political, and personal concerns. They demonstrate Berry's development as a moral thinker and his commitment to the Thoreauvian tradition of social protest that begins with a transformation of one's personal values and lifestyle. Berry defines his understanding of the moral and ethical responsibilities of a purely local citizenship, an understanding that had grown from his love of his native region.

Despite Oscar Cargill's warning that "you can't go home again," Berry left New York after only two years and returned to Kentucky (*Long-Legged House*, 175). To some degree, Berry's decision to forsake a teaching career at New York University and return home to teach at the University of Kentucky in 1964 was motivated by regional loyalty. But his decision also reflected the pattern of 1960s social activism, which moved from active opposition to the Vietnam War in the early 1960s to the disillusionment with political protests and growing interest in personal and spiritual renewal that had led some to return to the land by the late 1960s. Berry was an outspoken opponent of the Vietnam War, especially after his return to the University of Kentucky, but his essays reveal a skepticism about the political activism in which he felt compelled to take part.[5]

Berry's thinking also reflected the decade's increased environmental awareness, which culminated in the first Earth Day in 1970. He became one of the major voices in the growing environmental movement of the 1970s, especially on the subject of the connection between agriculture and the environment. His particular genius was in his ability to combine

Thoreau's passionate commitment to a particular place and to personal renewal with Aldo Leopold's more general articulation of a land ethic—an ability that led to Berry's own practice of responsible farming and land stewardship. One of his principal concerns is misuse of the land, whether through misguided government policies, poor farming practices, strip-mining, land speculation, development, or absentee ownership. His view of land ownership is intensely moral, combining careful stewardship and restoration to correct prior misuse.

The Long-Legged House is an important theoretical work in which Berry defines the *local* responsibilities of citizenship that underlie his environmental ethic. He is careful to limit the moral responsibilities of the state and to emphasize those of the individual and the community. His tradition of individual protest finds its roots in Thoreau's *Civil Disobedience* and in a Jeffersonian mistrust of big government. Berry shows a keen sense of social justice, but he is mistrustful of bureaucratic liberalism and attacks Lyndon Johnson's War on Poverty as misguided, wasteful, and ultimately ineffective.

The essays in *The Long-Legged House* move from the general to the particular. Those in part 1 deal with government charity, strip-mining, leisure recreation, and the decline of American optimism. Part 2 articulates Berry's position on the war in Vietnam and his understanding of the responsibilities of citizenship; part 3 is primarily autobiographical.

In "The Tyranny of Charity" (1965), Berry attacks federal antipoverty programs in Appalachia as misguided and ineffective. Using the example of a skilled furniture maker who is forced to accept food stamps to feed his family, Berry criticizes the logic of federal programs that reduce the poor to government dependency instead of helping them to become self-sufficient. He demonstrates that the furniture maker has the skills and means to earn a living but cannot produce a large enough volume of rockers to earn a livelihood from his work. Not only does he lack an adequate market for his furniture, but ultimately he is dependent on the economic health of his region. East Kentucky was economically depressed because it had been dominated by the big coal companies, with their absentee owners, extractive economic practices, and failure to pay adequate taxes or make constructive contributions to local communities. In effect, the entire region was an economic colony dominated by the greed and indifference of the big coal companies and the graft and corruption of state politicians. Berry argues that relegating people like the furniture maker to the category of the "rural poor" and offering them food stamps insults their skills and dignity; moreover, doing so overlooks the ultimate causes of rural Appalachian poverty. Despite the best of intentions, government bureaucracies put programs before individuals and treat people as abstractions. From Berry's perspective, the people of eastern Kentucky are capable of economic self-reliance and should be encouraged to provide for themselves through the development of their skills and handicrafts.

Berry continues this regional economic analysis in his next essay, "The Landscaping of Hell: The Strip-Mine Morality" (1966). Citing the same arguments made in Harry M. Caudill's *Night Comes to the Cumberlands* (1963), Berry recounts the terrible legacy of environmental damage done in the region by strip-mining and reviews the feeble efforts of the Kentucky State Legislature to pass laws to regulate strip-mining and the state courts' unwillingness to enforce those laws. He is particularly irate at the Kentucky Court of Appeals decision in 1968 to uphold the notorious "broad deed form," which permitted strip-miners to destroy the surface of the land as they extracted coal without compensating the landowners—from whom they had often purchased mineral rights for a pittance—for the damage done to their property from mine waste or stream pollution. These practices resulted in a kind of war on the environment, waged with greed and indifference to the small landowners whose property was ruined. Steep hillsides were strip-mined and left to erode, barren and unreclaimed. This terrain, Berry argues, should never have been mined in the first place, and the coal companies should be required to restore the land they destroyed. The 1966 reforms in the Kentucky strip-mining regulations were supposed to require land restoration, but in "Postscript, July, 1968: A Land Set Aside" (1969), Berry concludes that these reforms have had little effect on strip-mining practices in the region. Berry brings the same passion to his critique of strip-mining's role in environmental devastation that Thoreau brought to the fugitive slave laws in 1848.

The recreational practices of boat owners on the Kentucky River receive Berry's close scrutiny in "The Nature Consumers" (1969). The thoughtless, careless behavior of a few threatens the quality of river recreation for everyone. Berry calls attention to excessive noise, trash and litter dumped into the river from pleasure boats, and the eroding effect of speedboats on the steep, sandy riverbanks. On summer weekends, speedboats with powerful engines monopolize the river. The irony is that vacationers who come for the peace and quiet of the river destroy that possibility for others. A river that could support hundreds of responsible river users is diminished by the carelessness of a few. Motorboaters are consumers of the river who invariably leave it a little worse than they found it. Lacking what Aldo Leopold would call a "conservation esthetic," many Americans are unaware of their destructiveness.[6] Their attitude is that they should be free to do what they please on the river and anywhere else in nature because they are "public" places. In treating the outdoors just as the original settlers treated the wilderness, Berry argues, we ensure its eventual destruction. We are a restless people, he observes, who cannot feel at home anywhere. We fear the solitude and silence of nature because it forces us to confront ourselves, so we fill it with noise. But we cannot exist independent of nature. We treat the outdoors as another consumer commodity to be used up and thrown away, expecting that it will replenish itself. Berry presents us with two alternative attitudes toward nature: that of the frontiersman, or that of Thoreau.

In "The Loss of the Future" (1968), Berry continues his social criticism of American attitudes about citizenship and responsibility, commenting on the relationship between the breakdown of small, rural communities and the loss of a sense of personal responsibility for one's neighbor. One result of the great migration in America from farms to cities has been a shift from personal to institutional responsibility for the welfare of others. But charity, Berry argues, can never really be effectively institutionalized. The effect has been to free people in cities from any sense of personal responsibility for each other. While we retreat into the inflated language of personal "rights," reflecting our selfishness, fear, and isolation, the moral responsibilities abdicated by individuals for feeding, clothing, and sheltering others are assumed by the government. But public welfare thrives on the faulty assumption that our personal responsibilities can be assumed by bureaucratic "specialists." The best government, he affirms, governs least. Berry contrasts the impersonality of the modern city with the cooperative ethic of the small, rural farming community, where everyone has a stake in the well-being of the community. Such a community exists through a shared understanding of limits and the need for cooperation and mutual assistance. At its best, this concern extends to the unborn and to the land itself and thus ensures a commitment to the future, which is lacking in our modern industrial (or postindustrial) cities and suburbs. Berry ties this loss of a sense of the future to the heedless, wasteful consumer ethic that grew out of frontier attitudes toward the land.

In part 2, Berry links these cultural criticisms to his opposition to the Vietnam War. "A Statement against the War in Vietnam" is the text of a speech delivered at the "Kentucky Conference on the War and the

Draft," held at the University of Kentucky in Lexington on 10 February 1968 (66). In his address, Berry offers a carefully reasoned set of antiwar arguments, based upon his personal pacifism. The advent of the atomic bomb, he argues, has completely changed the logic of war. We must transform the ways in which we resolve international conflicts because a thermonuclear war threatens all life on the planet. Moreover, Berry considers the war in Vietnam the result of a failure of imagination, the abandonment of our principles to the logic of power. World War II has made us a more warlike nation, but he does not believe that American ideals can be preserved by force. He announces his opposition to the war as both a teacher and parent, and he calls for Americans to reduce the violence in their own lives, to learn to be at peace with themselves, and to make their homes and communities more peaceable through personal reform. Berry's moral sincerity and deep personal convictions raised the tone of his remarks above the shrillness of much antiwar rhetoric.

In "Some Thoughts on Citizenship and Conscience in Honor of Don Pratt" (1969), Berry returns to the question of the meaning of citizenship. He proposes a model of citizenship beginning at home and based upon the total health of the household. Like Thoreau, he asserts that personal conscience precedes the law because it is based upon a higher moral authority. Government, he reminds us, governs by the consent of the people. Appealing to a tradition of civil disobedience based upon conscientious objection and allegiance to a higher moral law than civil authority, Berry supports the decision of a young University of Kentucky student, Don Pratt, who went to jail in 1968 for refusing to be drafted (82). Berry wonders whether he himself should be in jail as well, but he argues that he can most effectively bear witness to his beliefs through his lifestyle.

As a pacifist, Berry repudiates all the violence of his time, including violent civil disobedience. Disavowing allegiance to any political abstractions, he insists that we embody the quality of our beliefs in our lives. Before we can promote an idea, we must live that idea. Peace with ourselves and our neighbors will not be possible, he argues, until we are at peace with our place in the world.

Berry would extend his definition of pacifism to include the earth and all forms of life. Environmental destruction is an act of violence, he argues, "not only against the earth but also against those who are dependent on it, including ourselves" (87). Our capacity to destroy the environment has been enhanced by modern technology and weapons. This heedless wastefulness of land and resources is a particularly American problem, a legacy of the frontier attitude that there would always be more land to use, leading to restless spiritual nomadism. Environmental degradation and the Vietnam War are linked as examples of our cultural propensity for violence. This violence, Berry observes, appeared during the 1960s in urban unrest and violent demonstrations as well.

The wisest practice during violent times, Berry counsels, is to remove oneself from the source of the evil and retire to the countryside to live a simple, virtuous life. Practice subsistence agriculture, he urges, and become as self-sufficient as possible. Use less, consume less, waste less—avoid being enticed by consumerism. The presence of a sizable number of people living this way would exert a profound influence on the life of the country and the world. But is this merely naive, wishful thinking?

Berry anticipates the counterarguments about "dropping out." He acknowledges the risk of sounding "merely wishful or nostalgic or absurd" (91). But in fact he is grounded in a tradition of moral idealism that includes Thoreau, Tolstoy, Gandhi, and King, as well as a number of lesser-known American reformers who have advocated a return to "the simple life" as a means of moral and ethical reform.[7] Peace must transcend political slogans; it must become a permanent condition of one's life. But how is peace to be accomplished in a violent world? One must attach oneself to the earth, Berry asserts, and fulfill oneself on life's terms, through the earth's meanings and demands. Berry voices an almost mystical attachment to the permanence of one's local place, but how permanent is the earth? Isn't life in a process of constant dynamic change as it adjusts to the changing conditions of the environment? And doesn't even the most benign agriculture profoundly change the local environment? Berry would probably brush aside these objections by pointing out that his loyalty to his native region is personal and experiential, not philosophical. His decisions reflect a pastoral tradition—reaching back to the Latin poets, particularly Virgil and Horace—of retreating to one's country home in times of chaos. This emphasis on his native roots becomes apparent in the long autobiographical essays of part 3.

In part 3 of *The Long-Legged House*, Berry turns to nature writing and the personal essay, becoming less strident and polemical and more at peace with himself. "The Rise" (1968) was first published in a special limited edition by the University of Kentucky Library Press.[8] The essay is based on a canoe trip that Berry and a companion took in the winter of 1967 from the mouth of Drennon Creek, downstream along the Kentucky River, to his home in Henry County. They set out on the river during a winter rise, or flood, when the river had crested and flooded swamps and woodlands. In a nice metaphorical touch, Berry compares their launching into the floodwaters to launching into life. Thoreau's *A Week on the Concord and Merrimack Rivers* (1849), about a similar trip taken by Thoreau and his brother John in August 1839, echoes throughout the essay.[9]

Berry describes their fear and exhilaration as they learn to steer their canoe on the swift currents. But once they become accustomed to the river, they feel as amphibious as ducks. At water level, the canoeists directly experience the river's power. The eddies and whirlpools constantly threaten. The floodwaters are silent, powerful, implacable— beyond human control. The canoe trip conveys hints of a male initiation experience—something primitive and atavistic—but without the horrors of James Dickey's novel *Deliverance* (1970). The river's wildness is primarily unannounced, silent to the ear, except at the banks. The pleasure of being out on a winter rise lies in seeing the country from a strange new perspective. Passing well-equipped quail hunters on the shore, Berry expresses his opposition to those who hunt without ever knowing the habits of the game they kill for sport. In a nice Thoreauvian paradox, Berry and his companion witness the life of the bobwhite in the brush along the swollen river. The rise readjusts the ecological margins of land and water, forcing the observer to recognize in the flood the untamable powers of nature. The cries of a pair of pileated woodpeckers in the flooded woods serve as "the intimation of another wildness that will not overflow again in *our* history" (109). "The Rise" concludes with a sense of having been in a different world, offering a rare glimpse of the wildness of nature.

The title essay, "The Long-Legged House" (1969), is a long personal essay describing Berry's own gradual process of enlightenment: it is his account of how he learned to be at peace with himself through appreciating the legacy of the Camp, his Uncle Curran's cabin. As symbolically important as Thoreau's cabin on Walden Pond, the cabin on the river becomes both the genesis and a symbol of Berry's decision to return to Kentucky and become a writer. He has long associated the Camp, which had become a family gathering place for summer outings, with a sense of freedom. Originally built by Uncle Curran for health reasons and as a fishing camp, it also reflected his love of solitude and nature. The small, faded green-blue building with two rooms and a screened porch was set on stilts on the wooded bank above the river. It had been flooded in 1937, 1945, and again in 1961.

As discussed in chapter 1, Berry turned to the Camp as a teenager
seeking retreat from the confusions of adolescence—a function that
became even more important to him after he was sent away to the strictly regimented Millersburg Military Institute. He did his first serious
reading at the Camp, and it was there that he learned to appreciate the
natural world. The cabin was neglected during his college years, but he
and Tanya would spend the first summer of their marriage at the Camp,
which came to serve as the center of the "sacred hoop" of their marriage
and life together.

Like Thoreau at Walden Pond, the newlyweds discovered what the
true essentials were by simplifying their lives and experiencing the quiet-
ness and completeness of life on the river. Berry wrote his first long
poem, "Diagon," that summer and discovered the importance of close
and accurate description through his reading of Andrew Marvell's poetry.[10] That summer he began the hard and difficult task of seeing his
native region clearly and accurately, of discarding the false and dishonest
clichés of Kentucky local-color regionalism. He came to realize that as a
writer he had found his subject matter—this place was his fate—but he
had to discover what to do with what he had. Beyond the literary falsifi-
cations, his home region was, from a writer's point of view, an undiscov-
ered country. One of his most important literary models was William
Carlos Williams, whose poems had grown out of his life in his native
Paterson, New Jersey. Berry gradually developed a humble sense of his
place as he came to appreciate the complexity of the life around him.

After a series of floods inundated the Camp, Berry decided in June
1963 to move it to higher ground. With the help of two friends, he dis-
mantled the cabin and rebuilt it between two large sycamores. In
1964–65, the winter he spent commuting back and forth between
teaching in Lexington and solitary writing at the Camp, he was writing
A Place on Earth and the Camp helped him to find his voice as a writer.
For instance, he was particularly attuned to the variety of bird life on the
rich margins of the riverbanks. His descriptive passages show a keen
interest in the natural history of the seasons at the Camp. But in addition, his bird-watching taught him the lessons of quiet observation,
watchfulness, and silence. He learned that the most worthwhile knowledge comes simply through watching and waiting—being attentively
present.

That year he consummated his "marriage" with the place, buying the
Lane's Landing property adjacent to the Camp in November 1964 and
moving there permanently with his family by the following summer.

The "Long-Legged House" concludes with a series of Zen-like paradoxical insights as Berry arrives where he always has been and learns to
put aside distractions and be fully satisfied with what he has in the present moment. This discovery was perhaps his most valuable legacy from
Curran Matthews. It is in this essay, surely one of the classics of
American natural history writing, that Berry explains himself most
clearly, in which he is by turns personal essayist, natural history writer,
environmentalist, social critic, and philosopher.

In the last essay in the volume, "A Native Hill" (1969), Berry continues to explore his native roots. He points out, with some pride, that five
generations of his family have farmed in the same locale, tracing his lineage back to Ben Perry, who settled in Port Royal in 1803. Berry grew
up working alongside his grandfather and other men who still farmed
with mules and horses. Learning traditional farming skills, such as harnessing and working a team of mules, taught him invaluable self-discipline. The proper methods of farming his region took many generations
to develop, however, and market pressures constantly tempted farmers
to overtax the land in order to hold onto their farms. Moreover, the reck-
lessness of early pioneers was incompatible with the necessary disciplines
of farming. Berry quotes from a historical sketch, "The Battle of the
Firebrands" (1874), which describes an incident from Kentucky frontier
life in November 1797.[11] A group of about 100 young men were called
upon to assist in building a new road from New Castle, the county seat,
to the Kentucky River. After doing violence to the land by felling the
trees and mounding them in huge piles, they set bonfires and com-
menced telling stories and singing. This led to rowdiness and eventually
to a free-for-all, with the men tossing lighted firebrands at each other for
two or three hours until the captain of the group broke up the brawl.
Berry finds the incident representative of frontier violence and ignorance
and contrasts the frontiersmen unfavorably with the Native Americans.

Berry walks these same woods almost 200 years later and recalls the
great tracts of beech woods that once covered the land. "It is no longer
possible to imagine how the country looked at the beginning, before the
white people drove their plows into it," he concludes (190). Too much of
it is gone, literally eroded away. He marvels at the slow, steady work of
clearing the land but regrets that the frontier culture assimilated so little of the wisdom of the natural world. Humans must become conscious
of creation, he warns, or the spirit of creation will go out of them. Even
the paths he takes on his habitual winter walks grow from his easy famil-
iarity with the land.

As Berry wanders along the wooded slopes and ridges of his land, his thoughts become more speculative; he marvels at a created order so full of mystery that "we will never fully understand it" (196). He criticizes organized religion for its lack of reverence for the immanent creation and for its destructive dualism between humanity and nature. Christian eschatology focuses so exclusively on the next world, he complains, that we miss the sense of holiness and the presence of creation all around us. His glimpse of a clump of spring bluebells reminds him that much of the world is beyond his understanding. In the midst of such natural beauty, he feels himself merely a fragment of the natural order.

The land, he believes, is the ultimate reality, and like the giant Antaeus, Berry derives his strength from the earth. "Until we understand what the land is," he warns, "we are at odds with everything we touch" (207). He uses the image of a rusted lantern discarded by a frustrated hunter to represent the need to discard our exploitative attitudes toward the land. "In order to know a hill it is necessary to slow the mind down, imaginatively at least, to the hill's pace," he concludes (208). Great peacefulness and joy are to be gained from a clear understanding of the earth, of the humus that is our origin and our fate, and from having the courage to accept that clear and simple understanding. Berry literally traces his lineage and his origins back through the five generations that have sprung from the soil of his native hills.

In Berry's reverence for the natural world, one hears echoes of Thoreau, John Burroughs, John Muir, Aldo Leopold, and other American natural history writers, but Berry adds a unique historical perspective and a clear awareness of the need for a comprehensive land ethic that will instill a reverence for life.

The Hidden Wound

The Hidden Wound (1970) is an extended personal meditation on the legacy of slavery and racism. Writing in the first person, Berry recounts the story of the unique friendship between himself as a young white boy and an older black couple, Nick Watkins and Aunt Georgie Ashby, tenants on his grandfather's farm.

The book was written during the troubled period following the assassination of Martin Luther King, Jr., in Memphis on 4 April 1968, an event that forced white Americans to confront the reality of racism. According to the afterword, Berry wrote *The Hidden Wound* "in the Bender Room of the Stanford University Library during the Christmas holiday of 1968–1969."[12] The immediate inspiration for the book was the controversy on the Stanford campus regarding the establishment of a black studies program. The anger that surfaced over this issue inspired him to try saying something "too complicated and laborious to say at a public meeting, then, or perhaps now" (110). Berry articulates the personal meaning of racism for a white southerner as honestly and straightforwardly as he can, without guilt or sentimentality. His observations on the "hidden wound" of racism parallel the comments of writers such as Richard Wright, Ralph Ellison, James Baldwin, Martin Luther King, Jr., and Malcolm X on the psychological burden of racism on whites.[13] Berry writes in a confessional mode, combining autobiographical reminiscence, history, and moral reflection in a powerful rhetorical discourse. His observations combine intellectual honesty and moral urgency on the issue of race. Berry calls *The Hidden Wound* "in some ways the least satisfying essay that I have written" (111), perhaps because the issue of racism remains so complicated and intractable. He has said that he wrote the book "because it seemed to me that the psychic wound of racism had resulted inevitably in wounds in the land, the country itself" (112).

Berry confesses in his introduction to having had surprisingly little to say about blacks in his writing, although his life has been greatly influenced by them. This comment is certainly true of his fiction, in which blacks are mentioned, if at all, mainly as minor characters in what seems to be primarily a white rural community. He attributes this absence to the historical legacy of slavery: whites have largely repressed or denied their moral complicity in the continuation of racism. Both races have suffered for this silence, though white southerners have suffered less visibly and more subtly from the lingering impact of racism. The spiritual cost of racism for the South has been the attenuation of the moral conscience, the hardening of segregationist attitudes, and the perpetuation of a racially divided society.[14]

Berry examines the impact of racism on his family, whose ancestors on both sides owned slaves, although they did not have large plantations. When Berry was a child, his parents and grandparents dealt directly with blacks, who worked for them as farm laborers. Berry wonders about the moral consequences of slavery. What is the moral cost of holding another person in bondage and forcing him or her to work for you? How does slavery debase work? Berry focuses his meditations on racism around the complex extended metaphor of the "hidden wound," implying a cultural wound that lies festering below the surface of the mind. The slaveholder inflicts suffering on others that inevitably wounds himself because evil invariably rebounds on the doer. The slave system—human beings held against their will, reduced to things or possessions—is innately violent. Slavery is especially pernicious when it follows racial lines. Berry wants to heal the hidden wound of racism and avoid passing the contagion on to his children.

Berry acknowledges that his paternal grandfather was a slaveholder who was once forced to sell a defiant and intractable slave to the notorious slave trader Bart Jenkins. What was the moral impact, Berry wonders, of the sale and violent removal of another human being from his grandfather's farm? Southerners masked the brutality of slavery in the sentimental rhetoric of medieval chivalry, as evinced in Berry's excerpts from George Dallas Mosgrove's *Kentucky Cavaliers of Dixie* (1895), a romantic reminiscence about Gen. John Hunt Morgan's Confederate Fourth Kentucky Cavalry Regiment, of which Jenkins was an officer (9–12). He led a company of freelancers who lived off the countryside and terrorized the local population. Berry speculates that Jenkins was conditioned for his role in warfare by his involvement in the violence of slavery.

The greatest impact of slavery was in fostering moral hypocrisy and corrupting southern Christianity. How could you preach the Sermon on the Mount to a mixed congregation of masters and slaves, Berry asks, without resorting to a selective interpretation of Scripture? Part of the cost derived from shifting the focus of faith to the next world and creating a "bogus mysticism." Berry criticizes the Southern Baptist Church's doctrine of salvation by faith for its avoidance of the painful social issues involved in dealing with one's neighbor. The early Kentuckians gave their most fervent support to the doctrine of separation of church and state, Berry observes, because of "the clergy's insistence upon attacking the institution of slavery" (15). Southern clergy learned to confine their sermons to the next world and to ignore the social implications of the Gospel.

Throughout *The Hidden Wound*, Berry emphasizes how much he learned from Nick Watkins and Aunt Georgie Ashby. Nick had a "somber open dignified face and gentle manners, was quick to smile and to laugh" (28). He wore old, stained work clothes, and his hands were hard and callused from work. He was tied to the fields and animals and loved to foxhunt with dogs. Berry remembers with fondness the close companionship between Nick and his grandfather, who would stay in the fields with Nick even after he could no longer physically do the hard farm work. His grandfather refused to accept any limits, Berry recalls, and was constantly in danger of hurting himself, so Nick had to look after the old man as well as Berry and his younger brother. But after work there was the pleasure of good conversation around the barn as they fantasized about the future. Berry and his brother were Nick's inseparable companions, and they emulated him in their play. Berry recalls coming up against the complex racial taboos of his culture when he was rebuked for impulsively kissing Nick's hands and for inviting him to his birthday party.

Aunt Georgie, in contrast, was "short and squat, bowlegged, bent, her hands crooked with arthritis, her two or three snaggling front teeth stained with snuff" (30). She was a strong, formidable personality, full of a mixture of Scripture and the occult—by turns imaginative, superstitious, and primitive. Berry acknowledges that the character of Aunt Fanny in *A Place on Earth* is to some extent modeled after her (32). She told the boys many stories about Africa, and Berry gained from her his first awareness of the civil rights issue. She was full of hair-raising Gothic tales with the "straightforwardness and innocence of a Rousseau painting" (34) and of the lore of snakes. She took a kind of delight in scaring the two gullible little boys, who nevertheless enjoyed visiting her cabin. Berry recalls that she was a tireless gardener, botanizer, and herbalist who knew all about healing herbs, tonics, poultices, and ointments. She called Nick "Nickum-Nackum," and he called her "Miss Georgie" (38). They never married but lived together amiably. Berry emphasizes that Nick and Georgie implicitly challenged the values and assumptions of white society by living contentedly with values radically different from the monetary success ethic of white society, with its estrangement from the land and consequent artificiality.

Berry acknowledges that his recollections of Nick and Georgie may be inaccurate and that he risks sentimentality and nostalgia in depicting their lives as better than they actually were, but he stresses that his aim is merely to tell the truth as nearly as he can recall it, even if it is a very personal truth shaped by a child's mind. Berry praises the moral resources of childhood, particularly the moral candor that enables children to accept others as they are, without prejudgment. The subtext throughout *The Hidden Wound* is racism's estranging power, which caused him gradually to sense the difference between the races as he grew older. His intention in maturity is finally to free himself and his family from the destructive forces in their history.

Berry's quest to be at home in his native region necessitates coming to terms with its legacy of slavery and racism. Yet, as he indicates in his

new afterword, four problems associated with racism have resisted reso-
lution in the 20 years since Martin Luther King's death: the displacement of racial problems from the country to the city, with the resulting
loss of rural black self-sufficiency; the dispossession of black American
farmers from their land, along with high urban black unemployment;
the degradation of useful work by our society and the consequent lack of
economic justice for manual workers; and the widespread social disintegration of our communities—characterized by high crime rates, drug
addiction, violence, poor education, and poverty—that disproportion-
ately affects black Americans.

The Unforeseen Wilderness

In the 1960s, the Army Corps of Engineers proposed building a dam on
the Red River Gorge in Powell County, Kentucky, near the western edge
of the Cumberland Plateau. The purpose of the dam was ostensibly to
control floods and to create a man-made lake for recreation. The proposed dam, however, would have flooded the scenic Red River Gorge,
with its magnificent wilderness landscape. In 1967 Matthew Hodgson,
then at the University Press of Kentucky, asked Berry if he would be
interested in doing a book on the threatened gorge. Berry agreed, on the
condition that the book include photographs by his friend Ralph Eugene
Meatyard, a Lexington photographer. The project was approved, and the
two men, separately and together, began making trips to the gorge.[15]
    Berry had often hiked and camped in the region, and he became
active throughout the next 20 years in the political battle to preserve the
Red River Gorge. As late as April 1975, as chairman of the Cumberland
Chapter of the Sierra Club, Berry helped to organize a rally in Frankfort
to present to Gov. Julian Carroll a petition with 44,200 signatures
opposing the dam.[16] Such actions eventually helped to delay a $1.5 mil-
lion congressional grant for the project.
    Berry's most important contribution to the campaign to save the Red
River Gorge, however, was the publication of The Unforeseen Wilderness:
An Essay on Kentucky's Red River Gorge, a long nature essay by Berry com-
bined with stunning black-and-white nature photography by Gene
Meatyard. Published by the University Press of Kentucky in 1971, the
collaborative effort by Berry and Meatyard earned critical acclaim and
helped publicize the efforts to save the gorge.
    The original edition of the book combines 5 chapters of text with 48
photographs. The revised edition includes a preface by Berry in tribute to

Meatyard (who died of cancer in 1972) and 10 additional photographs, as well as extensive revision and shortening of the original text. The shift in emphasis in Berry's text between the two editions of *The Unforeseen Wilderness* is subtle but important. In the original edition, he presents a relatively straightforward description of the natural beauty of the gorge and an appeal to preserve it. The revised edition is shorter and more analytical, especially in its elaboration of the reasons the gorge was threatened by the Army Corps of Engineers project. Most important, when the first edition of the book was published in 1971, the fate of the gorge hung in the balance; by the time the book was revised in 1991, the battle had been won: the gorge had been saved.

Both versions of Berry's text are divided into five chapters. Chapter 1, "A Country of Edges," takes the reader into the gorge through accounts of various hiking and canoe trips. Chapter 2, "A One-Inch Journey," is a Zen-like parable of greed, blindness, and ignorance of the natural beauty of the gorge, based on the historical legend of John Swift's silver mines lost somewhere in the mountains of Kentucky. Apparently many early settlers preferred to hunt for silver rather than plant corn, just as their descendants would rather dam a river than understand why it floods. "And the world cannot be discovered by a journey of miles, no matter how long," Berry concludes, "but only by a spiritual journey, a journey of one inch, very arduous and humbling and joyful, by which we arrive at the ground at our feet, and learn to be at home" (29–30).

The thick mollusk shell of our civilization prevents us from appreciating the natural world on its own terms. Politicians propose engineering solutions to moral and ecological problems of land abuse and soil erosion that cause flooding. A dam is a human simplification of a complex natural process, the tendency of water to follow the route of least resistance in its downward drainage. A healthy ecosystem acts like a sponge to absorb the excess water. Once the land is strip-mined, deforested, or plowed, nothing remains to hold back the water. The political pressure to dam the Red River Gorge and create an artificial lake for tourism and development promised to turn an ecological disaster into an economic bonanza.

Chapter 3, "An Entrance to the Woods," is about a solitary camping trip that Berry took late one summer into the Red River Gorge—a kind of Native American vision quest to encounter the nonhuman world and purify his senses. The wilderness provides a temporary retreat from mechanical civilization, out of range of the constant sound of machinery. As he adjusts to the woods, he feels himself slowing down to a walking pace. The nonhuman world is our true home, he insists, but we live encased by the shell of our civilization. Going into the wilderness forces him to confront forces greater and more mysterious than himself. The "tonic of the wilderness" refreshes and renews him, much as it did Thoreau in *The Maine Woods* (1864).

Chapter 4, the title essay "The Unforeseen Wilderness," contains a subtle metaphoric image. The key word is *unforeseen*. We are blind to nature as it is and unable to notice small natural details because we are always in a rush. We come to nature as tourists or sightseers, expecting to find a fixed natural order and unprepared for the eternal flux of nature. But the person who enters the wilderness on foot or in a canoe is stripped of these illusions and finds the natural world endlessly changing in front of his or her eyes. The wilderness can also teach us the humility of knowing our limits. Berry shifts to an extended anecdote about a solo canoe trip that almost ended in disaster. Having misjudged the river, Berry turned back only at the last minute from a plunge into rough, impassable rapids. He discovered later that at the bottom of these rapids lies Dog Drowning Hole, aptly named for the foaming, churning water sucked between large boulders as the swift current boils and rushes over the precipice.

During another trip in which Berry and Meatyard waded down the river, they came upon a boulder covered with mosses, lichens, and liverworts, like an exquisitely scaled, miniature Japanese garden, forming a microcosm of the gorge, itself a microcosm of the world. The scene calls to mind one of Berry's favorite quotations, William Blake's mystical aphorism about finding the world in a grain of sand.

Berry's excursions into the Red River Gorge become the source of his gradual realization that nothing in nature is permanent—"there is only everlasting process" (58). The process of natural change is worth valuing as an absolute, Berry intimates. We must find a way to break through to a new level of consciousness in our ability to value and appreciate nature in and of itself. "For the wilderness, which is to say the universe, we have no words" (58). It simply is; one must deal with its stones, trees, and water as they are.

The final chapter, "Journey's End," opens after a five-year interval (much like Wordsworth's "Tintern Abbey") during which Berry's appreciation of the Red River Gorge has deepened and matured. He speaks in almost religious terms of the peace and certainty of his relationship with the gorge—it no longer feels "strange" for him to be there. He has reached an enhanced awareness of his close, unmediated kinship with nature—of the continual immanence of creation—that reaches beyond our customary inattentiveness to nature. Though he has learned to be "at home" there, its mysteries have increased. Having experienced the threat to the gorge as a threat to himself, Berry finds that the gorge has become a part of his life.

The Unforeseen Wilderness ends on a note of warning of the impending ecological catastrophe. The entire Kentucky River Valley, Berry notes, is deteriorating rapidly because of widespread strip-mining, poor farming practices, uncontrolled pollution, and sewage contamination. In less than 200 years, Americans have polluted what was once a pristine watershed. Trash is everywhere—what Edward Abbey calls the "world's grossest national product" (55). And now economic forces seek further recreational development that will destroy the natural beauty of the gorge. Berry's tone is a bit polemical at times, but he is justifiably angry at the wholesale destruction of the natural environment. He offers profound cultural criticism of our attitudes toward the natural world. He compares the tourist-photographer, who wants merely a scenic "snapshot" of a place, with the genuine artistic photographer, who takes the time to study and get to know a place. The aesthetics of mere scenic beauty attempt to extract something of value that is really inseparable from the natural order. One of Berry's major themes is that we are not separable from nature; it is us and we are it. We *are* the world, and we must take responsibility for its preservation. *The Unforeseen Wilderness* is a modern masterpiece of nature writing—profound, subtle, metaphysical, and ultimately religious in its sensibility.

Chapter Four
An Agricultural Critic

In 1971 Wendell Berry was named Distinguished Professor of the Year by the College of Arts and Sciences at the University of Kentucky. As the 27th recipient of the honor, he was released from his academic responsibilities for one semester to write, but he was also expected to give an address at the university. His talk, "Discipline and Hope," later became the keynote essay in his new collection, *A Continuous Harmony: Essays Cultural and Agricultural* (1972).[1]

A Continuous Harmony

The eight essays in *A Continuous Harmony* continue Berry's distinctive style of cultural criticism, with personal and literary reflections. Some of the topics he covers are nature poetry, regionalism, economics, consumerism, and farming. The development of Berry's thought during the 1970s reflects the multitude of intellectual influences on the burgeoning environmental movement, including Eastern religious thought, the economics of scale, ecological awareness, and consumer activism.

The first essay in the collection, "A Secular Pilgrimage," is important both as a tribute to contemporary American nature poets and as a self-definition of Berry's own work as a nature poet. He singles out for praise the nature poems of three of his contemporaries, Gary Snyder, Denise Levertov, and A. R. Ammons. Not only have these poets turned to the natural world for subject and inspiration, Berry explains, but for them nature is of primary interest; they sense within nature a shaping and sustaining spirit. These contemporary nature poets "approach their subject with an openness of spirit and imagination, allowing the meaning and the movement of the poem to suggest themselves out of the facts." Their poems express "a wish to be included in the natural order rather than to 'conquer nature,' a wish to discover the natural form rather than to create new forms that would be exclusively human" (4). This kind of poetry arises out of a "religious" mindset that senses the "presence of mystery or divinity in the world" and expresses "attitudes of wonder or awe or humility before the works of the creation." A better term for this sensibility, Berry concedes, might be "worshipful"—"in the sense of *valuing* what one does not entirely understand, or aspiring beyond what may be known" (5). The particular aspiration of contemporary nature poetry may be called a "secular pilgrimage" because it traces a journey that takes place outside of and without reference to any religious shrine or holy place. That journey is nevertheless a "pilgrimage" because it is a religious quest.

In an argument that parallels Lynn White's "Historical Roots of Our Ecologic Crisis" (1967), Berry traces contemporary attitudes toward the environment back to the medieval Christian doctrine of *contemptus mundi*, which devalued this world in favor of the next.[2] Western Christianity drew a sharp distinction between the Creator and the Creation, fostering an unfortunate dualism and making it possible to worship God while despising the natural world. Both Berry and White argue that this conceptual distinction has been one of the great disasters of human history.[3] By pursuing the chain of reasoning that follows from the initial assumption of a God separate from Creation, Berry shows how that assumption gave humans license to exploit and misuse the natural world, since it was not sacred or worthy of respect. Christians were taught to live for the next world and to ignore or despise this one. One might even argue that institutional Christianity has inadvertently fostered materialism by failing to value Creation sufficiently. Christianity, capitalism, and the environmental crisis form a logical sequence, since the instinct to devalue the physical world encourages the impulse to exploit it.

This contempt for the world has reached its climax in our time, for with the power of modern technology, humans have the ability utterly to destroy the natural world, so great is the discrepancy between our power and our needs. No other creature has fouled its environment so thoroughly as to make it unfit for other forms of life. We pay a spiritual price for our destructiveness, however. "A man cannot hate the world and hate his own kind," Berry argues, "without hating himself" (11). And those who are unable to view the earth as good in and of itself are unable to imagine a future that protects the health of the earth as God's Creation. Berry echoes Thomas Merton's warning of the loss of wisdom inherent in self-conscious estrangement from the natural world and our consequent inability to understand our proper place in the complex order of life, upon which we are totally dependent.[4]

Contemporary nature poetry may be a source of our healing and renewal. Through its ecological vision, it can point out the inherent connectedness of all life in nontechnical terms and encourage a worshipful attitude toward the nonhuman world. It can articulate a vision "that incorporates the essential double awareness of the physical presence of the natural world and of the immanence of mystery or divinity in the physical presence" (17). Berry praises the line of descent from such English nature poets as Chaucer, Marvell, Blake, Wordsworth, Hopkins, and Lawrence, and American poets such as Whitman, Pound, Frost, and Williams. He also cites the influence of the directness, brevity, and physical tangibility of Oriental poetry. Modern poetry, which has suffered from the self-reflective preoccupation of modern consciousness, can help to heal our schism with the natural world through its use of open forms, myth, and ritual, drawing us outward into contemplation of the nonhuman world. Contemporary nature poetry can teach us that each living creature is a separate, intact "center of life" worthy of reverence and respect. It can help to replace the notion of human dominion over creation with Saint Francis of Assisi's ideal of the equality of all creatures.[5]

In his essay "The Regional Motive," Berry complains of being burdened by the critical misunderstandings of the term "regionalist" that arise either from local chauvinism or a sentimental and nostalgic mythology. The South, in particular, has been prone to false literary or cultural generalizations that transform myth into fantasy, and fantasy into exploitative regionalism. Berry pays tribute to the love of the land implicit in the writings of the southern Agrarians but complains that too often this love remains a theoretical sentiment rather than a practical reality. The regionalism Berry would "adhere to could be defined simply as *local life aware of itself*" (67). It evokes the habits, memories, and associations produced by generations of stable community life rooted in one place. Such collective folk wisdom is the best way to guarantee protection of the land, and it offers a richer way of life than the restless urban nomadism of contemporary America.

In "A Homage to Dr. Williams," Berry cites the poet William Carlos Williams as an example of responsible literary regionalism. Berry confesses that he has always been attracted to Williams's work "because of his use of the art of writing as an instrument by which a man may arrive in his place and maintain himself there" (56). Williams understood that poetry is as necessary a part of the settlement of a new country as the axe or plow. To be at home in a particular place, one must spiritually identify with it, as Williams did with his native Rutherford, New Jersey (and nearby Paterson), where he spent a lifetime as a pediatrician and poet. His poems, often written hurriedly on prescription pads between house calls and hospital visits, celebrate the small moments of ordinary, local life. "What he accomplished," Berry affirms, "was a sustained and intricate act of patriotism in the largest sense of that word" (57). During a discouraging period in the late summer of 1962 when Berry was looking for a house to rent before he started his fall teaching at NYU, he realized that life in suburban New Jersey *was* possible when he recalled Williams's memorable poetry about it. Williams also demonstrated to Berry that poetry could be useful in a practical sense by helping people to understand themselves and their culture. As Williams writes in "Asphodel, That Greeny Flower":

> It is difficult
> to get the news from poems
> yet men die miserably every day
> for lack
> of what is to be found there.[6]

People are most human, and the best citizens, Berry concludes, when they are most humanely exact in their use of language. Berry would later pay further tribute to Williams in the poem "In a Motel Parking Lot, Thinking of Dr. Williams" in *Entries* (1994).

In "Think Little," an essay that originally appeared in *The Last Whole Earth Catalogue* (1970), Berry argues that an essential quality of local, self-sufficient communities is the proper scale of economic activity.[7] Berry attributes much of the current environmental crisis to the wastefulness of our national (and global) economy, whose pervasive consumerism encourages helplessness and dependency. Berry complains that most people have lost the skills and knowledge to provide the necessities of life for themselves and have become totally dependent on large corporations. Such dependency is a drain on local communities, which could remain self-sufficient if local markets were not being squeezed out by big producers. According to the Confucian *Great Digest*, wealth is produced chiefly when "the producers be many and . . . the mere consumers be few" (76). Berry cites the example of the American farmer, who is economically hard-pressed to earn a decent living because of the shortage of farm labor and his dependence on expensive equipment, chemical fertilizers, and petrochemical pesticides and herbicides. A self-sustaining farm economy would be based upon the land and would by necessity encourage sound environmental practices. The remedy, claims Berry, is to think small. We need to think local, produce more, consume less, and waste less. The principles of ecology should remind us that our lives are depen-

dent on the health and vitality of the other living systems, which we can
neither fully understand nor control. Berry praises the intensive, small-
scale agriculture that has been practiced in the Orient for millennia
without sacrificing the fertility of the land. Drawing on F. H.
King's *Farmers of Forty Centuries* (1911), Berry cites the example of a Chinese
farmer who could support a family of 12 on two and a half acres of land
with a donkey, a cow, and two pigs.[8] Many of Berry's arguments here
anticipate those of the British economist E. F. Schumacher, whose *Small
Is Beautiful: Economics as If People Mattered* (1973) also supports small-
scale, regional self-sufficiency as the best economic model, especially for
developing countries that cannot afford to duplicate Western capitalism.[9]

"Discipline and Hope," the longest essay in *A Continuous Harmony*, is
a kind of moral manifesto—a call to renewed discipline in personal life,
family, work, and community. Berry believes that we live in a time of
"general cultural disorder," and his purpose is "to examine to what
extent this disorder is a failure of discipline" (86). Our cultural disorder,
he argues, reflects a personal disorder. Berry's view of ecology—the
economy of nature—is intensely moral; for Berry, as for Thoreau, the
contemplation of nature leads to moral philosophy. Much like Thoreau
in "Life without Principle," Berry intends here "to invoke the use of principle, rather than partisanship, as a standard of behavior" (87). Berry
evinces the same moral vigor and intensity of purpose as Thoreau, practicing an environmental evangelism, rhetorical and exhortative in tone.

Directed to a University of Kentucky audience, "Discipline and
Hope" was delivered on 17 November 1971 at the ceremony honoring
Berry as Distinguished Professor of the Year. Written during the period
of public confusion and uncertainty surrounding the end of the Vietnam
War, the essay tries to establish a corrective moral tone of rectitude and
renewal. Berry offers an agrarian vision based on self-restraint, work, and
conservation as antidotes to the social and environmental chaos he fore-
sees. Berry's criticism has so many targets—dishonest political discourse,
the specialist mentality, farming and education policies, the youth culture, drug use, and the bureaucratic mindset—that his essay risks losing
its focus. His broadly cast arguments are divided into 11 sections that fit
roughly in a problem-solution format. In the first five sections, Berry
criticizes five "kingdoms" or root causes of our cultural disorder—politics, efficiency and specialization, consumption, abstraction, and bureaucratic organization. The remaining six sections offer his proposals for
reform: moral discipline, ecological awareness, rejection of consumerism,
a strong work ethic, atonement, and revival of community.

Lacking traditions of discipline and restraint, our culture demands quick answers and easy solutions, which in turn create additional problems. Our land is sick, our environment is polluted, and our society is disintegrating. Berry analyzes the root causes of our present cultural crisis and suggests remedies. Beginning with politics, Berry accuses our leaders of acting in bad faith. The political right defends not the best of the past (as true "conservatives") but economic privilege; the left permits its methods to contradict its aims; and the center has become "extreme" in its self-righteousness and defensiveness. Berry compares the level of contemporary political discourse with that of the Founding Fathers, especially Jefferson and Adams. Perhaps it is a measure of how far we have departed from their values that the comparison seems quaint and almost irrelevant. Television has debased political discourse by reducing complex positions to slogans. Lacking an adequate medium for public discourse, our cultural values have become trivialized and distorted. Without discipline, he emphasizes, there is no hope.

Everywhere, Berry complains, the old standards of skill and quality have been replaced by efficiency and specialization. "Nowhere are these tendencies more apparent than in agriculture" (95), he continues. The so-called Green Revolution of the agricultural specialists has revolutionized farming methods with hybrid seeds, chemical fertilizers, pesticides, and herbicides. These biological shortcuts boost production temporarily. But in the long run, they rob the soil of its fertility, and the only real efficiency, according to Berry, is long-term. Agricultural specialization leads to fragmentation of knowledge and decline in the discipline that protects communities and the land; hence, it is both socially and ecologically destructive. Specialization results in an intensive monocrop agriculture intended to extract the maximum short-term profit from the land. A healthy, ecologically sound agriculture is highly diversified and returns all organic wastes to the soil to maintain its fertility. The proper discipline for agriculture is ecology, not economics, Berry argues. Much of Berry's inspiration comes from the British agronomist, Sir Albert Howard, a pioneer in the methods of organic farming who promoted his ideas in *An Agricultural Testament* (1943).[10]

Unfortunately, the American agricultural tradition has been inadequate from the beginning. We need a truly indigenous American agricultural tradition, not one borrowed from Europe. It should promote methods of farming appropriate to the native soil and climate, methods dependent on naturally occurring ecological processes, not on modern technology. Our agricultural model should be the forest, which renews its fertility, not the laboratory. Farming is an art, not a science. It grows out of a cultural tradition, it requires a long apprenticeship, and it demands style as well as expertise. The cultural union of a land and its people should be like a stable and lasting marriage. We need an ecological approach to agriculture, Berry continues, modeled after the great wheel of life, which sees all natural processes as interrelated.

Berry has three criticisms of our faith in technological solutions, especially as applied to agriculture. Technological triumphs such as the moon walk do not necessarily translate into better scientific methods of agriculture, he complains, because good agricultural methods evolve slowly through long practice. Moreover, the best measures of good farming methods are ecological rather than economic. The traditional, organic methods—including crop rotation, intercropping, and use of animal manures—produce a sustainable yield without large inputs of energy or synthetic fertilizers. And finally, because we are unable to distinguish between training and education, we assume that it is as easy to produce a good farmer or a good citizen as it is to train an astronaut. Training is a process of conditioning, whereas education is that "obscure process by which a person's experience is brought into contact with his place and his history" (103).

Democracy needed two disciplines, according to Jefferson: education and land. Education would produce the "natural aristocracy" needed to govern, and ownership of land would produce civic loyalty to democratic customs and values. Universal public education would raise the standards of citizenship, and the widespread possession of land would create just, orderly, and stable communities. But far from fulfilling the Jeffersonian vision of a virtuous, self-reliant, agrarian Republic, we have produced a culture of violence, ignorance, consumer dependency, and wastefulness. The moral dangers of consumerism manifest themselves in various ways: in habits of wastefulness and idleness, in misuse of leisure, in drug and alcohol dependence, and in the fragmentation of the consumer market, which isolates the generations and creates a separate youth market. We need to change our cultural mindset, according to Berry: we should think of ourselves not as "consumers" of the world but as fellow creatures who share in its bounty and preserve its health.

An essential virtue for an enlightened citizenry is self-reliance, according to Berry. How can a person be free who can do nothing for himself? Work is inherently valuable in affirming one's dignity and self-respect and should not be shunned. Berry questions our culture's avoidance of manual labor, from the time of slavery through the most recent labor-saving technology. There is a danger in "the pseudoaristocratic notion . . . that one is too good for the fundamental and recurring tasks of domestic order and biological necessity" (115), according to Berry. Not all work is drudgery, and avoiding necessary work does not eliminate it but merely degrades it by our social attitudes. Berry insists on the distinction between meaningful and meaningless work. According to the traditional work ethic, accepting life's necessary work teaches valuable self-discipline. Mastering the necessary skills of self-provision, and doing them well, is also valuable. "A man who would not be the slave of other men must be the master of himself—that is the real meaning of self-government" (129), Berry concludes. A consumer is a specialist in dependency and helplessness, at the mercy of large corporate producers. For Berry, "the most able are the most free" (130).

Berry warns us against making the consumer economy an absolute standard of value, for "its principle is to waste and destroy the living substance of the world and the birthright of posterity for a monetary profit that is the most flimsy and useless of human artifacts" (122). A better economy would be one that values the quality and durability of necessities rather than the quantity and useless luxury of consumer goods. It would be one that values good work, quality products, and ecological health. Prices would reflect a set of values different from mere supply and demand, values that account for how and under what conditions an item is grown or produced. A less exploitative economy would create a society of producers rather than consumers. Correct economic discipline would bring us into line with natural processes and allow us to live with minimal impact on our environment. In attempting to accumulate material wealth, we have confused means and ends. A moral economy would value the life and health of communities and guarantee hope for future generations. It would not treat the land as a factory or people as spare parts. We would value farming and teaching as a commitment to the future, as stewardship of the land and of the young. Our values must become more communitarian so that we do not encourage individuals to put their own interests ahead of the general good.

Using the images of the road and the wheel, Berry compares the linear Western view of history as progress with the Native American view of life as a series of interlocking natural and human cycles. He describes the cyclic vision in *Black Elk Speaks* (1932): the basic and necessary patterns of life are repeated in a circular dance. Happiness and prosperity do not lie ahead or behind but *within* the sacred hoops of land, family, and tribe. Within Black Elk's vision, all things have inherent value and a right to exist; they do not exist merely to be appropriated and used by humans. It is a humble vision that acknowledges the mystery and sacredness of life. The world is not to be conquered for human use but lived within. There is no taking without giving back in return, since all things are ultimately united. There is no undue worry about the future or about social disintegration because the culture has established equilibrium with its environment and learned to live within renewable limits.

A truly ecological culture would be based upon two kinds of community discipline: the living memory of the collective experience of the community, and fidelity to the living community (152). Berry rejects the cliché of "rugged individualism" as adolescent bluster and argues that we must learn to reconcile the tensions between American principles and practice. To choose loyalty to community over principle is to diminish the community's moral inheritance, but to choose principle over community is even worse, because such a choice isolates a person from the community. Berry cites the example of Robert E. Lee as someone who felt a greater loyalty to his region, finally, than to his principles, and who would not turn his back on his people. Berry seems to prefer the Jeffersonian vision of community and regional loyalty over the Thoreauvian vision of individual moral protest. Berry finds in the community a necessary discipline controlling our egotism and selfishness.

Berry sees all the essential human relationships—ecological, social, and personal—expressed in the "expansive metaphor of farming and marriage and worship" (159). These three kinds of relationships are interdependent, and all are rooted in the concept of atonement, which Berry redefines as "at-one-ment." Berry's concept of atonement, which serves as a model for human behavior, contains pastoral, biblical, and theological overtones. It prescribes a nurturing, caring relationship with all of life, focusing and channeling human energy in healthy and constructive ways. The neglect of any of the three relationships threatens the whole social fabric: there is a connection between the mistreatment of the land, of women, of Native Americans, and of blacks. Social constraints depend on our awareness of the metaphor of atonement in our relations to our work, our families, our environment, and our religious beliefs. This awareness grows from our roots in a particular place; it is not portable. The social mobility of modern American life has caused us to lose the unifying vision of atonement in all our relationships.

Finally, Berry emphasizes that his moral, ecological, and spiritual vision is also practical. Ultimately, there is only one value: "the life and health of the world" (164). Practical and spiritual values are identical; beauty is wholeness; health is ecological balance; and ecology is long-term economics. Moral value is not separable from other values, Berry argues. An adequate morality would be both ecologically sound and morally pleasing. Morality defines practical human limits, found in the balance between personal interests and the overriding interests of the community and the environment, and it describes the penalties for violating those limits. The basic moral issue for Berry is one of character. We need to demand more of ourselves and expect less of institutions. "Goodness, wisdom, happiness, even physical comfort, are not institutional conditions," Berry reminds us. "The real sources of hope are personal and spiritual, not public and political" (168).

Berry concludes *A Continuous Harmony* with two short essays. "In Defense of Literacy" argues that language and literary training are more than specialties; they are necessities for responsible citizenship, enabling people to defend themselves against the hucksterism of advertising and the deliberate misuse of language by the media. Illiteracy is both a personal and a public danger, according to Berry. We must teach our children to use language precisely and articulately enough to tell the truth about the world as we know it. The best guarantee for democracy is an intelligent and well-informed citizenry.

In "Mayhem in the Industrial Paradise," Berry revisits the coal fields of Kentucky and finds no evidence that the new strip-mining laws are reducing the wholesale destruction of the land. There are two competing philosophies of land use, he concludes: stewardship and care versus exploitation and ruin. He condemns the enrichment of absentee coal interests at the cost of the impoverishment of the local communities and points out that the costs of reclaiming one section of the Coal River watershed in West Virginia will be as much as the total value of the coal strip-mined there (178). Kentucky and much of the rest of rural Appalachia have become a colony of the coal companies. Since coal companies justify the damage of strip-mining as the cost of supplying electrical power, the best way to reduce strip-mining is to reduce our demand for and consumption of electricity. Our comfort is paid for by someone else's distress. Culturally, our greatest sin has been to despise our most precious gift—a fruitful land—and it is a sin for which we will inevitably pay.

The Unsettling of America

In 1977 Wendell Berry left the University of Kentucky to serve as a writer-in-residence for a semester at Centre College in Danville, Kentucky. He would also spend the next two years as a contributing editor for Rodale Press. Berry wanted to devote himself full-time to farming and writing, and he had come to dislike the technological emphasis of the university. He had also become disillusioned with the decline of the traditional liberal arts curriculum, the increasing specialization of academic disciplines, and the inability of the university to fulfill its mission to pass on the cultural and intellectual inheritance of the past.

In his association with Rodale Press, he wrote occasional articles for *Organic Gardening* magazine and served as a contributing editor for *The New Farm*, a magazine devoted to organic farming. For a time, Berry associated himself with the organic farming movement as he sought alternatives to the wastefulness of modern American farming practices. Robert Rodale and his father were the founders of the organic farming movement in the 1930s and had done much to promote methods of organic farming and gardening.

The Unsettling of America, published by the Sierra Club in 1977, is probably Berry's most influential book.[11] Subtitled *Culture and Agriculture*, it is really a long jeremiad against corporate agribusiness. The nine chapters of close argument constitute an expansion and elaboration of Berry's arguments in "Discipline and Hope." In his attack on agribusiness, Berry returns to basic principles. Agriculture, he points out, means "cultivation of land," not a form of science or business (87). He attacks the basic premises of modern American agriculture: that bigger is better; that small farms are inherently inefficient; that farming is a business; that the concentration of more land in fewer hands is good for American agriculture; that the land should be forced to produce as much as possible, regardless of the ecological consequences; and that food can be thought of as a "weapon" in the cold war. Berry's basic argument, constructed almost like a syllogism, is that the ecological crisis and the agricultural crisis are linked together as part of a general crisis of culture and character: if the ecological crisis is a crisis of culture, and if the agricultural crisis is an ecological crisis, then the agricultural crisis is also a crisis of culture. The targets of his attack are Secretary of Agriculture Earl L. Butz of the Nixon administration and the "agricultural specialists" of state schools of agriculture who formulate agricultural policy.[12] As Berry notes in his preface, over 25 million Americans had left the farm since 1940 (viii), and the problems in American agriculture had been compounded by the high costs of land and farm equipment and the low price of farm commodities. The economic destruction of traditional agriculture would only intensify America's ecological crisis. Berry dedicated the book to his good friend Maurice Telleen, an Iowa draft-horse farmer and founder and editor of the *Draft Horse Journal*, a publication dedicated to preserving the traditional skills of working with draft animals.[13]

American farming has faced a slow, steady industrialization that has replaced handicraft and human skill with machine labor and mass production of a few basic cash crops pegged to future commodity prices. When Berry wrote, the average American farmer fed himself and 56 others; 96 percent of American workpower was freed from food production; and by 1974, 4 percent of American farms produced almost 50 percent of farm products (32). Berry rejects the basic premise that having fewer farmers cultivating more land is a sign of progress, for such consolidation of farming marks a destructive simplification of a complex cultural practice. The ideal of the gigantic, fully automated farm of the future is frankly totalitarian in its aims and practices. When ownership of farmland is concentrated in ever fewer corporate hands, the professional managers do not have the same commitment to land stewardship and conservation as the farmer who owns his own land. There is also a danger that large-scale corporate agriculture will simplify and disrupt the complex ecological cycles of nature, leaving the land vulnerable to insect pests and crop diseases that will require ever larger doses of pesticides, herbicides, and chemical fertilizers. A healthy ecosystem, Berry argues, is marked by diversity, stability, balance, and complexity—the exact opposite of the conditions created by large-scale agriculture. Our attempts to dominate and control nature can result only in the destruction of the fertility and health of the land.

Berry finds an ironic connection between agribusiness and the military-industrial complex. Many of the most commonly used pesticides were originally developed through chemical warfare research. After the end of World War II, as the defense industry and the petrochemical industry made the transition from wartime to peacetime production, they were forced to look for new applications for their technologies. One obvious market for machinery was in farming, which was still relatively unmechanized. Farmers were urged to buy bigger and more expensive machinery and were forced to extend their credit in order to afford it. Energy expenditures also increased in the switch from horse-drawn to fossil fuel–powered machinery, owing to the loss of the solar-powered energy produced by the farm-grown hay and grains used to feed draft animals. Thus, the farm lost its self-sufficiency and became not only a net importer of energy but, like the rest of America, energy-dependent.

Likewise, in place of the organic farming practices of crop rotation and animal manuring that had maintained soil fertility and helped crops resist insect damage and disease, farmers gradually became dependent on chemical fertilizers and petrochemical pesticides and herbicides. The conversion of the output of chemical plants from war explosives to ammonia- and nitrate-based fertilizers was a relatively simple operation, and such plants were able to create a large and dependable new supply of these products. Petrochemical plants likewise switched their production to farm chemicals that could be used in the "war" on pests and plant diseases. As Rachel Carson points out in *Silent Spring* (1962), powerful new synthetic chemicals—like DDT, originally developed for wartime use to eradicate the mosquitoes that spread malaria—were now applied widely and indiscriminately to crop pests.[14] The Green Revolution did boost American farm production, but at a cost: farmers had to import their energy in the form of fossil fuels, their fertility in the form of inorganic nitrogen fertilizer, and their crop protection in the form of synthetic insecticides.

In his discussion of the Morrill Act of 1862, which established land-grant colleges, Berry points to the differences between Jefferson's largely idealistic agrarian vision of the citizen-farmer and Cong. Justin Morrill's more practical and utilitarian vision of farming and the "mechanic arts." Through its emphasis on the purely practical, the Morrill Act inadvertently encouraged an impermanent agriculture destructive of land and rural communities. Jefferson believed in the need for a liberal education to create an informed citizenry capable of protecting democracy, whereas Morrill emphasized the purely practical aspects of education. The standards of liberal and practical education are fundamentally different. Berry likens a liberal education to the bequest of a cultural legacy, whereas a practical education is merely a commodity to be exchanged later for wealth or status.

As American agricultural policy shifted from expansion to productivity, the state agricultural colleges emphasized those policies that would favor large producers, often at the expense of small farmers. Berry condemns land-grant colleges and state schools of agriculture for abandoning the small family farmer in favor of large-scale agricultural interests. The very institutions that were created to protect farmers have been instrumental in discouraging traditional farming practices and ruining rural life. Part of the problem, Berry believes, is that the study of "scientific agriculture" has been divorced from the humanities and from the needs of ordinary farmers and become beholden to business and corporate pressures. As agriculture has become more "industrial" in scope, the emphasis has shifted from the farmer alone to a network of farming "inputs" (farm machinery, fertilizers, pesticides), the farm as a production unit, and the food-processing industry (where the profits are made). Berry wonders whether it is indeed possible to halt the trend toward fewer but larger farms. Does not the steady decrease of the farm population raise questions about the long-term survival of small family farms?

In his last chapter, "Margins," Berry offers some thoughts about avoiding the farm crisis, beginning with a repudiation of "agribusiness orthodoxy." Large agricultural enterprises, he points out, are able to make a profit by selectively externalizing certain costs, such as maintaining water quality and soil fertility and controlling erosion; these costs are passed on to the larger community. Agribusiness takes the benefits and passes on the costs. Berry draws an implicit distinction between internal (conventional) accounting and external (ecological, social, moral) accounting. Scientific agriculture has become an extension of modern scientific thinking—a dominant paradigm, in Thomas Kuhn's terms, that is gradually changing.[15] As an orthodoxy, the impulse of scientific agriculture is to protect itself rather than to examine its assumptions and methods critically. Change or reform comes not from within but from without, from the "margins."

Berry finds some reason for hope in the "marginal places" overlooked by progress. He cites the self-sufficiency and diversity of the Amish community and the skillful small-scale agriculture of the Peruvian peasant farmers of the Andes. The agricultural principle they follow is to accommodate diversity within unity, through various methods of traditional organic farming: maintaining the genetic diversity of many different plant varieties, crop and field rotation, using cover crops and organic manures, and producing sustainable yields. These examples of traditional farming are "healthy" by virtue of their diversity and independence.

Unfortunately, orthodox agribusiness has marginalized whatever practices are not immediately profitable, including traditional methods of organic farming. As a result, Berry claims, everywhere in rural America are the signs of greed, neglect, and the abandonment of small farms that do not lend themselves to modern "scientific" farming practices. What are the signs of a healthy, well-maintained farm, Berry asks?

It has trees on it—a woodlot—and an ordered diversity of plants and animals, and it renews its own fertility, provides its own energy, makes full use of human and animal power, and practices every possible self-sufficiency. "The healthy farm sustains itself the same way that a healthy tree does," Berry writes, "by belonging where it is, by maintaining a proper relationship to the ground" (183). He praises the Amish farms for maintaining land and people in a healthy balance. A farm that depends on large corporations for its energy, machinery, fertility, and crop resistance is no longer a farm; it has become an economic colony.

What Berry offers in *The Unsettling of America* is a cultural history and a criticism of American farming as an essential cultural activity. A lasting human culture is one that establishes a permanent ecological balance with its native soil, climate, and natural resources. To achieve this balance, it is necessary to reform our present agricultural practices and institute appropriate methods of small-scale, organic agriculture. The history of our land use, unfortunately, shows hasty, careless, and wasteful practices, the effects of which will not heal for generations, if ever. What we need is an agriculture guided by reproduction (which unites the male and female perspectives) rather than merely production (which is exclusively male-oriented). Berry concludes the book with 12 remedies: repudiating the specialist mentality; maximizing the use of human and animal energy; limiting the role of government in agriculture; lowering the price of farmland; establishing production and price controls; promoting local self-sufficiency; recycling local organic wastes; reviewing sanitation laws; encouraging technological and genetic diversity; reforming state schools of agriculture; considering the problem of appropriate human scale; and affirming the absolute value of the health and wholeness of the land.

The Gift of Good Land

Berry's third essay collection, *The Gift of Good Land* (1981), was published the same year as *Recollected Essays: 1965–1980* by his new publisher, North Point Press in San Francisco. The collection includes 24 new essays, most reprinted from *The New Farm* and *Organic Gardening*. These essays elaborate and apply Berry's more extensive criticisms of industrial agriculture, as set forth in *The Unsettling of America*. *The Gift of Good Land* draws on a variety of examples of good farmers and sound farming practices to demonstrate that "an ecologically and culturally responsible agriculture is possible" (ix). However, two obstacles stand in the way of responsible agriculture: the discipline of farming has low public standing, and good farmers are hard to find.

Both of these problems are related to a much broader cultural criticism that Berry makes with increasing frequency: our economic reasoning is based upon the wrong premises. We expect the economy to provide unlimited growth based on increased production and consumption of limited resources. Furthermore, the only economic value we respect is monetary value: for profit, we are willing to sacrifice every other value and to count the sacrifice as no loss. But inevitably we will approach a point of diminishing returns as we push ecological systems to the point of collapse. In a profit-driven system, small, healthy, ecologically sound producers are not desirable because they consume too little. Disease is more profitable than health; land is more valuable for development than for farming; divorce is preferable to marriage, since it multiplies needs; and consumer debt is preferable to savings. Our growth-oriented economy is killing us and destroying our land, families, and communities, though we persist in believing that big is better.

In his foreword to *The Gift of Good Land*, Berry offers a set of alternative economic assumptions to create a sustainable agriculture *and* economy. He defends the small farm as appropriate in both size and scale, because smallness encourages diversity and ecological complexity, which in turn sustain the health of people and land. The present system of industrial agriculture is failing because monocrop cultures eventually destroy farmland and watersheds. What if we used as our basic economic indicators the health of the land, the watershed, and the community, rather than the cash value of the crops produced? What if we emphasized sustainable production of food and other renewable resources and minimized consumption? What if everything produced eventually had to be recycled, as it is in nature, rather than thrown away or wasted? And what if we encouraged self-sustaining communities of small, local producers rather than a nation of consumers dependent on large corporations?

Berry discovered through his association with Rodale Press that what makes ecological sense may not be sufficiently profitable for a commercial publication. Although *The New Farm* and *Organic Gardening* were originally intended to address the needs of small farmers, producers, and gardeners, articles on repairing used farm equipment, working with draft horses, and limiting consumption, he implies, were discovered to be insufficiently profitable. The editors gradually changed their focus to bigger farmers, who consume more and provide a more receptive market for advertising for pickup trucks, big tractors, and expensive farm equipment. The Rodale magazines eventually grew to resemble more mainstream farming publications, such as *Farm Journal* and *Successful Farming*. Articles on how not to buy things may be ecologically responsible, but they do not attract big advertisers, who unfortunately pay a magazine's bills. When Rodale Press "sold out" to corporate financial interests, the small farmer lost another defender. Berry severed his association with Rodale Press after two years, and *The New Farm* eventually folded.

The essays in *The Gift of Good Land* examine a cross-cultural variety of examples of responsible farming practices. In his discussions of peasant farmers in Peru, Papago and Hopi farmers in the Southwest, and Amish farmers in Pennsylvania, Berry ventures into the area of cultural anthropology. In other essays, he discusses the impact of public health laws on small dairy and poultry producers, the economics of subsistence farming, the use of draft horses, new crop prospects in agricultural research, and the value of nonmechanized farm tools. Many of these essays are practical in tone rather than literary or theoretical, but all are written with Berry's customary grace and style.

As he makes clear in his essay "Agricultural Solutions for Agricultural Problems" (1978), Berry is continually searching for practical solutions for farm problems—solutions that are appropriate in size and scale, do not result in a net energy loss during crop production, and do not erode or degrade the land. The machine metaphor and the factory model do not work well in agriculture because they tend to oversimplify natural ecological systems and impose crude and destructive solutions on both farmers and their land. Industrial production cycles are never complete because there is no return of waste materials—hence the exhaustion of the land and the contamination of the environment. Good agricultural solutions, Berry argues, should meet the criteria of scale, balance, diversity, and quality.

The major problem with industrial agriculture is that large energy inputs are needed from fossil fuels once the farmer's traditional connection with the sun has been broken. Berry points out that by substituting petroleum energy for solar, human, and animal energy, American agriculture has become one of the largest net consumers of energy in the economy, although much of this energy use is hidden in the food-processing system. Cheap fossil fuel caused Americans to abandon the traditional economies of subsistence farming and local food production in favor of a larger but more inefficient system of industrial agriculture. Rather than using solar energy concentrated in forage and fed to draft animals, which is endlessly renewable and essentially free, the farmer began to import and pay for his energy in the form of petroleum. Cheap domestic petroleum sources hid the true costs of this change until the energy crisis of the 1970s, when farmers discovered that they could no longer afford the high costs of imported petroleum. A bushel of corn produced by using one gallon of gasoline costs six times as much as a bushel of corn grown by a farmer using horse-drawn equipment (260). After subtracting the large energy inputs of the industrial farm, one discovers that the small, diversified, Amish farms are much more efficient. For Berry, energy self-sufficiency is one of the cornerstones of his proposal for reforming American agriculture.

America's insatiable demand for cheap energy had already created a number of environmental problems from conventional coal-fired power plants—especially in the Ohio Valley, where air pollution was already severe and plans were afoot to build two nuclear power plants. Berry's concerns about the environmental impact of nuclear power plants in the Ohio River Valley led him to take part in a nonviolent sit-in demonstration on 3 June 1979 at the site of the Marble Hill nuclear power plant that was being built near Madison, Indiana, across the Ohio River from his farm in Port Royal, Kentucky.[16] For Berry, nuclear energy is perhaps the ultimate example of the dangers inherent in the quest for cheap energy. Living just 20 miles downwind from the proposed plant and mindful of its potential dangers, especially after the Three Mile Island accident in Pennsylvania, Berry chose nonviolent protest as his way of registering his vote against the risks of living so near a nuclear power plant. In his essay "The Reactor and the Garden" (1979), Berry outlines his reasons for protesting, but he makes it clear that a single, symbolic, nonviolent action will not solve the greater problem of the inherent wastefulness of the automobile and the modern household, both of which depend upon cheap energy. He proposes the garden as the best counterpoint to the reactor, since it does not try to solve one problem— the demand for cheap energy—by creating many more problems in the form of radioactive wastes. His motto is, Think small, think local, and think self-sufficient.

Berry examines another possible means of harnessing more solar energy by genetically improving some of our native prairie grasses to create new perennial grains and improve warm-weather pasture yields. In "The Native Grasses and What They Mean" (1979), he mentions some of the promising research being done by three Kentucky researchers in selecting native prairie grasses and herbs to improve pastures. In "New Roots

for Agricultural Research" (1981), he describes the research being done
by Wes Jackson at the Land Institute in Salina, Kansas, to create an agriculture based upon perennial grains. Jackson began with the assumption
that a self-sustaining Midwest agriculture should be based upon the ecological model of the prairie. Raising annual grains like corn requires
extensive fossil energy and results in massive soil erosion. To stop the soil
erosion, the land must be covered at all times. Corn is a heavy feeder
that depletes the soil and, as a monocrop culture, requires pest control,
whereas the balanced diversity of a prairie's polycrop culture is self-
renewing, creating its own fertility and discouraging pests. Jackson is
optimistic about the long-term prospects for discovering improved varieties of perennial crops.

The use of petroleum or nuclear energy instead of human energy
deprives people of the meaningful, craftsmanlike work they could do on
farms or in rural communities and forces them to take up mindless factory labor or low-skill service jobs; their displacement in turn generates
other social problems. Berry asks the same questions of modern agricultural technology that John Ruskin, William Morris, and their followers
asked of Victorian industrialism:[17] What is the difference between useful
work and useless toil? Between work and labor? How is human work
degraded by the machine? Factory labor is measured in man-hours, the
sum of human energy plus human time. Preindustrial work traditionally
implied a vocation, careful training, an apprenticeship, and high standards of quality and craftsmanship. These standards were maintained by
the community or the craft guild. Traditional farming at its best was
highly skilled work whose pace was set by the demands of the seasons,
not the time clock. It demanded long hours, close attention to detail,
and continual concern for the well-being of one's land and animals.
American culture, with its crassly utilitarian concern for technique, has
emphasized speed and efficiency with a resulting decline in the care and
quality of work. The modern American farmer in his air-conditioned
tractor cab may work faster than his predecessors, but not better. His
work, or vocation, has been reduced to a kind of factory farm labor measured in man-hours, not in the enjoyment of good work done for its own
sake or for the improvement of his farm.

One sees the results of this transformation, Berry notes, in the run-
down appearance of so many contemporary American farms, with their
neglected barns and sheds, broken fences, plowed windbreaks, lack of
woodlots, and absence of farm animals. With the consolidation of small
holdings into large farms, much of the midwestern farming country has

come to resemble an agricultural desert, homes and churches abandoned, the rural population gone. Berry contrasts this emptiness with the small, diversified farms of Amish country. Not only are Amish farms thriving, and their population growing, but they have survived as agricultural communities at a time when millions of conventional American farmers have gone bankrupt. The Amish better survived the agricultural crisis of the 1980s because of their low production costs and low farm debt. But most important, in Berry's view, "the Amish have steadfastly subordinated economic value to the values of religion and community" (261). They have practiced good stewardship of their land and farmed on a scale appropriate to the needs of their families and communities.

Whenever possible, Berry would prefer the simplest technology with the lowest impact on the environment. Many traditional hand tools are actually better designed for their work than modern "labor-saving" power tools. One hand tool perfectly adapted to its use is the grass scythe, which Berry ordered when he became fed up with his power scythe. The power scythe was clumsy, noisy, dangerous, and undependable; Berry found the grass scythe to be light, graceful, quiet, cheap, and efficient. The power tool, as a technological "solution," became a labor maker rather than a labor saver. Sometimes to get ahead, Berry observes, one has to go backward.

The best example of traditional farming methods is the use of horse-drawn equipment, which Berry found to work slower but often better than tractor-driven equipment. The tractor makes it possible to do more work, he observes, but not better work. At a certain point, more becomes worse. When we consider technological innovations and ask what is a good tool, we need to ask: How well does it work? What are its effects? Does it promote care and good workmanship, or speed and carelessness? Is the technology labor-saving, or does it replace or displace human labor? And who benefits from the displacement of farmers? In "Horse-Drawn Tools and the Doctrine of Labor Saving" (1978), Berry attacks the whole concept of labor-saving technology for substituting machines for human labor, thereby saving labor costs by reducing farm labor. From 1946 through 1976, he points out, the American farm population declined from 30 million to 9 million (108). But what happened to these people who were displaced from farms? Most of them emigrated to urban centers, eventually to become part of the growing urban crisis.

In his title essay, "The Gift of Good Land" (1979), Berry examines the theological implications of land stewardship and offers a biblical argument for ecological and agricultural responsibility. Berry emphasizes the incarnational dimension of Christianity, complaining that it is not *earth-ly* enough and that a valid spiritual life must have "a practice and a practicality" (267). Conventional Christianity is often too otherworldly; it needs an equivalent of the Buddhist notion of "right livelihood" or "right occupation." In addressing the question of the Judeo-Christian responsibility for the environmental crisis, Berry points to the moral difference between God's instructions to Adam and Eve to "have dominion over" the earth and "subdue it" *before* the Fall, when they lived in harmony with the rest of creation, and His commands to the pair *after* the Fall, when they had been separated from the rest of Creation and had to work and toil by the sweat of their brows.

For Berry, the story of the giving of the Promised Land to the Israelites is more instructive as an ecological parable than the story of the Garden of Eden, because God's gift was more strictly conditional on the continued obedience of the Israelites, an undeserving and disobedient people. They were warned against excessive pride or hubris and told that the gift was dependent upon their good stewardship and continued worthiness. "The Promised Land is not a permanent gift" (270), Berry observes, but a loan of that which belongs to the Lord and which He loves for its own sake. The Israelites can prove their worthiness for this gift of the Promised Land by their faith, gratitude, humility, charity, and good husbandry.

But God's love for the Creation is ultimately mysterious and absolute. It is not to be qualified by human selfishness or greed. The most dangerous human motives are intellectual pride and abstraction. Heroic pride makes human desires absolute, recognizing no limits to its Promethean ambition. The forerunner of this kind of romantic, secular heroism is Milton's Satan, who embodies abstract intellectual pride. The remedy for such pride, and the way to prove oneself worthy of "the gift of good land," is modest dedication to one's daily work and to the work of good stewardship.

Recollected Essays: 1965–1980

When Berry decided to move to North Point Press, one inducement was the opportunity to reprint in one volume the best of his nonfiction. These essays were originally printed with four different publishers, and many had gone out of print. His *Recollected Essays: 1965–1980* (1981) contains 11 selections, all but one reprinted from his first five nonfiction works—*The Long-Legged House, The Hidden Wound, A Continuous Har-*

mony, *The Unforeseen Wilderness*, and *The Unsettling of America*. The one new essay, "The Making of a Marginal Farm," first appeared in *Smithsonian* magazine.[18]

As he indicates in his foreword, Berry took the opportunity to revise many of the essays, deleting some passages and qualifying others, as well as making minor editorial changes. The collection spans about 17 years of Berry's career. During that time, as he indicates, his work "has been motivated by a desire to make myself responsibly at home both in this world and in my native and chosen place" (ix). Perhaps the best expression of that regional loyalty is "The Making of a Marginal Farm," which concludes the edition. In this short autobiographical piece, Berry discusses what motivated him to return to his native Henry County in the summer of 1964 and to buy the Lane's Landing farm. He recalls another summer day in 1956 when, just before leaving for school, he stopped on a road above the house in which he now lives and said to a friend, "That's all I need" (*Recollected Essays*, 330). His words proved prophetic, for Berry did return to buy the "twelve acres or less," gradually adding to it as it changed from a summer house to a farm and permanent residence. Berry describes how he and his family slowly transformed the farm, restoring and healing the land. His reclamation project increasingly captured his imagination as a way of living out the values he believed in and practicing what he advocated in his books. Though not an economic success at first, his farm eventually began to produce a modest return. Berry expresses some reservations about his practical accomplishments, however: such marginal, hilly land requires constant, careful management, and he made some early mistakes, such as trying to dig a pond on a steep hillside, which slipped above and below the pond. Also, because his farm lay at the lower end of the Kentucky River watershed, it was subject to flooding and erosion from strip-mining and overdevelopment upstream, which had depleted the land's capacity to hold water. Nevertheless, he can point with pride to the restored health of his fields and pastures and realize that he is still farming where one of his great-great-grandfathers settled in 1803.

Chapter Five

A Cultural Critic

During the 1980s, beginning with *Standing by Words*, Berry gradually shifted from agricultural criticism to broader cultural criticism, based upon his same fundamental premises: the insidious relationship between corporate greed and the consumer economy, the decline of the work ethic, the vulgarization of popular culture, the pernicious influence of the mass media, the debasement of language, the trivialization of education, the destruction of family and community life, and the degradation of the environment. Berry saw these trends as ultimately interrelated, all of them symptomatic of the loss of connection between nature's Great Economy and human economics.

Central to his argument is the importance of meaningful work that enables us to take part in the cycles of nature rather than ignoring them by shifting work to labor-saving machines dependent upon petroleum energy. Meaningful work ensures human health, dignity, and self-reliance for individuals, families, and communities. In his next four essay collections, Berry would set forth a new cultural and economic vision based on a combination of ecological, populist, and traditional values and would demonstrate how it is possible to be at home as part of the earth's household.

Standing by Words

Standing by Words (1983) examines the decline in language and sensibility evident throughout modern life. Dedicated to his friend and fellow poet Gary Snyder, this collection of six previously published essays criticizes modernist poetics and offers an extended definition of Berry's more traditional poetics.[1] A primary issue for Berry is the role of language in our cultural decline: language became debased as words shifted from their original meanings and language itself came to serve the needs of specialists. Berry examines the relationship between the loss of audience and the increasing specialization of modern poetry and the decline of language. He demonstrates the connections between personal and cultural disintegration in the corruption of language by the specialist mentality, which he finds in both literature and technology. According to Berry, the degeneration of language is manifest throughout our culture, from poetry to politics, and the ever-widening cleft between words and their referents mirrors the increasing isolation of individuals from their communities.

What is so impressive about these essays is the breadth of Berry's interests as a cultural critic: he moves knowledgeably from poetry and literature to farming and environmental questions, demonstrating his concern for all that nurtures and enhances rather than destroys human and biological communities. His argument that the technological mentality is equally destructive to the health of language and the health of the land finds support in a series of examples drawn from the obscurity of much modern poetry, the evasive jargon of Three Mile Island technicians, and the futuristic megalomania of technological planners such as Buckminster Fuller. In each case, Berry argues, we find a mind divorced from the external world of nature, a private sensibility feeding upon itself, lacking any accountability to audience or community.

As the title of this collection implies, Berry's concern is our fidelity to words and their meaning. The dust-jacket design features the Chinese character for "man" standing beside the sign for "word." This ideogram, borrowed from Ezra Pound, means "fidelity to the given word"; hence, the man is "standing by his word."[2] Perhaps this concern seems merely quaint or old-fashioned, but Berry draws convincing examples of the decline of public discourse and its implications for our culture. His arguments are closely reasoned, and he quotes extensively from classic Western texts, including Homer, the Bible, Dante, Spenser, Shakespeare, Milton, Dryden, and Pope. Though not specifically denominational, Berry demonstrates a profoundly Christian sensibility, grounding his aesthetic, cultural, and ecological judgments in the Medieval and Renaissance idea of the Great Chain of Being, with its explicit hierarchy and order of creation.[3] Berry defends the neoclassical poetics of scale, decorum, propriety, balance, order, form, discipline, and responsibility— also grounded in the Great Chain of Being—and applies these standards to a broad range of cultural issues, from economics to the environment. The work of poetry, he implies, is not fundamentally unlike any other kind of cultural work. Throughout these essays, he defends tradition against the cult of progress and the assumption that the past has nothing to teach us.

In his keynote essay, Berry argues that "we have seen, for perhaps one hundred and fifty years, a gradual increase in language that is either meaningless or destructive of meaning" (24). Furthermore, he continues, "this increasing unreliability of language parallels the increasing disintegration, over the same period, of persons and communities" (24). The thrust of his argument resembles George Orwell's in "Politics and the English Language" (1946), although Berry's target is not the totalitarian and bureaucratic abuse of language but the relationship between literature and culture.[4] Both writers are concerned with the corruption of language that follows from the split between words and their meaning, particularly when meaning is consciously distorted to defend the indefensible, whether it be political totalitarianism, environmental pollution, manipulative advertising, or literary obscurity. In each case, the triumph of propaganda leads to the degradation of language and withdrawal into private sensibilities, with a consequent decline in the quality of public discourse. Orwell warned of the political consequences of the erosion of language in his famous "Newspeak" in *1984* (1949); a generation later, Berry finds that the destruction of public language, like the destruction of our environment, has proceeded apace.

In "The Specialization of Poetry" (1974), Berry questions some of the key assumptions of modernist poetry: for instance, that the poem is primarily a self-referential verbal construct, and that the poet must necessarily be alienated from his or her work. He rebukes modern poets for their lack of interest in form and tradition; nor does he agree with the prevailing assumption that the personality of the poet can serve as the primary focus of modern poetry. This largely unrestrained cultivation of self-consciousness and narcissistic self-expression has diminished the estate of poetry, as exemplified by the current vogue for interviews with poets, which demeans poetry by presenting it as merely another specialization in a culture of specialists. Berry also objects to the celebrity quality of the interview genre, which tends to focus on poets' private lives and on what they say and do rather than on what they write.

Berry points out that withdrawal from ordinary life and a resulting lack of responsibility for anything but oneself are evident in much modern poetry. Poets offer no vision of social betterment, he charges, only the refinement of private sensibility. Modern poets have made a private religion of their art, with their small coteries of devoted followers, and in the process they have lost the general audience that Frost and Sandburg enjoyed. Instead of creating poetry that remains prominent in the general culture, a generation of minor poets are writing for an increasingly narrow, academic audience that tends to mirror their own tastes and concerns. This loss of audience and increasing poetic specialization are dangerous both to poetry and to society because, as Berry observes, "one of the first obligations of poets is certainly to purify the language of the tribe—but *not* merely to write poems in it" (10). Instead, advertising and the mass media shape our general language, while poets remain ignored. The so-called practical disciplines—engineering, agriculture, business—ignore ethics and aesthetics in their narrow functionalism, and our general culture suffers from a disregard for beauty, goodness, and truth.

Another of Berry's concerns is the modern poet's lack of interest in tradition—particularly the literary traditions that in the past helped to shape public discourse. He attributes this lack of interest to four false assumptions: that all closed forms are false; that traditional forms are the *only* forms; that all forms are necessarily restrictive; and that organization by itself implies order (11). Open verse, he argues, is not to be preferred to conventional forms; too often it is not organic but chaotic. Berry in fact suggests that the distinction between traditional and open form is misleading; better to distinguish between organic and mechanical form, each with a recognizable principle of order and coherence.

Another reason the wholesale dismissal of our literary past is unhealthy is that contemporaneity by itself too often implies mere novelty, while "what is needed is work of durable value" (13). Berry condemns our preoccupation with novelty as a cultural obsession. "Why is it necessary for poets to believe, like salesmen, that the new inevitably must replace or destroy the old?" he asks (18). Why cannot poetry renew itself and advance by adding to a durable tradition? "The past is our definition," he asserts, not a burden to be discarded (14). The past is valuable because "there is much that we need that we cannot get from our contemporaries" (13–14). Tradition conveys a sense of our perennial nature, of the longevity of human experience, and of the central values and necessities of human life.

Without such a tradition to build upon, modern poets are forced to turn in on themselves, either drawing upon their personal pain and torment or depending upon drugs or alcohol for stimulation. Berry reminds us of James Dickey's warning against the dangers in the "overcultivation" of our sensibilities (14). Berry condemns the romantic aesthetic of self-destructiveness, claiming that the past offers more examples of poets who wrote from joy than from torment. "A fragmented, diseased people cannot make a whole and healthy art out of their fragmentation and disease," he asserts (16). The isolated self becomes the exclusive preoccupation of much modern poetry—to the exclusion of song, lyric, rhythm, narrative, and storytelling. The loss of interest in narrative poetry implies a lack of interest in responsible action. Instead, modern poets continually allude to what Berry calls "that debased tale of futility, victimization, and defeat" (19). Berry condemns the overrefined sensibility he finds in so much modern poetry: the paralysis of intellect, the moral indifference, the unwillingness to make choices, the decadence or helplessness apparent in the work of many of the alienated poets of our age. Instead of languishing in self-indulgent introspection, poetry has the responsibility to tell the truth, to address the social order, and to insist upon right and responsible action. We should turn to the example of poets such as William Carlos Williams and William Butler Yeats, who served their communities and their nations without withdrawing entirely into their art. Poets, in Berry's opinion, should aim for perfection in their lives *and* their art.

In his title essay, "Standing by Words" (1979), Berry argues that the disintegration of persons and communities is related to the disintegration of language. This reciprocal decline can be checked, however, by holding language and the users of language to clear standards of both internal and external accountability. The specialist mind thinks only in terms of external accountability and sacrifices language to the interests of power and quantity while ignoring internal problems of quality and restraint. The danger of specialization is that it isolates us from our fellow man and from the unity of the natural world; this mindset in turn leads to a bureaucratic language of containment and control. Berry suggests three tests for the responsible use of language: language must have a clearly designated object; its speaker must believe it and be willing to act on it; and the relation of speaker, word, and object must be clear to the community. In other words, we must assume "that language is communal and that its purpose is to tell the truth" (26).

For language to function responsibly, we must have clear prescriptive standards for grammar and usage. Berry opposes linguistic relativism, which assumes that, because changes in language are inevitable, it is futile to establish standards of correctness, and which presumes to make the study of language "scientific" by eliminating concern for value or quality. Without standards of correct usage, changes lead to degeneration of the language. Again, the parallels with Orwell's "Politics and the English Language" are instructive. Both writers are opposed to jargon, cant, obscurity, imprecision, excessive generalization, and careless thinking. Both men believe that language does not merely reflect a debased culture but helps to create it. And finally, the assumptions of both are basically moral: in Berry's words, "fidelity between speaker and word" is essential for political health (30).

The remainder of the essay is devoted to a long historical argument in which Berry traces the gradual decline in the use of language over the past 150 years, beginning with the British romantic poets and using Shelley's poetry as a special case in point. He then considers various examples of both clear and muddled writing from linguistic and rhetorical claims in freshman English textbooks, literary selections from the *Norton Anthology of English Literature*, transcripts of the Nuclear Regulatory Commission (NRC) reports during the Three Mile Island crisis, an agriculture article on dairy cattle, and the writings of Buckminster Fuller. In each of these cases, Berry criticizes vague, loose syntax for often reflecting equally vague thoughts; after all, *sententia*, the Latin root of the word *sentence*, "means, literally, 'a way of thinking'" (53).

Berry's concern is maintaining the quality of communal speech, since the health of language and the health of the community are intimately related and a decline in one must affect the other. Berry warns against the tyranny of technology—that is, against the specialist intellect detached from any sense of responsibility or humility and elevated by a false sense of pride and self-importance. He objects to large-scale technological planning as implicitly totalitarian: a few planners make long-range choices for many others, who have no practical say in the matter. Too often these planners disguise their motives behind bureaucratic jargon that evades responsibility and denies the ethical concerns of the community. Berry advocates a language of clearly designated responsibilities to maintain the health of both language and community. Responsible language and behavior could be visualized as grounded in a series of concentric circles, broadening from the individual ("ontogenetic") to the family and community ("phylogenetic"), and finally to all of nature ("ecogenetic") (48).

The third essay in the collection, "People, Land, and Community" (1983), deals with the complex interrelationships that create a thriving culture. Berry draws a parallel between healthy, productive farms, stable marriages, and an enduring culture—in each case, love, patience, labor, and discipline are essential. Using one of his familiar themes, he likens farming to marriage: each requires devotion, mutual respect, and sustained effort. Much of the essay is devoted to working out the elaborate analogy between farming and marriage. As with a couple about to marry, a farmer's connection to a farm begins with love. In each case,

Berry asserts, we choose in good faith, unable to foresee the consequences of our choice. Knowledge alone is insufficient to establish a lasting commitment to a marriage or to a farm. We begin with an ideal
vision of a relationship or a place. Our original vision, to some degree an
imposition, is gradually tempered by the actual possibilities of work and
life, as thoughts are translated into acts. Both farming and marriage
require the commitment of keeping one's word and standing by one's
work. To live on a farm and maintain it productively over a lifetime is a
labor of love, dependent upon appropriate scale of farming, correct discipline, and right understanding. Good farming practices create an agricultural harmony that reflects the greater ecological harmony of nature.
For Berry, small is better in farming because it more nearly approximates
the scale of nature. Furthermore, to be sustained for more than one generation, good farming must take place in a stable and enduring farming
community. At least three generations of settled farming families need to
work the same land in order to develop a cultural memory for good
farming practices. The present American farm typically changes ownership at least once a generation.

As a society, Berry argues, we need to find the means to preserve the
traditional farming culture of our rural communities. A healthy community sustains its culture, just as good soil holds its fertility. Berry praises
the stability and continuity of Amish culture, which is built upon a field-
crop-horse-farmer-family-community relationship. By maintaining a
proper scale of farming, the Amish have been remarkably successful, but
the introduction of mechanized equipment would destroy their culture.
Unfortunately, much of rural American culture has already been lost
through the imposition of industrial agriculture, as small family farms
are gradually sold and consolidated into large corporate holdings. A culture that destroys its farmers, land, and communities is behaving as
though it has no future—which it well may not.

In "Notes: Unspecializing Poetry" (1983), Berry returns to his earlier
critique of modernism in a series of short journal entries and observations
about modern poetry. He objects to the New Critical premise that the
poem is a self-contained artifact; this attitude encourages the specialist
mentality, and a refinement in poetic specialization leads eventually to
self-absorption and obscurity. "Unspecializing" poetry would liberate the
imagination and return it from the self back to the community—back to
daily life—to imagine better possibilities for farms, families, and communities. Berry wants to make poetry practical again. The world, not

oneself, is the proper subject for poetry, he argues. The same values hold for poetry as for farming—balance, scale, propriety, order, form, discipline, responsibility—and these are ultimately drawn from nature. Both poetry and farming should reflect the universal and permanent in human nature, rather than the merely temporary or expedient.

"Poetry and Place" (1983), the longest and most complex of Berry's essays in *Standing by Words*, examines the question of the human *place* in the great order of life. He raises the central philosophical question of human nature as it has been understood in Western literature. Berry draws a parallel between current ecological concerns and the loss of a clear understanding of the human place in the natural world. He presses into service as an ecological metaphor the medieval and Renaissance concept of the Great Chain of Being, which grew out of a hierarchical understanding of the natural world that superimposed the order and decorum of an aristocratic worldview onto the world of nature, where a similar order and pattern of relationships were supposed to exist. The structure of meaning, however, was God-centered, not human-centered. Berry traces the development of the idea of the Great Chain of Being in poetry from Dante through Shakespeare, Spenser, Milton, Dryden, and Pope, to its breakdown with the romantic poets. He examines the deductions about human nature that can be made from the idea of the Great Chain of Being: human status in the scale of life, a proper understanding of human nature, and the ethical implications of this order.

According to Berry, the Great Chain of Being offered a unified, coherent worldview that checked human pride and ambition. The Great Chain of Being discouraged a merely instrumental or exploitative view of nature by insisting that humans have a fixed place midway in the chain, that human nature partakes of both the animal and the spiritual, that human reason and intelligence have limits, and that this order has moral and ethical implications for human behavior. According to this scheme, all creatures have intrinsic value and the goodness of life cannot be understood simply in terms of its human utility. The principle of plenitude was inherent in the fecundity of life. All creatures had their assigned place, and order was maintained by the kinship and correspondence of life. As Berry concludes, "If we understand this concept of place carefully and fully enough, we can simply say that to be in place is good and to be out of place is evil, for where we are with respect to our place both in the order of things and on earth is the definition of our whereabouts with respect to God and our fellow creatures" (178).

A sense of human place in the Great Chain of Being helped to check the aspiring individual mind and maintain a coherent social order. Berry views the growth of individualism as inimical to social and ecological order. Cartesian dualism shifted the locus of certainty from the external world to the subjective self and resulted in a pernicious mind-body dualism. The rise of the heroic rebel, which Berry traces to Milton's Satan in *Paradise Lost*, resulted in the severing of the imagination from reason and from the material world, a trend reflected in Shelley's poetry and—continuing to the present day—in much contemporary verse.[5] When imagination turns in on itself and abstract reason becomes deified, the ultimate result is what Berry calls "the ferocious equation between abstraction and materiality" (166). The mind freed from restraint is also free to expand human domination over the rest of nature.

The Great Chain of Being also supports the aesthetic values of balance, decorum, and propriety. Berry prefers the formal structure of neoclassical poetry to the formlessness and disregard for tradition so often evident in contemporary verse. Poetry can no more exist for its own sake, as a separate artifact, than a creature can exist apart from its place in the hierarchy of the chain of life. Berry's defense of poetic tradition shows some resemblance to T. S. Eliot's arguments in "Tradition and the Individual Talent" (1920), although Berry and Eliot value different sets of poets, for different reasons.[6]

The final essay in the collection, "Poetry and Marriage: The Use of Old Forms" (1982), elaborates the metaphorical argument that Berry makes in "The Country of Marriage" (1973). Berry's great theme is domestic economy or husbandry—putting our own homes and lands in order to make them productive and fruitful by eliminating waste and destruction. Marriage and poetry both promise satisfaction through artificial constraints—fidelity to forms and words, and the willingness to make those forms work. "This word-keeping, standing by one's word," Berry asserts, "is a double fidelity: to the community and to oneself" (208). Such forms define us as human beings. To have a life, a marriage, or a poem that is formless is to allow impulsiveness and caprice to triumph over order and decorum; it is to be faithless to our words.[7] Therein lies the problem in the decline of language: our tolerance of formlessness and chaos and our lack of fidelity to words ultimately corrupt both our language and our culture. Marriage, too, is the rhyming of two lives within the same form, a form indispensable to our mature fulfillment as human beings. Here and elsewhere in his writing, Berry offers one of the most thoughtful modern commentaries on the institution of marriage.

Home Economics

In the fall of 1987 Berry returned to teaching in the University of
Kentucky's English Department, after a decade's absence. He had first
been approached by then-Chairman Robert Hemenway in 1985, but he
was unsure and took about two years to make his decision.[8] Berry's academic schedule was arranged to allow him time both to teach and to
farm. He taught two courses a semester: a course in agriculture and literature and a composition class for future high school English teachers,
both areas that reflected his strong interests in agricultural reform as
well as clarity of expression.

During the 1980s Berry gradually came to realize that the reforms he
had been advocating for so long in farming and agriculture would not
come about without a more comprehensive change in economics and
public policy. Hence, for his next collection, *Home Economics* (1987),
Berry assembled a series of essays that focus in one way or another on the
root meaning of the word *economics*, which is derived from the Greek
oikonomikos—relating to household management or stewardship.[9] As
Berry explains in his preface, the title refers not to the high school course
but to the environmental stewardship that begins in the home, farm,
and community and, by extension, ultimately affects the entire planet.
Aristotle distinguished between "*chrematistics*" and "*oikonomia*" as short-
term versus long-term economic activity. As Herman E. Daly and John
B. Cobb note in *For the Common Good, oikonomia* can also be understood as
including those economic policies that view "the market from the perspective of the total needs of the community" (158)[10]

In his pursuit of agricultural reform, Berry has gradually developed a
coherent social philosophy that values stable farm ownership, home-cen-
tered family life, self-sufficient communities, small-scale technology,
decreased energy use, sustainable agriculture, protection of the natural
environment, comprehensive educational reform, and a decrease in government and corporate interference in local affairs. In broad terms, he
favors a change away from the self-centered individualism that has led
Americans to favor careers, professionalism, and upward mobility over
service to their communities. For Berry, these changes represent not so
much a political agenda as a social agenda for the renewal of sustainable
agriculture. His arguments attempt to define an agricultural ethic based
upon an appropriate understanding of humanity's place in the world.

Berry dedicated *Home Economics* to Wes Jackson, his good friend and
the founder of the Land Institute in Kansas.[11] As Berry indicates in his

preface, these 14 essays are a series of "trials" or "attempts"—reflecting the etymology of the word *essay* (French: *essai*, to try or attempt)—to construct an argument that he began 20 years before, one that articulates his sense of human dependence upon "a pattern, an all-inclusive form, that we partly understand. The argument, therefore, is an effort to describe responsibility" (ix). This effort necessarily involves a study of connections, which Berry finds both endlessly fascinating and an essential part of our self-preservation. He acknowledges that the book may repeat some themes and topics, but he also points out that his pattern of argument is like an "irregular spiral": he revisits old subjects with new insights (x). Berry likens his essays to extensions of conversations he has had with books, friends, and strangers. Once again, most of these essays first appeared in magazine publications.

Berry's short "Letter to Wes Jackson" (1982), which opens the collection, stresses the randomness and unknowability of nature, which Berry speaks of as a "mystery" (4). There is a pattern to nature, Berry asserts, and we must respect it even if we do not fully recognize it. Any comprehensive definition of agriculture must take account of this mystery.

"Getting along with Nature" (1982) emphasizes that the natural and the human are not two separate estates. Each realm by itself is insufficient for human life and needs the other. Unfortunately, humans cannot live in nature without changing it, but in this respect we are no different from other creatures, from termites to beavers, who also alter their environment. In fact, all creatures both depend upon nature and alter it. "What we call nature is," Berry observes, "in a sense, the sum of the changes made by all the various creatures and natural forces in their intricate actions and influences upon each other and upon their places" (7). But unlike other creatures, humans are capable of choosing "the kind and scale of the difference they make" (7). Too small a difference may diminish their humanity, while too great a difference diminishes nature and ultimately destroys humans themselves. Nature, Berry concludes, is "our limit and measure" (8). Our proper relationship with nature should be cooperation, not opposition. What Berry seems to be introducing here is an idea of nature based on the dynamic equilibrium of ecosystems and on the optimal carrying capacity of the land. Healthy ecosystems maintain their diversity. We cannot have a healthy agriculture apart from the health of the soil, which includes all of the invertebrates and microorganisms that carry out "the fundamental work of decomposition, humus making, water storage, and drainage" (11). The appropriate scale of human use enriches the environment, especially at the margins of fields and woods and in desert oases, hedgerows, streams, and marshes. Humans and animals can work for each other's mutual benefit, but doing so requires wisdom, restraint, and the proper scale of activity, embedded in cultural traditions. Wilderness must be preserved locally as well as nationally, in small lots and corners of vacant land where nature can be allowed to take its course. Our agricultural practices need to imitate those of nature as much as possible. "It is good to have Nature working for you," observed an old sheep breeder, because "she works for a minimum wage" (19).

In "Preserving Wildness" (1985), Berry extends this argument, asserting that, for humans, wildness and domesticity are actually inseparable. Having eliminated most of their competitors, humans are now the top predator in most of the world's food chains, and we have directly or indirectly appropriated almost 40 percent of the terrestrial food supply.[12] To polarize the environmental debate between wilderness preservation and development is not helpful, Berry argues, because it blurs the fundamental issue of our necessary connection with the rest of life. To some degree we must live at the expense of other creatures, but the rest of creation does not exist primarily for our use. Nature and culture, wildness and domesticity are complementary influences. Since we are social, not solitary creatures, we derive our humanity from our culture, not from nature, yet we depend upon nature for our survival. Though we cannot return to nature entirely, we must try to preserve wildness as the source of our domesticity. "The only thing we have to preserve nature with is culture," Berry observes, and "the only thing we have to preserve wildness with is domesticity" (143). Preserving nature means more than protecting wilderness areas; it involves the careful and thrifty use of raw materials and the encouragement of good workmanship so that our products are well crafted and durable. Instead of depleting the world's resources, we should use no more than a sustainable yield.

Our present economy, in contrast, preys upon both nature and human society. We are not even honest materialists, Berry observes, since we do not value material products for their quality, as did the Shakers, but rather value the consumption of disposable items, which boosts the gross national product (GNP). Our economy is hardly spiritual, but neither is it, according to Berry, materialistic; he labels it abstract, based upon money and power. It thrives upon the creation of endless consumer wants that can never be satisfied. A better economy would unite the practical and the spiritual. It would look to nature to determine the proper economic use of a place.

In "Two Economies" (1983), Berry criticizes our money economy for not being comprehensive enough. Dependent upon systems it does not comprehend, our economy tends to destroy them. He proposes instead a broader economy of life that he calls "the Kingdom of God," the Tao, or the Great Economy, suggesting that "we live within order and that this order is both greater and more intricate than we can know" (55). This order is at once ecological and moral. Within the Great Economy is the little economy of human monetary transactions, but the Great Economy would always have priority and determine the kind and scale of human activity. Value would originate in the Great Economy rather than in our monetary economy. Human restraint would be imposed by respect for this greater order of which we are a small part. Cultural sanctions would enforce necessary limits on individual greed and selfishness. Thus envisioned, the Great Economy could last indefinitely, unlike the human economy, which diminishes what it uses without replenishment. Berry likens the contrast between the human economy and the Great Economy to the difference between the golden egg and the goose that laid it.

Berry also draws an analogy to the use and regeneration of topsoil. A healthy ecosystem can both live upon and generate new topsoil, which is produced by the life dying into it. Humans, by contrast, use and deplete topsoil but cannot make it without the assistance of nature. Furthermore, good topsoil is only a small part of the complex ecosystem of a farm. One of the basic principles of ecology is that diversity increases carrying capacity. Nature enriches itself within its physical limits by diversification, by reaching out into every available niche that will support life. Within this vast diversity is an overall harmony and unity. The human economy, by contrast, divides, simplifies, and ultimately destroys this great web of life. We are willing to sacrifice the diversity of life in the Great Economy in order to sustain the growth of our little economy.

As Berry indicates in "A Nation Rich in Natural Resources" (1985), we do not manage Earth's household very well because we lack a comprehensive measurement of economic gains and losses. Too often the gains are made by the wealthy and powerful, who are far removed from the full impact of their activities. Waste is institutionalized because our false accounting withholds value from human or natural resources until they are transformed into a market commodity. There are two opposing meanings of resource, Berry indicates, something renewable and something expendable, and we choose the latter. Nature is seen merely as a source of raw materials to be transformed into something valuable. "But when nothing is valued for what it is," Berry observes, "everything is destined to be wasted" (135–36). Instead of being recycled, industrial and agricultural "waste" becomes a primary source of pollution.

A major theme that emerges in *Home Economics* is the defense of the home and the community against rampant individualism and careerism, which would sacrifice healthy local economies to abstract market values. In "Higher Education and Home Defense" (1983), Berry points out the irony of NRC members appearing at a local hearing to defend the building of a nuclear power plant in Marble Hill, Indiana, even though not one of them lived within 50 miles of the proposed plant. Their professional interests dictated that they support this proposal, regardless of its impact on the local community. Unfortunately, such behavior is not at all unusual. Local life is continually being disrupted by the actions of powerful people who live beyond the bad effects of their work. "A powerful class of itinerant professional vandals is now pillaging the country and laying it waste," Berry concludes (50). Unfortunately, these "professional vandals" are practicing the intellectual and elitist careerism they learned in college. Instead of encouraging selfish upward mobility, higher education ought to encourage young people to return to their communities. Americans view education as a commodity, however, as something to be gained in order to make money, not to promote the general good.

In "Property, Patriotism, and National Defense" (1984), Berry examines the root meanings of these terms. What quality of life is worth the ultimate sacrifice of one's life? Humans will instinctively defend their homes or communities, but they have to be conditioned to accept broader abstractions such as patriotism and national defense. As Berry evaluates the impact of the cold war, he observes that the nuclear policy of mutually assured destruction (MAD) may have defeated Leonid Brezhnev and brought about the demise of the Soviet Union, but we have paid a heavy domestic price in the form of high taxes, inflation, spiraling national debt, and the increasing gap between rich and poor. The major beneficiary has been the military-industrial complex, while the nation as a whole has suffered a decline in character and morale.

Berry objects not to the idea of national defense but to a policy whose "economic and moral costs have all become so extreme as to be unimaginable" (101). Our nation was well defended from the Revolutionary War through World War II because we had a country that was worth defending. It was a nation of small communities and small businesses with "a broad, democratic distribution of usable property" (103). Since

World War II, land and wealth have become concentrated in ever fewer hands, with a corresponding loss of opportunity and vitality in small communities. A sound defense policy ought to be based on widespread and equitable economic opportunities rooted in local communities. Exactly the opposite occurred during the 1980s as millions of Americans lost their jobs, homes, farms, and land as a result of the economic dislocations caused by corporate mergers, layoffs, plant closings, and bank failures. Above all, the growing national debt puts the federal government in direct competition for capital with ordinary people. Berry demonstrates his economic populism in his perceptive criticisms of the economic trends of the 1980s and their impact on middle- and working-class Americans.[13] "People, as history shows, will fight willingly and well to defend what they perceive as their own," Berry observes. "But how willingly and how well will they fight to defend what has already been taken from them?" (111).

Chief among those values worth defending is the idea of the family farm. As Berry observes in "A Defense of the Family Farm" (1986), it is an idea that should not need defending but has in fact been debated since Jefferson and Hamilton argued over whether America would be an agrarian or mercantile society. Would the land and wealth of America be shared equitably or held by a small elite? The family farm embodies the agrarian ideal of a nation of small, independent landowners. Democratic property ownership ensures that political power will be shared equally as well. When market forces redistribute land and property, wealth is often concentrated in corporate hands, in accord with the legal fiction that a corporation has the same standing as a private citizen.

With the demise of the family farm, property ownership and political power have shifted from individuals to corporations, and the very nature of work has been demeaned as well. A small farmer or craftsman who is fully responsible for his or her work lends a dignity and quality to that work. Berry cites the remarks of the English social critic Eric Gill about the decline of labor from *making* to *doing*, which results in degradation both of products and of workers' minds (165–66). Industrialization depreciates work, a trend that began in eighteenth-century England with the Enclosure Acts, which destroyed rural self-sufficiency and community and forced the landless to seek work in the mines and urban factories.[14] The implication is clear: division of labor destroys communities. An analogous movement occurred in America for 25 years after World War II when one million farm families were forced from their land each year. About 72,800 families still leave their farms each year, leaving only 3 percent of the American population on the farm (104).

Through the dismemberment of work and the degradation of our minds as workers, we are denied the realization of our vocation through our labor. Ideally, our spiritual calling is answered through our work; we become artists by working with our hands on a task from start to finish. The family farm is one of the last places left where such unity of work is still possible. For Berry, this realization of ourselves through our work constitutes one of the primary values of the family farm. If the family farm is failing, then the values and the community that supported it must also be failing. Our culture has changed by accepting industrial values, which assert that value equals price; that all relations are mechanical; and that competition is the primary human motive (168). For Berry, to use the industrial economy as the universal standard is to commit what Alfred North Whitehead called "the fallacy of misplaced concreteness."[15] The problem with economic indicators such as the GNP, as some economists warn, is that "conclusions are drawn about the real world by deduction from abstractions with little awareness of the dangers involved."[16] When the health of the economy is measured by the abstract circular flow of national product and income in a competitive market that ignores the well-being of the individual, the community, and the biosphere, then one ends up measuring an abstraction— money—as an absolute value. Such an economy will be divorced from all restraining principles of government, morality and religion. "We assume that we can have an exploitive, ruthlessly competitive, profit-for-profit's-sake economy," Berry muses, "and yet remain a decent and a democratic nation, as we still apparently wish to think ourselves" (169). Perhaps the destruction of the family farm over the past 40 years indicates that we are neither.

Berry blames the demise of the family farm on collusion between land-grant colleges, agribusiness corporations, and government agencies to support policies that actively discourage small family farms. But farmers themselves have also subscribed to the fantasy that "big is better" and have chosen to borrow heavily at high interest rates to expand their land and production instead of practicing thrift and self-reliance and showing concern for their neighbors.

In a related article not included in *Home Economics*, "Whose Head Is the Farmer Using? Whose Head Is Using the Farmer?" (1984), Berry demonstrates that the industrial "solutions" to the farming crisis are no solutions at all.[17] Good traditional farming demands close attention to one's work. It calls for a continuous set of complex judgments about when and how much to do given the variables of soil conditions, climate, weather, and market. The agricultural industry and experts from the U.S. Department of Agriculture are ready to do that thinking for the farmer, but he must do it for himself. A good traditional farmer must understand the details of crop rotation, livestock breeding and rearing, and sound conservation practices. He must understand the carrying capacity of his land and not overextend himself, and he must constantly maintain a balance between crops and livestock. The able farmer must be a master of both economics and ecology. Sustainable farming practices must come from his direct experience on his own land. No one else can do his thinking for him. A farmer who owns, works, and knows his own land obviously has more of a commitment to good farming practices than a salaried farmer working for an absentee or corporate owner.

But even in the best of circumstances, good farming practices must be supported by the community. In his essay "Does Community Have a Value?" (1986), Berry reminisces about his native community of Port Royal, Kentucky, in the years before World War II. This neighborhood consisted of 9 subsistence farms and households, ranging from 37 to 100 acres, with an average gross income of no more than $1,000 a year (180–81). Berry's friends Loyce and Owen Flood moved into this neighborhood as newlyweds in 1938 and were immediately accepted by their neighbors. The women taught Loyce domestic skills, while the men taught Owen farming skills. Each family kept a separate household, but some of the hardest work was done communally. Made durable and strong through the local customs of close interdependence, this subsistence economy could have continued indefinitely, but unfortunately, it no longer exists. After World War II it was gradually absorbed into the greater regional and national economy, and the local community declined. Port Royal is still inhabited, but its citizens are no longer a close-knit community. "The place is no longer central to its own interest and its own economy," Berry observes (184). The fate of Port Royal is the fate of much of rural America, which has become, in Berry's words, a "colony" of the industrial economy (185). Colonialism is by its very nature extractive and exploitative; it has no interest in maintaining strong local economies or communities. Its interest is in promoting individual consumption by destroying "the principle of local self-sufficiency" (186). In contrast, the Amish have resisted these pressures by maintaining their economic interdependence within their local communities. Berry compares two farms: a large Ohio industrial farm of 640 acres has a gross income of $200,000 and an average net profit of 2 percent; the 123 acres of the Amish farmer David Kline gross only $50,000, but 50 percent of that is net profit (187–90). If the 640-acre farm were broken up into five small farms the size of Kline's and were run by the Amish, the human population would increase from 5 to about 25, and more important, each small farm could net $5,000 more than the corresponding portion of the original large farm, with a total increase of $25,000 in farm income for the region (190). Such a transition would impose limits of scale on each individual, but in exchange it would strengthen and rebuild the local economy. Berry concludes, "The local community must understand itself finally as a community of interest" in which the natural and human communities support each other (192).

What Are People For?

What Are People For? (1990) turned out to be the last new title that Berry published with North Point Press; the publishing house issued no more new book titles after the publication of its spring 1991 list.[18] North Point had been founded in 1980 by William Turnbull and Jack Shoemaker in an attempt to create a small, high-quality American publishing firm, but financial difficulties, stemming in part from their insistence on high standards, forced them to seek a buyer by 1990.[19] When they could not find a buyer, the firm decided to fold.

By 1990 North Point Press held the publishing rights to all of Berry's books; once it ceased publishing new titles, distribution of those books became a problem. If his in-print books were to continue to be sold, Berry needed to find a new publisher. He first tried the University Press of Kentucky, then settled with Pantheon Books, a division of Random House. In the meantime, Farrar, Straus & Giroux agreed to acquire North Point's backlist titles in 1992.[19] In addition, Gnomon Press in Frankfort, Kentucky, has republished some of his books.

What Are People For? is a collection of 22 poems, essays, reviews, and literary appreciations, dedicated to Berry's friend and colleague at the University of Kentucky, Gurney Norman.[20] The book is divided into three sections, the first containing "Damage" and "Healing," each a set of short proverbs and observations—resembling William Blake's proverbs—that describe Berry's consternation and regret at having too hastily decided to

dig a stock pond on a steep hillside on his farm. The land above the pond
slid into the pond and damaged the hillside. Berry used this incident to
reflect on man's destructiveness and nature's healing.

The second part of *What Are People For?* contains six reviews and
essays. The theme of regionalism, or a community of the soil, unites
these works—some of Berry's finest literary criticism—in which he honors the Alabama sharecropper Nate Shaw, the Kentucky lawyer and
writer Harry Caudill, and Edward Abbey, Wallace Stegner, Norman
Maclean, and Mark Twain. All of these men tenaciously loved their
native regions and were willing to defend and honestly express the life of
those regions. Berry also admires the character and integrity of each
man. One is struck by the range and power of Berry's literary criticism,
in both his attentive reading and his ability to enter into a text and
amplify its meaning for his readers.

"Wallace Stegner and the Great Community" is a courteous tribute to
the writer who was Berry's teacher and mentor at Stanford. The essay
conveys a sense of Berry's desire to live up to Stegner's high expectations
for him. Berry praises Stegner as a talented and influential creative writing teacher who taught by example. Stegner set high standards for all his
students and expected work to be completed without excuse. "He com-
mended generously where commendation was due" (51), Berry recalls,
but "one thing he did not do was encourage us too much" (52). Stegner
knew enough about the art of writing to know how much his students
still had to learn. In Stegner's classes, there were no formulas or shortcuts to becoming a good writer. The emphasis was always on good
workmanship. Stegner had been teaching at Stanford since 1946 and
had had hundreds of students, but he never claimed any credit for their
success. How does one measure the influence of such a teacher? "A
teacher, finally, has nothing to go on but faith," Berry concludes, "a student nothing to offer in return but testimony" (54).

Berry praises Stegner as a responsible regionalist who has extensively
studied the history of the American West and both watched and protected his region.[21] For Stegner, history is both immediate experience and
cultural memory. Rather than exploiting his region, he has written about
it in a precise and distinctive way, avoiding the dangers of "regionalism." Berry acknowledges his debt to Stegner in his tribute: "I feel
strongly the need for the sort of regional identification and commitment
that is exemplified in Mr. Stegner's work" (56).

"Style and Grace" offers an incisive comparison between Hemingway's "Big Two-Hearted River" (1925) and Norman Maclean's *A River*

Runs through It (1976). Berry demonstrates how Hemingway's story eludes grace by refusing to deal with the protagonist's pain and bewilderment, while Maclean's novel reveals the working of grace through its clear and forthright treatment of the mystery of a human life gone wrong. Berry announces, "Works of art participate in our lives; we are not just distant observers of *their* lives" (64). Sometimes this reciprocal relationship can take the form of a conversation with a work of art. Berry considers the moral and aesthetic dimensions of Hemingway's story; while finding it a triumph of modernist style, he finds it deficient in moral perception because of Nick Adams's refusal to face himself. The moral problem lies in the story's ending. Through his close reading, Berry focuses on Hemingway's choice of the word *tragic* to describe Nick's fishing prospects had he not turned back from the river running into the dark swamp. Berry asks, why would the fishing be "tragic"? The reader has not been given enough information about Nick Adams to validate this claim. Nick has no personal history, no family or community, no personal attachments. By avoiding the issue of what troubles Nick and focusing on the specific details of fly-fishing, Hemingway creates a pure but reductive style. The story's refusal to go into the dark swamp separates aesthetics from ethics. As Berry concludes, "It deals with what it does not understand by leaving it out" (66).

On the whole, Berry prefers Maclean's *A River Runs through It*. Here, fly-fishing is considered as an art form to be thoroughly mastered, not as an escape. It also represents the connective power of culture, passed on from father to son. The whole story takes place in a moral "swamp" of sorts, in the tangle of human relations. But Berry argues that the narrator's struggle to be his brother's keeper makes Maclean's novel a profoundly religious story. It is also a story about grace and redemption, as they are understood within Presbyterian doctrine. The father is a good fly fisherman and a minister; Paul, the younger son, is a superb fly fisherman but also a compulsive gambler with a self-destructive instinct. In the triumph of his art, his mastery of fly-fishing, Paul recovers the grace necessary for redemption. A halo of reflected mist hangs over his head as he fishes from a rock in the middle of the river. Maclean draws an explicit parallel between fishing and religion, art and grace. Despite the tragedy of Maclean's story, catharsis is to be gained in the joy of memory and retelling. In Hemingway's story, art triumphs over life, while in Maclean's story, art remains subordinate to the moral perspective of the story. Berry's preference tells us much about his attitude toward his own art.

"Writer and Region" (1987) offers a provocative criticism of the conclusion to Twain's *Huckleberry Finn* (1884). For Berry, the last 11 chapters fail not because of any artistic lapse but because of Huck's failure to accept any version of community life. While his earlier escape from the pieties of Miss Watson may have been understandable, his decision "to light out for the Territory"—that is, the book's failure "to imagine a responsible, adult community life" (77)—had profound consequences for subsequent American writers. Berry delineates various intellectual territories of escape that American writers have chosen— alienation, expatriation, self-righteousness, despair, abstraction—and contrasts these evasions of community with the warm portrait of Maine community life in Sarah Orne Jewett's *The Country of the Pointed Firs* (1896).

The 12 essays in part 3 of *What Are People For?* all broadly deal with the issue of ecology and economics. "God and Country" marks an escalation of Berry's criticism of institutional Christianity for its failure to address the environmental crisis. Berry charges that "organized Christianity" has avoided dealing with economic justice because of its dependence on the economy. The problem stems from the institutional nature of the modern church, with its denominational hierarchy organized like the spiritual counterpart of a modern corporation. As an institution, the church is living off the land rather than teaching people how to live with it. Berry excoriates the practice of tithing, which amounts to an expropriation of the labor of others and a tax on the land. And he questions the practice of sending young ministers to rural congregations, which they promptly leave as soon as they have gathered enough experience to qualify for more affluent suburban churches. Berry calls for a renewal of Christian stewardship in the form of usufruct, the responsible use of property belonging to God. Usufruct builds community; usury, in contrast, destroys community by substituting greed for generosity and charging a price for one's neighborliness.

In "A Practical Harmony," Berry honors the work of three outstanding horticulturists, Liberty Hyde Bailey, J. Russell Smith, and Sir Albert Howard, all of whom stressed the importance of organic farming and arboriculture on hilly land.[22] Each taught that the *"farming should fit the land"* (106). Trees are an ideal crop for steep or eroded land because they are perennials and their roots hold the soil, which does not need to be disturbed. Each of these agricultural writers—Bailey, Smith, and

Howard—viewed nature as an instructor and judge of the most appropriate agriculture for a given region. Berry honors them for seeking "a harmony between the human economy and nature" that will best preserve each (107).

"An Argument for Diversity" restates the need for greater human and natural diversity in the natural landscape. Diversity follows from quality and care of the land, so that as the scale of use declines, tools become simpler and human skills become more complex. We use well what we care for, Berry argues, and we care for what we know well. The abstractness of modern life prevents us from gaining intimate knowledge of our natural environment, and specialization prevents us from gaining enough practical knowledge to practice good stewardship.

The title essay argues that unemployment is a logical consequence of our national ambition to avoid work by replacing humans with machines. "What Are People For?" points out that the acceptance of structural unemployment is too high a price to pay for economic growth. Furthermore, Berry argues, there is nothing shameful about work; on the contrary, decent work lends dignity and meaning to human life. A leisure society disdainful of work and abstracted from the land inevitably looks down upon farmers, but it is ill equipped to restore farms, forests, towns, and communities. Leisure, properly understood, is the fruit of labor and the basis of culture, not an occasion for idleness, boredom, and consumption.[23]

Not only does our culture waste human lives, it generates huge amounts of garbage from excessive consumption. As Berry notes in "Waste," the local landfill in Henry County receives 50–60 large truckloads of garbage each day from other states. Much of this waste is generated by machines that replace human labor and process and package everything we buy. Fast-food companies are responsible for a large portion of this waste, Americans having become ever more dependent upon this industry for their food and drink. Our garbage inevitably litters the countryside as the cities spread their detritus. Trash is the tangible evidence of good work not being done. "The ecological damage of centralization and waste," Berry observes, "is thus inextricably involved with human damage" (128).

What we need instead of an economics of consumption, Berry argues, is an economics of pleasure. In "Economy and Pleasure," he objects to the elevation of economics as the ultimate science, with competition as its sovereign principle. Competition, which always implies winners and losers, destroys human community because it sets us against each other; it destroys natural communities as well because it recognizes no limits. The destruction of life is accepted as a necessary cost of economic growth. The ultimate danger lies in the concentration of economic power with no social restraints. Competition also requires constant change, while community aspires to stability and continuity. Unrestrained competition leads to social chaos, with the inevitable dominance of the strongest and most ruthless.

Berry invites us to consider instead an economy driven by pleasure—affection in action—rather than by competition. By pleasure he means not self-indulgence but the sheer pleasure of existence, as expressed in our economic life. Such pleasure often derives from work well done. "The nearly intolerable irony in our dissatisfaction," Berry observes, "is that we have removed pleasure from our work in order to remove 'drudgery' from our lives" (141).

One of life's great pleasures, Berry acknowledges, is eating, but that too has been rendered passive by consumerism. In "The Pleasures of Eating," he notes that Americans are largely ignorant of how their food is produced. Most have never lived on a farm, and few grow or prepare the food they eat. Severing the ties between producing and eating food is one more effect of the industrial economy. Direct knowledge of how our food is grown ensures not only that our food will be healthful but that we will not be enslaved by pervasive consumerism. What can be done? "Eat responsibly," Berry advises (145). Buy fresh food, buy local, prepare your own food, and learn as much as possible about good nutrition.

The symbiosis of ecology and economics is reflected in Berry's "The Work of Local Culture." That work is represented by the slow accumulation of humus in an old bucket hanging from a fence post. Berry compares the process of building soil to the way a community slowly develops its customs and traditions over time. Aware that he is living in a diminished culture, Berry compares the loss of local culture to the erosion of fertile topsoil from the land. A community is built upon trust, and people do not trust each other when they do not know each other's stories. Communities gradually lose their distinctiveness as they lose their memory of themselves and become part of a national consumer culture, with television linking everyone in collective loneliness. In a society where people are meant only to consume, technological and economic "progress" inevitably produces social and environmental decline.

Sex, Economy, Freedom and Community

In Berry's most recent essay collection, *Sex, Economy, Freedom and Community* (1993), he shifts his attention from the natural to the human environment, focusing on the process of community disintegration implicit in the self-liberation that began in the 1960s. Berry continues to view small, self-sufficient communities as the best protection against the pressures of rampant consumerism, which leaves individuals dependent on large corporations for the necessities of life. But small, local economies have been largely replaced by an impersonal global economy of multinational corporations that colonize and extract resources without benefiting local communities. Fragmentation of life and a pervasive loss of moral responsibility are the results of unrestrained global economics. Meaningful economic reform must begin with personal responsibility.

Most of the eight essays in *Sex, Economy, Freedom and Community* were previously published in magazines or as pamphlets.[24] Berry refers to himself as an essayist in the dissenting tradition of the Protestant reformers, a prophetic tradition that bears witness to truth and speaks out against corruption. His epistolary preface, "The Joy of Sales Resistance," announces the theme of the book. Since the essential art of our culture is salesmanship—advertising and marketing products and services that people do not need—the essence of freedom lies in resistance to such blandishments.

"Conservation and Local Economy" (1992) continues a familiar Berry theme. The story of our nation lies in the fate of our land. Having dispossessed the original inhabitants, Americans now find themselves being dispossessed by the large corporations that control much of the land and wealth. Sounding a populist note, Berry claims that corporate America has destroyed the culture of rural America as thoroughly as any totalitarian government. Berry alludes to an article by the journalist William Allen White, who pointed out that, in 1912, Marion County, Kansas, had the largest per capita bank deposits in the nation, illustrating the success of the Jeffersonian dream of a democratic distribution of wealth through equitable land distribution (9). Today that dream is long gone. Berry argues that we must return "economic self-determination to the people" (17). He proposes "a kind of secession" from corporate America to re-create a more democratic capitalism (17).

In "Conservation Is Good Work" (1992), he returns to the theme of limiting personal consumption as a precondition for environmental health. Conservation is not merely saving spectacular scenery, conserving resources, and preventing pollution. Conservation also derives from our good work, which connects us to the earth, he explains, and begins in our homes and communities. Berry opposes the General Agreement on Tariffs and Trade (GATT) because he believes that food should be produced and consumed locally. He fears that free trade will put American farm producers at a disadvantage against foreign competition.

Berry has shown an increasing willingness to speak out on religious issues. His "Peaceableness Towards Enemies" (1992) offers a thoroughgoing pacifist critique of U.S. policy in the Gulf War. He argues that it was not a war to "liberate Kuwait" but a war of self-interest to protect our sources of cheap Middle East oil. In terms reminiscent of Mark Twain's "The War Prayer," Berry criticizes the inevitable jingoism and militarism that accompany any imperialistic venture.[25] Such expressions of power run counter to our highest national purposes.

"Christianity and the Survival of Creation" was first delivered as a chapel talk at the Southern Baptist Theological Seminary in Louisville, Kentucky, on 22 March 1992. In his talk, Berry examines the "culpability of Christianity in the destruction of the natural world" (93). He accuses Christianity of fostering a destructive body-soul dualism that tends to denigrate this world in favor of the next and creates an artificial division between "sacred" and "secular." Berry argues that the world is whole, and that Creation itself is sacred and not to be disdained. Our self-consciousness divides us from the world, and we act as though that division were reality. Neither the materialist nor the gnostic sufficiently values the sacredness of Creation. If Christianity is contained within churches, which are the only holy places, then Christians are free to desecrate the rest of Creation. Furthermore, when we separate the sacred from the secular, we separate our religious lives from our economic lives. But faith cannot be separated from works. "What sort of economy would be responsible to the holiness of life?" Berry wonders (100). It would not be an exploitative economy, but one that "hallowed the everyday," in Martin Buber's words, and valued the spirituality of work. "Work connects us both to creation and to eternity," Berry points out (111). Some religious sects have valued work as prayer, as did the Shakers, who cultivated fine workmanship in furniture and crafts. In denying holiness to the body and the world, Berry argues, we discourage good work that would unify the sacred and the secular. By becoming a specialist creed that concentrates on saving souls and getting people to heaven, "Christianity connives directly in the murder of Creation" (115).

The challenge for modern Christianity is to rethink its relationship to Creation in terms of biblical teachings about the sacredness of the world.

Berry's long title essay, "Sex, Economy, Freedom and Community" (1993), examines the changing relations between men and women in our culture.[26] Berry argues that the "sexual revolution" of the 1960s was an unmitigated disaster, for instead of making sexual relations between men and women easier and more natural, it has made them more fearful and uncertain. "Seeking to 'free' sexual love from its old community restraints," Berry observes, "we have 'freed' it from its meaning, its responsibility, its exaltation" (142). A strong believer in community-based moral standards, Berry argues that communities have a legitimate interest in regulating sexual conduct, which is not simply a private affair. The community has an abiding interest in maintaining the unity of marriages and families against predatory sexuality that would destroy human bonds for selfish reasons. The community teaches the young sexual mores through stories, customs, and traditions. Now standards of sexual behavior are determined by television and the media. "Communities are being destroyed both from within and from without," Berry observes, "by internal dissatisfaction and external exploitation" (125).

Chief among these casualties has been marriage. Marriage is a giving of oneself to another that must be protected by the community from disintegration into self-seeking. The community uses the potent energy of sexuality as a bonding force to keep the family intact and to provide for the nurture of children. Freed from community restraints, that energy destroys the trust and respect essential to human relations and threatens the community. Economic and sexual exploitation are closely related: liberated from the sanctity of marriage, sexuality becomes the ultimate consumer commodity. "Just as the public economy encourages people to spend money and waste the world," Berry observes, "so the public sexual code encourages people to be spendthrifts and squanderers of sex" (142–43). Berry also views the rise in sexual harassment and crimes against women as related to the use of sex in marketing and advertising manipulation. "Starting with economic brutality, we have arrived at sexual brutality," he concludes (143).

The preoccupation with romantic love also encourages people to withdraw from community life into self-willed isolation. "Lovers must not, like usurers, live for themselves," Berry warns (137). As the divorce rate rises, families are fragmented as parents use children as hostages in their emotional battles. Child abandonment and child custody battles proliferate; parents refuse to pay child support. Berry marvels at how uncharitable we have become. "The proper question, perhaps, is not why we have so much divorce," he observes, "but why we are so unforgiving" (140).

Berry views the disintegration of marriages and families as the ultimate failure of community and an indication of the triumph of individual rights and self-assertion. "Much of the modern assault on community life has been conducted with the justification and protection of the idea of freedom," he notes (144). As a culture, we have tended to absolutize individual rights at the expense of community. Our culture tends to depict the community as a repressive force associated with narrow, old-fashioned, puritanical values and to glamorize the individual rebel. Individual self-realization, however, too often involves a flight from all personal responsibility (except the obligation to consume). "The individual life implies no standard of behavior or responsibility," Berry comments (149). Most Americans today are rootless nomads, displaced from their communities of birth by ambition or necessity. The nuclear family has not been able to withstand this restlessness. Separated from family and childhood friends, husbands and wives turn to each other for virtually every social need. But with the economic pressure on both parents to work, careers grow more important than family ties and family life diminishes. The warm, neighborly life of American communities has all but disappeared. Berry laments these changes, showing the same loyalty to his community that the ancient Athenian felt for his city-state.

For Berry, community is the touchstone for economic, aesthetic, environmental, and moral values. He opposes our drift toward community disintegration as the result of an unrestricted market economy that preys upon human vulnerability. Community values, he argues, are more than public values, because they tend to be reinforced by daily life. Public values, in contrast, are the values of anonymity and isolation. Communities promote trust, which protects our human dignity against forces that exploit human weakness. Above all, a community is a placed and rooted people who understand themselves as part of their natural environment. Berry calls for a true pluralism of settled communities that would encourage a genuine cultural diversity of arts and crafts emerging from indigenous local cultures wed to the land.

Chapter Six

Harlan Hubbard and More Stories of the Port William Membership

After a 12-year hiatus, Berry returned to fiction with the publication of *The Wild Birds* (1986), six new short stories about the lives of the characters in the Port William Membership, the fictional Kentucky farming community modeled after his native Port Royal.[1] These stories, spanning a period from 1930 to 1967, involve the lives of the Catletts, Penns, Feltners, Beechums, and Coulters and are primarily portraits of a living farm community. Berry's characters share a strong work ethic; in fact, their work defines their lives. Most of the stories are told from the perspective of Wheeler Catlett, a shrewd country lawyer with strong ties to the land. The stories are low-key and realistic, with strong thematic emphasis. In fact, Berry's stories tend to be glosses of his essays. Seldom has an American writer used essays, fiction, and poetry to develop so consistent a set of themes.

In "Thicker Than Liquor," Wheeler Catlett is summoned to rescue his besotted Uncle Peach, laid up in a seedy Louisville hotel. The story traces Wheeler's changing attitude toward his uncle as he himself matures, from admiring his uncle as a boy to despising him as a teenager, finally to accepting responsibility for him as he is. Uncle Peach is a ne'er-do-well bachelor farmer, a sometime carpenter, and a binge drinker. A likable person when sober, Uncle Peach has become an increasingly fumbling, incompetent worker who misplaces tools and tangles himself in his rope. Wheeler's mother Dorie has devotedly cared for her brother because "blood is thicker than water," and now that care has devolved upon Wheeler. The story's title, "Thicker Than Liquor," comes from Wheeler's sarcastic comment to his mother about her devotion to Uncle Peach, although Wheeler eventually learns to put aside his irritation with Uncle Peach and take responsibility for his care. Uncle Peach somewhat resembles another wastrel, Roger Merchant in *A Place on Earth*, who is cared for by his cousin Mat Feltner.

"It Wasn't Me" picks up where *The Memory of Old Jack* ends, with the public auction of Jack Beechum's farm after his death. Wheeler tries his best to keep the farm with Elton and Mary Penn, the young couple who have been farming it as Beechum's tenants. Wheeler's adversaries are Beechum's daughter Clara and her husband, Gladston Pettit, a wealthy Louisville banker. Jack Beechum has left the Penns a legacy sufficient to buy the farm, if Clara will accept a reasonable price. But Clara, who hated the farm and left it as soon as she could, holds out for the highest price she can get for the land. Wheeler tries to act as an honest broker but is rebuffed by the Pettits. Out of respect for Jack's wishes, Wheeler must persuade Elton Penn to bid for the farm against two competitors, a neighboring farmer and the local doctor. For Clara, the sale of the farm represents merely the disposal of a valuable asset to the highest bidder, but to the Penns it represents the continuity of a way of life. They are Jack Beechum's true heirs and successors because they have inherited his values: his love of farming and land. Elton finally gets the farm but has to pay $300 an acre, more than he can afford. He is reluctant to accept Wheeler's help or advice because he longs to be independent, but he cannot bear to be ungrateful. Wheeler patiently explains that Elton was chosen by Old Jack to be a steward of the farm, the latest in a succession of good owners. Elton must accept that the most important gifts cannot be repaid.

By far the most powerful story in the collection is "The Boundary," a story about work, aging, and the acceptance of one's mortality, told with subtle foreshadowing. Berry reintroduces Mat and Margaret Feltner, the central characters of *A Place on Earth*, 20 years later, in their old age. Mat can no longer actively work his fields, but he still works around the barn and in his garden. Despite his growing frailty, one spring afternoon he decides to check on his livestock fencing in a lower pasture below the barn. Following the stream down from the fields to the woods is easy, but he soon grows tired and confused. Here, the title becomes significant as the story assumes a figurative meaning: "The descent beckons and he yields eagerly to it, going on down into the tireless chanting of the stream" (79). Memories of the dead return to him as he walks along the fence he helped build 75 years earlier. Mat discovers that Nathan Coulter has already mended the broken section of fence.

The exertion of the walk has tired and confused him. Mat brought his cane from the barn, a small concession to Margaret, but he suddenly realizes that he is an old man. He begins to let go of his life and returns to the freedom of the woods. It is late spring and the dogwoods are past, but the mayapple is still blooming beneath the trees. Visions of the dead appear to Mat, and he evokes the communion of men at their work—his father Ben, his uncle Jack Beechum, his son Virgil, and Joe Banion. "Gone. All of them are gone," he thinks (80). But he can still affirm that his life has been blessed. Mat is 80, but he can still feel the wonder and mystery of nature in a thrush, woodpecker, or hawk. He rests himself beside a spring that he and his son Virgil built beneath the roots of an old sycamore one dry summer. "'I could stay here a long time,' he thinks" (82). Mat's memories of his son, killed 20 years earlier in World War II, evoke echoes of Wordsworth's "Michael," a pastoral narrative about the disappearance of the English rural farming class. Like Michael and his son building the stone sheep-pen, Mat and Virgil built a stone wall to contain the spring. Virgil left an old earthenware water jug there, beneath a sycamore root; finding it 20 years later, Mat momentarily grieves for his son.

Mat turns to leave, becomes dizzy, and suddenly feels the heaviness of his body. He is uncertain whether to follow the stream up or down the hill, but he chooses the difficult way—up—as he has done all of his life. He knows that Margaret is waiting for him at home, and he thinks of their common life together. Then he sees his father and son approaching on the other side of the stream as darkness clouds his vision. Mat faces another kind of "boundary," one that beckons to him, but he is not yet ready to cross. He climbs heavily up the ravine and stumbles but does not remember falling; an "overmastering prayer" comes to his mind (96). He realizes that something has happened to him, and he worries about Margaret, who will be alarmed by his absence. Partially paralyzed by a stroke, he crawls to the base of a large walnut tree, where he rests and falls asleep. Sometime later he is awakened by the sound of an approaching car. In the gathering dusk he is spotted and rescued by his son-in-law, Wheeler Catlett, returning home from his office.

"That Distant Land" describes Mat Feltner's death at home later that summer after his stroke. The story is narrated by Andy Catlett, Mat's grandson, who sits by his grandfather's bedside as Mat prepares for death. An active man all his life, Mat makes no effort to get out of bed, eats very little, and just looks out his window at the ridges above the river valley. The townspeople—friends and relatives—drop in each day to see Mat and Margaret because, as Andy remembers, "we were a membership" (102). As Andy sits with him, Mat recites the Twenty-Third Psalm and a stanza from Milton's "Lycidas." As the summer progresses, Mat weakens, but he holds out until the tobacco harvest begins. One hot afternoon, as the neighbors are cutting the long rows of Elton Penn's tobacco, Burley Coulter sings out, jokingly, "Oh, pilgrim, have you seen that distant land?" (110). At the end of that day's work, Wheeler Catlett brings the news of Mat's death.

"The Wild Birds," like "It Wasn't Me," deals with the disposition of farmland, in this case, Burley Coulter's farm. One Saturday afternoon Burley visits Wheeler's law office to ask Wheeler to draft a will leaving his farm to Danny Branch and his wife. Danny, it turns out, is Burley's illegitimate son by Kate Helen Branch. Burley has long looked after Danny and has all but acknowledged his paternity. Now, after Kate Helen's death, Burley wants to make official his relationship with his son. At first, Wheeler hesitates at the seeming impropriety of the act, although he recognizes that Burley is following his conscience. Since Wheeler's eventual cooperation is inevitable, the story's only dramatic conflict lies in the conflict of character and values between Wheeler and Burley. Wheeler is a conventional man, committed to order and propriety, while Burley has led an unconventional life, yielding to freedom and impulse, never marrying, farming indifferently, and sowing his wild oats about the town. Wheeler is a lawyer who would rather be farming, while Burley is a farmer who would rather be coon hunting.

The most interesting part of the story—Burley's relationship with Kate Helen Branch—is hinted at but never fully told. The story picks up from *Nathan Coulter*, in which we learn of Danny's birth, but we never find out much about Kate Helen's character or why she and Burley never married. Their story is told entirely from Burley's perspective, with a long digression on his love of hunting. We are given only a glimpse of Kate Helen as Wheeler remembers her: barefoot on her porch, with a guitar on her lap and a red ribbon in her hair.

Wheeler disapproves of Burley's "wayward" life and his divided loyalties: "He has been a man of two loves, not always compatible: of the dark woods, and of the daylit membership of kin and friends and households" (127). Yet Burley's waywardness makes him an attractive and sympathetic character and gives him a palpability that other characters lack. Wheeler seems to disapprove of Burley's love of hunting as an atavistic impulse that pulls him away from community, yet it also ties Burley strongly to the land. Burley's waywardness challenges the strong work ethic of the Port William Membership, but he is always there to lend a hand with anyone's work. He tries to remain a free spirit within the confines of what his community will tolerate, and his transgressions are mostly common knowledge. The story's title perhaps comes from Burley and Kate Helen's long-standing relationship: are they the "wild birds?"

Remembering

Berry's next fictional work, *Remembering* (1988), was largely written during his time as writer-in-residence at Bucknell University during the winter of 1987.[2] In this novella, Berry picks up the story of Andy Catlett, Wheeler's son, who is now a farmer with a wife and two children. The fourth novel in the Port William Membership series, the story recounts in seven chapters a period of crisis in Andy's life after he loses his right hand in a corn picker. Despondent, he quarrels with his wife Flora and is impatient with his children. As he leaves for a midwestern agricultural conference, ironically titled "The Future of the American Food System," he feels estranged from his farm, his family, and his community. After embarrassing himself at the conference with an impromptu outburst, Catlett continues west to San Francisco, where he is scheduled to give a college talk. At the airport, he walks past the student waiting for him and checks into a hotel instead. There, in a "dark night of the soul," he spends a sleepless night, walking the San Francisco streets, reexamining his life, his values, and his connections with his past. By rejecting his past and denying his identity as a farmer, Catlett creates "the little hell of himself alone" (45).

Remembering is something of a roman à clef in which Berry creates a fictional persona to dramatize many of the arguments he sets forth in his essays. Much of the plot involves Catlett's recollections of his career as an agricultural journalist and his "conversion" from industrial to traditional agricultural methods. His disillusionment began when, as a staff writer on the trade journal *Scientific Farming*, he interviewed an Ohio farmer, Bill Meikleberger, who farmed 2,000 acres "scientifically" and spoke candidly of his ulcers. Catlett compared Meikleberger with the Amish farmer Isaac Troyer in terms virtually identical with Berry's examples in his essay "Does Community Have a Value?" in *Home Economics*. The conference Catlett attends, supposedly concerned with the "Future of the American Food System," provides an opportunity for Berry to satirize the assumptions of industrial agriculture.

Andy Catlett eventually returns home to Port William, to his family and his responsibilities, reconciled to the loss of his hand. This theme of returning home links Andy to his father, Wheeler Catlett, who passed up a lucrative law career elsewhere to practice law at home, and his grandfather, Mat Feltner, who returned home from college to farm. Catlett's night in San Francisco allows him to imagine the urban life he might have enjoyed, but he is repelled by the lack of trust and community in the city. In his predawn wanderings, he encounters weary lovers, a tall blond streetwalker, a hip panhandler, a frightened matron, and an old Chinese couple—nameless minor characters who seem to function merely as representatives of the urban life that Catlett rejects. In a moment of despondency, Catlett recalls his grandfather Mat Feltner's story about cooling off in a creek after working in a cornfield on a hot summer afternoon and realizing that all he wanted in life was right there.

As a fiction writer, Berry is most successful as a regionalist, within the fictional realm of the Port William Membership. In his first three novels, Berry creates convincing portraits of the Coulters, Feltners, and Beechums, but in *Remembering*, set largely in San Francisco, his narrative skill as a storyteller is blunted by his discursive tendency to make the novel a forum for his agricultural arguments. No matter how much one sympathizes with Berry's arguments against corporate agriculture, those arguments do not belong in his fiction. The purpose of the novel is to tell a good story, with believable characters engaged in a credible dramatic conflict. When the fiction writer subordinates art to polemics, narrative becomes argumentative discourse and the work lapses into didacticism. Despite the elaborate allusions to Dante, *Remembering* seems less a story of Andy Catlett's redemption than an extension of Berry's agricultural criticism.[3]

Another Port William sketch, published separately as a small offprint, is "The Discovery of Kentucky."[4] Told in the tall-tale tradition, this sketch involves Burley Coulter and four of his friends, who plan an elaborate prank during the inaugural parade in Frankfort for Kentucky's new governor. Burley and his friends are recruited by the horse breeder John T. McCallum to dress as early Kentuckians and march alongside his covered wagon and prize Percherons. Burley decides to upstage the pompous McCallum by spiking the jugs they carry with Kentucky Pride and by having the group fire blank cartridges in the air during the parade. The sketch satirizes Kentucky boosterism and self-promotion and makes a trenchant point about who *really* controls Kentucky politics: the big coal companies.

Fidelity

Berry's next collection of short stories, *Fidelity* (1992), presents five new tales of the Port William Membership.[5] A story of remarkable emotional power, "Pray without Ceasing" tells of Ben Feltner's murder at the hands of his friend Thad Coulter in July 1912. It presents a moving story of murder, forgiveness, and reconciliation of two families through the renunciation of vengeance.

At the age of 60, when Thad Coulter had worked all of his life to pay off the mortgage on his farm, he made the mistake of offering his farm as collateral on a loan to set his son Abner up in the grocery business in Hargrave. Abner disappeared after his business failed through mismanagement, the bank called in the loan, and Thad Coulter stood to lose his farm. Despondent, Thad begins drinking heavily and goes to his friend Ben Feltner for help. Thad is so drunk and incoherent that Ben asks him to leave and return when he is sober. Feeling insulted and rejected by his friend, Thad returns home to get his pistol and, still drunk, rides into Port William on a hot Saturday morning in July. In a scene reminiscent of the Colonel Sherburn–Old Boggs episode in *Huckleberry Finn*, Coulter shoots Ben Feltner down in the middle of the town's main street.

When Ben's son Mat learns of the shooting, he wants to kill the man who has murdered his father. As Mat pushes through the crowd of bystanders, he is caught by his older friend Jack Beechum and constrained until his rage subsides. Jack, twice Mat's age, struggles to hold onto the younger man, saving him from an act that he would surely regret. Later that day, as he sobers up, Thad Coulter is filled with grief and remorse, and he turns himself in to the sheriff in Hargrave, the county seat. When his daughter Martha Elizabeth comes to the jail to visit him, Coulter is overcome with grief, his hands over his face. Two days later he hangs himself in his jail cell.

Ben Feltner's friends fetch his body back home, where it is laid out for viewing. Neighbors come with food to pay their respects to his wife Nancy and the children, Mat and Bess. Beechum's old schoolteacher, Miss Della Budge, brings a cake. As she hobbles in, she remarks to Jack Beechum that we never know when we will be called, so we must "pray without ceasing" and, by implication, forgive our enemies as we would be forgiven (54). That evening, a crowd of townspeople appear at the Feltners' home with a rope, offering to ride over to the Hargrave jail and take matters into their own hands, but Mat and his mother ask them to disperse. Mat Feltner never talks about the event afterwards, but he goes out of his way to be friendly to the Coulters. Eventually the families are reconciled when Thad's nephew, Wheeler Catlett, marries Ben's daughter Bess. Mat Feltner reunites the two families, and his grandson, Andy Catlett, the narrator of the story, is "the child of his forgiveness" (59).

"A Jonquil for Mary Penn" describes the adjustment of a young farming couple as they are gradually drawn into a close-knit community that understands them well enough to meet their unspoken needs. When the young wife, Mary Penn, is sick with fever and despondent after a quarrel with her husband, she awakens to find a neighbor sitting at her bedside, embroidering jonquils. The account of how all the neighbors help each other reminds us of Berry's account in "Does Community Have a Value?" of how Berry's own neighbors, Lance and Owen Flood, were accepted by their neighbors when they moved to Port Royal in 1938.

Another emotionally powerful story, "Making It Home," describes Arthur Rowanberry's slow readjustment to civilian life as he makes the long walk from the bus station in Jefferson, on the north side of the river, to his father's farm near Port William. The story contains an implicit antiwar theme in Rowanberry's gruesome memories of field combat in Europe, which he mentally contrasts with the pastoral images of his home. Rowanberry, a World War II infantryman who fought in the Battle of the Bulge, has lost many of his friends and been wounded him-self by an artillery shell. His eager return to farming contrasts sharply with Nick Adams's inability to adjust to civilian life in Hemingway's *In Our Time* (1925).

The title story, "Fidelity," recounts the death of Burley Coulter after he is disconnected from life support systems and brought home from a Jefferson hospital by his son Danny Branch.[6] Danny and the other fami-ly members are deeply distressed by the sight of Burley with a feeding tube in his nose, breathing with the help of a respirator. They feel it would be treason to abandon Burley to an impersonal death at the hands of modern medicine. At 82, he is at the end of his life, and it is futile to try to prolong it. Danny's "rescue" of his father shows deep compassion and an instinctive understanding of what Burley would have wanted. Wheeling his unconscious father out of the hospital in the middle of the night, Danny takes him to an old, abandoned tobacco barn where they had often taken shelter while hunting.

The story expresses Berry's deep distaste for the impersonality of modern medicine. Burley returns home to his community, where family and friends gather at Wheeler Catlett's office to meet with the detective investigating Burley's disappearance from the hospital. In a gesture of solidarity, they refuse to cooperate in disclosing Danny's or Burley's whereabouts. As the protective circle of the community surrounds one of their own, the reader wonders why they agreed to hospitalize Burley to begin with. Another discordant note is in Berry's stereotyped depiction of Kyle Bode, the detective who futilely pursues the case.

The most moving part of the story is the account of Danny digging his father's grave in a stand of old trees on the morning after they leave the hospital. Leaving his comatose father resting in the tobacco barn, he digs the grave by hand and lines it with flagstones from a nearby creek, preparing a primitive but appropriate burial site as Burley nears death. Burley returns to consciousness only long enough to recognize where he is and dies peacefully soon afterward. Danny lays his father's body gently in the grave and drapes it with wildflowers before he places the flagstones over the stone casket. Burley's death and interment seem as natural and appropriate as the fall of a leaf. His body is returned to the woods he loved, and Danny senses his father's spirit lingering near the burial site. Despite some polemical notes in Wheeler's defense of community against the encroachments of the modern state, this story presents a moving end to the life of one of the Port William Membership's most notable characters.

Harlan Hubbard

On 10 April 1989 Berry was invited to deliver the annual Blazer Lecture Series talk at the University of Kentucky.[7] His address was entitled "The Achievement of Harlan Hubbard." Hubbard, a Kentucky painter, writer, musician, and naturalist who lived from 1900 to 1988, spent five years on a homemade shantyboat with his wife Anna. The Hubbards later homesteaded on seven acres in Trimble County, Kentucky, beside the Ohio River, leading a life notable for its independence, frugality, dignity, and elegance, as well as its unconventionality. Hubbard was the author of *Shantyboat* (1953), *Payne Hollow* (1974), and two posthumous works, *Harlan Hubbard Journals, 1929–1944* (1987) and *Shantyboat on the Bayous* (1990).[8] He was a talented musician and the creator of hundreds of paintings, prints, and drawings. Berry's two Blazer lectures were subsequently published as *Harlan Hubbard: Life and Work* (1990).[9]

Berry had first met the Hubbards 25 years earlier, on 26 July 1964, when he and his friend Pete Hammond were camping and canoeing on the Ohio. By chance, they stopped at the Hubbards' home in Payne Hollow to replenish their water and were welcomed by Anna Hubbard, a gracious, elegant woman who gave them water and ripe tomatoes for their dinner (88). Berry was much impressed with the dignity and integrity of the Hubbards' life and returned to visit many times afterward. In 1976 he wrote a foreword for a new edition of *Shantyboat* (91).

After Hubbard's death in 1988, Berry thought much about the significance of the lives of Harlan and Anna Hubbard, and when he was asked
to deliver the Blazer lectures, he resolved to write about them. At that
time, no one knew the full extent of Hubbard's work. Berry read over
2,000 pages of Hubbard's then-unpublished journals, a collection of letters, and the manuscript of an unpublished book, "Uncle Jim's Trading
Boat." He studied Hubbard's watercolors and graphic works and
arranged to see as many of Hubbard's paintings as possible (94). As a
result, *Harlan Hubbard* is a beautifully illustrated book that includes
Hubbard's line drawings, black-and-white photographs of the Hubbards, and color reproductions of 20 of his paintings.

Berry was clearly impressed with the clarity of Hubbard's values and
with the originality of the life he chose. His biography, one of the first to
be published about this remarkable man, attempts to capture the clarity
and simplicity of Hubbard's vision.[10] The Hubbards managed to combine economic simplicity and varied cultural interests in a life that
offered a remarkable degree of leisure and suggested possibilities for a
quality of life not often found in rural America. Hubbard mastered a
variety of skills—masonry, carpentry, boat-building, gardening, and bee-
keeping—that enabled the couple to remain largely self-sufficient. They
bartered for whatever they could not grow or produce for themselves,
avoiding the use of money. The life they gradually created for themselves
had an almost Oriental tranquillity and simplicity. They sought to live a
good life by reducing their basic needs to the barest essentials. The
Hubbards no doubt served as a model for much of what Berry later
wrote about household economy.

A shy, self-effacing man who gained little recognition for his artistic
achievements, Hubbard was a person of remarkable character and originality, and his life deserves to be better known. A dedicated student of
Thoreau's writing, Hubbard decided early that mainstream American
life could provide little satisfaction for him, so he chose to live an austere
and self-reliant life. A Kentucky native, he moved with his mother to
New York City at the age of 15 and studied at the National Academy of
Design. He returned to northern Kentucky at 19 and studied at the
Cincinnati Art Academy. Solitary by nature, he pursued his interests in
music, painting, reading, and hiking, supporting himself as a day labor-
er through his skill at carpentry and masonry.

Sometime after 1933, Hubbard met his future wife, Anna
Eikenhout, a librarian in the Fine Arts Department of the Cincinnati
Public Library. A graduate of Ohio State University, she was the second

daughter of a cultured Dutch family from Grand Rapids, Michigan. She and Hubbard discovered their common interests, began to play music together, and eventually married on 20 April 1943, when he was 43 and she was 41. (3).

After their marriage, they settled in Brent, Kentucky, on the Ohio River, and together built a shantyboat from materials scavenged from dumps and drift piles along the river. In six months the boat was finished, and on 11 December 1943 they embarked on a voyage down the Ohio and Mississippi rivers that would take them five years to complete. In no hurry, they were determined to enjoy the adventure, drifting downstream with the current. They would tie up for months at a time to raise a garden, barter for food, and enjoy their leisure. They read to each other, played chamber music, and worked at handicrafts. Hubbard painted and kept a daily journal. Anna cooked gourmet meals of whatever Harlan could catch, grow, forage, or barter. Often they went on bicycle excursions in the countryside and sought out local libraries. Such a life demands self-discipline, creativity, imagination, perseverance, and fidelity to one's principles and values. Like Thoreau, the Hubbards were determined to live more simply in order to enjoy life's pleasures. Their lifestyle may have isolated them from their families and friends, but their relationship was so rich that they never lacked for companionship until Anna's death in 1986.

In 1950, after they had reached New Orleans and spent several months exploring the Louisiana bayous, the Hubbards sold their shantyboat and bought a used car and a makeshift trailer. They worked their way back to Kentucky, camping along the way, and made several cross-country trips before purchasing a parcel of land on the Kentucky side of the Ohio River. Here they settled in 1951, building their own house and living in frugal self-sufficiency for the rest of their lives. On their seven acres at Payne Hollow, the Hubbards raised a large garden, took fish from the river, and kept goats, chickens, and bees. They built their home gradually, using local materials and locating it carefully to merge into its hillside setting. The Hubbards shunned electricity, telephones, and indoor plumbing, but they included in their home plenty of windows and bookshelves, a music room with a Steinway piano, a craft studio, and a barn. They shunned labor-saving devices, preferring hand tools, yet they enjoyed many of the refinements of life.

As Berry observes, the Hubbards' life was in many ways indebted to Thoreau, but they expanded on Thoreau's economics, supporting themselves for forty years—not just two, as Thoreau had done (24). The

Hubbards were careful to observe the proper scale of livelihood. By simplifying and unifying their lives, they were able to avoid the modern division of labor (28). In their daily life, the Hubbards rejected the modern dichotomy between art and work, between the useful and the beautiful. They believed that if a tool or object was useful, then it ought to be beautiful as well. Good use creates functional beauty. Like the British Pre-Raphaelites and the followers of John Ruskin and William Morris, they loved beautiful handicrafts and rejected machine-made artifacts. Besides his oil and watercolor painting, Hubbard enjoyed drawing and printmaking as well. His landscape paintings have the quality of naive folk art: expressing a sense of immediacy, they seem to have been executed boldly and quickly without excessive concern for theory or technique. He believed that all art is ultimately religious, and for him, painting expressed his great joy in life. The Hubbards strove to make their common life together a work of art.

Like Thoreau, Hubbard found direct revelation not in organized religion but in nature, which led him to an actively contemplative life. His was a practical, intuitive faith in immanence rather than transcendence. "'The beauty of the earth is Christ himself,'" Hubbard noted in his journals (39). As Berry observes, "making the most of what the earth offers" was Hubbard's religious vocation (38). As a Kentucky native, Hubbard had a deep sense of place and an affection for the Ohio River Valley that kept drawing him back from his travels. His love for the Ohio and Mississippi rivers is reflected in his journals and his paintings. In a large mural of the River Jordan that he was commissioned to paint for the Mount Byrd Christian Church in Milton, Kentucky, the Ohio River is clearly depicted, as if to suggest that the biblical sanctity of the Jordan is here at hand.

Berry was clearly drawn to the Hubbards by the affinity between their values and his own. He praises the exemplary quality of their lives and their marriage for offering a clear alternative to the heedlessly consumptive patterns of American life. Like Thoreau, the Hubbards tried to simplify their material needs in order to free up their time and energy for what mattered most to them. Their refusal to participate in the specialist division of modern labor lent clarity and coherence to their lives. "True simplicity," as Martin Lings has noted, "far from being incompatible with complexity, even demands a certain complexity for its full realization."[11] Paradoxically, the Hubbards' quality of life was achieved by their frugality: with little, they achieved much. Their lives were a direct rebuke to the dominant American assumption that the good life demands ever-increasing material consumption. As Berry concludes, the primary significance of the Hubbards' lives is that they managed to live a full and abundant life in a place that had been farmed over and abandoned (96). Hubbard's vision is expressed in his simple but trenchant comment, "I believe that whatever we need is at hand" (16).

Watch with Me

In Berry's most recent short story collection, *Watch with Me* (1994), he introduces two new characters from the Port William Membership, Ptolemy Proudfoot and his wife, Miss Minnie.[12] These seven sketches, which first appeared in the *Draft Horse Journal*, cover a 33-year period, 1908–41, and evoke the era of transition between the horse and buggy and the automobile. For the most part, they are light, humorous local-color sketches rather than short stories. They are built around amusing or disconcerting incidents, with little plot development or dramatic conflict. The characters are static rather than dynamic. "Tol" and Minnie Proudfoot are to some extent appealing caricatures, as their names suggest. Tol is a huge 300-pound farmer, somewhat reserved and deferential to his petite 90-pound wife, a former schoolteacher. They are a prosperous but childless farming couple of the early part of the century. Much of the appeal of these stories lies in the nostalgia of period pieces for a draft-horse magazine readership.

The opening story in the collection, "A Consent," dated 1908, recounts the story of Ptolemy's courtship of Miss Minnie. He is 36, a hardworking bachelor farmer; she is 34, a pert, diminutive grade-school teacher at the local school in the town of Goforth. Both are shy, and they avoid contact in public, although they secretly admire each other, as opposites sometimes will. The sketch describes the annual Harvest Festival, organized by Miss Minnie to raise money for books and supplies. This community event includes an auction of pies and cakes and recitations of poetry and songs by the awkward and embarrassed schoolchildren before their admiring parents. Tol dresses in his Sunday best for the affair but still manages to look untidy. He is shy and uncomfortable around the women until the auction begins, when he overbids on Miss Minnie's angelfood cake and earns the right to see her home. Very much a period piece, the sketch presents a charming picture of a self-sufficient rural culture in the time before radio and television.

In "A Half-Pint of Old Darling," the time is 1920, the start of Prohibition, and Ptolemy and Minnie are in Hargrave to shop for

Christmas presents. Ptolemy stops at the drugstore for a half-pint of whiskey to use as a stimulant for his new lambs. On the way home in their buggy, Miss Minnie, a teetotaler, discovers the bottle hidden under the seat. To spare her husband the ignominy of alcohol, she heroically drinks it herself and becomes quite animated before she falls asleep in the buggy and has to be carried indoors by Tol.

"The Lost Bet," set in 1929, delivers a sharp dig at the assumed superiority of urbanites over rural folk and at city slickers' sometimes contemptuous treatment of farmers. In this sketch, Ptolemy gets the best of a wisecracking grocer who tries to humiliate him. One November day, Tol rides into Louisville with Sam Hanks, his wife's nephew, to bring a load of livestock to sell at the Bourbon Stockyards. Tol enjoys his visits to the city, and after making his sale, he stops in a poolroom to eat fried oysters and engage the locals in conversation. This year, however, Miss Minnie has instructed him to bring home some navy beans, which were in short supply that year. Dressed in their farm clothes, Tol and Sam go on to a prosperous grocery store, where the proprietor tries to humiliate them in front of some salesmen. The owner, "a dapper fellow with a round face and round eyeglasses, his hair parted in the middle, with garters on his sleeves and a cigar in his mouth," deliberately insults Tol, calling him "Otis," "Timothy," "Mr. Wheatly," "Mr. Bulltrack," "Mr. Briarly," and "Spud," in response to his request for a two-bushel bag of navy beans (53–54). Tol quietly accepts the insults, though his eyes narrow somewhat. At the counter, after he has paid for the beans, he attempts an unsuccessful coin trick to disarm the proprietor. Then he offers him a bet, saying, "I'll bet you this quarter I can jump into that basket of eggs and not break a one" (57). The proprietor unwisely accepts the bet, and Tol jumps into the basket, breaking all the eggs. Now no one laughs. He pays up on his bet and quietly walks out on the open-mouthed proprietor.

In "Nearly to the Fair," the time is 1932 and Ptolemy and Minnie have bought their first car, a Model A coupe, which neither one of them can drive very well. When they decide to go to the state fair in Louisville at the end of the summer, they hire 12-year-old Elton Penn to drive for them. With only muddled directions from Sam Hanks, they inevitably get lost in Louisville and spend the better part of the day driving in circles. In a minor accident, they lock bumpers with a more expensive car, and Ptolemy rescues them by lifting the car to unhook the bumpers. After this incident, they are more than relieved to head for home, away from the confusion of city traffic.

"The Solemn Boy" is a poignant story, set in 1934, describing rural hunger and homelessness during the Depression era. Tol is harvesting dried corn in his bottomland one cold, late November day with a hint of snow in the air. As his team pulls the loaded wagon up the dirt road from the hollow, he spots a man and a boy walking along the road, poorly dressed and hunched up against the cold. He offers them a ride in his wagon and invites them to stay for lunch at his house. After warming up by the stove and washing, the strangers sit down with Tol and Minnie for lunch and begin to eat voraciously. They say little about themselves except to thank the Proudfoots for the meal. The boy sits solemn-faced and unsmiling until Tol inadvertently spills buttermilk down the front of his shirt, when the boy explodes into laughter. With the tension broken, they listen to Tol's stories until the meal is over, when Minnie finds a spare overcoat for the boy. The man and boy then thank them and take their leave. Tol and Minnie's simple and unassuming hospitality and generosity reflect their desire for the child they could not have.

"Turn Back the Bed," set in 1941, describes an incident from Tol's boyhood, when he was five. The occasion is an October get-together at the home of Tol's grandfather, the Proudfoot patriarch "Old Ant'ny," and his wife, Aunt Belle. This sketch evokes the lively frontier spirit in a humorous account of the boys' mischief-making after the noon meal, when the adults are resting. Tol's cousin Lester drops an old yellow tomcat down the stone chimney, where it gets stuck halfway down, so the boys drop a small, fierce feist down after it. Cat and dog drop down together into the fireplace ashes and proceed to chase each other through the house, causing pandemonium. Lester hides upstairs under a bed until Aunt Belle comes looking for him, and when she catches him by the leg to drag him out, he upsets an unemptied chamberpot, which spills through the cracks in the floorboards onto the head of Old Ant'ny, sitting below. The sketch is reminiscent of early southern humor, particularly chapters 31 through 43 of Twain's *Huckleberry Finn*, set at the Silas Phelps plantation, where Huck and Tom dream up a series of elaborate schemes to free Jim and make Aunt Sally and Uncle Silas miserable.

"Watch with Me," the title sketch and longest story, takes place in August 1916 and involves Ptolemy's encounter with a neighbor, Thacker Hample, a member of the large, shiftless Hample clan. Thacker Hample, nicknamed "Nightlife," is feeble-minded, wears thick glasses because of his nearsightedness, and is somewhat unpredictable, but Tol has always been patient with Thacker's "spells." On this particular August morning, however, everything starts badly for Tol. His cows escape through a gap in the fence, one of his Jerseys puts her foot in the milk bucket, and a snake threatens a nesting hen. Tol gets his 10-gauge shotgun, "Old Fetcher," to dispatch the snake but misses and blows a hole in the wall of his workshop. He reloads the gun, props it against the shop door, and begins hoeing cabbages. Tol is distracted by Sam Hanks coming to borrow a posthole digger and does not notice Nightlife approaching until he has picked up the gun. Thacker is distraught because he was not allowed to preach at the local revival in the Goforth church.

Tol does not trust Nightlife with the gun, and what follows is a long, comical chase after him to retrieve the gun and prevent him from shooting himself or someone else. Virtually all of the local farmers join in the chase, which is perhaps a bit overdrawn, but as with most southern humor, the pleasure is in the telling of the story. The men cannot approach too close for fear of provoking Nightlife, but neither can they afford to lose sight of him, so they follow through woods, fields, pastures, and tobacco patches, hot, tired and thirsty, missing lunch, dinner, and their evening chores. Nightlife seems to be wandering in a daze, but he never relinquishes the gun. The other men begin to grumble, but Tol, acting as his brother's keeper, remains steadfast in his concern for Nightlife. The men finally decide to bed down for the night and build a small fire to warm themselves. Early the next morning, they awake to find Nightlife standing over them, gun in hand, complaining, "Couldn't you stay awake? Couldn't you stay awake?" (198). Berry's sketch takes on biblical overtones as Nightlife leads the men back to Tol's farm, where they take shelter from a sudden downpour inside Tol's workshop. There, gun in hand, Nightlife finally gets a chance to lead his service, with hymn-singing and a sermon based on Matthew 18:12, the parable of the lost sheep. Nightlife tries haltingly to explain the nature of his affliction, and his simple words move the men. He inadvertently stands in front of the hen's nest, and she flies at him to return to her brood. Nightlife strikes out at the squawking hen, suddenly comes to his senses, and puts the gun down. Tol and the men had saved him from himself during his long ramble in the woods.

Berry's sketches in *Watch with Me* show many affinities with southern humor.[13] They are local, authentic, and detailed, usually focusing on one humorous incident retold by an anonymous first-person narrator, who recalls and closes each story. The stories are spun out with the slow pacing, lavish detail, and zestful exuberance of oral narratives and share with southern humor an oral style, burlesque humor, comic, mock-epic inflation, and tall-tale exaggeration. They capture the pace of ordinary rural life in a world governed by the seasonal rhythms of farm chores, harvest festivals, state fairs, and family get-togethers. As comic satire, Berry's sketches tend to defend rural community values—generosity, hospitality, neighborliness, family ties—against threatening outside forces—the automobile, politicians, city slickers. The sketches present an affectionate, nostalgic glimpse back to a simpler, less complicated time, to a self-sufficient rural culture that had largely disappeared by World War II. It is significant that the most recent sketch takes place in 1941, two years before Tol's death at 69, the last of his line. The style of Berry's fiction seems to be shifting from the straightforward, somber realism of his early novels to a more relaxed and expansive comic tone in these recent sketches.

Chapter Seven
A Prolific Poet

Berry has been without question a prolific poet throughout his career. Since 1964 he has published more than 10 volumes of poetry, plus his *Collected Poems* (1985) and numerous small, limited-edition volumes, chapbooks, and reprints, along with his uncollected poems. He has reworked many of the same pastoral themes in his poems, essays, and fiction, so that one finds a remarkable consistency of purpose in his use of various genres. Though basically a lyric poet, he has employed the narrative and dramatic modes on occasion. A traditionalist by instinct, he has used both open and closed forms, though he most often modifies conventional lyric forms to his own loose metrical style. He often writes in the first person, employing the persona of the farmer-husband-countryman. Above all, he is a discursive poet for whom the thematic structure of a poem predominates. There is little modernist formalism or postmodernist experimentation in his verse. As a regional poet, he celebrates the moods and seasons of his native Kentucky. In some respects, his verse seems deliberately anachronistic, expressing a sensibility at odds with the dominant "literary" mode of his age. Some of his poems resemble those of the Fugitive and Agrarian poets of the 1930s and 1940s— John Crowe Ransom, Allen Tate, and Robert Penn Warren—although there are certainly echoes in his style of William Carlos Williams, Robert Frost, William Butler Yeats, and Gary Snyder as well.

Berry has set forth his poetics in the essay "Notes: Unspecializing Poetry" in *Standing by Words*. He abhors specialization in poetry and makes it clear that art should not be divorced from culture, nor from work. The obligation of the poet is to tell the truth, using the "living speech" of the community to memorialize an event or insight. The poem is not an autonomous object but something that exists in a world of relations. He rejects self-reflexive poetry, insisting on the poet's obligation to relate to his or her community. Both the refinement of overspecialization and the subjectivity of self-absorption are destructive to poetry because they lead inward, not outward. "The right use of any art or discipline leads *out* of it," he asserts (85). Berry explicitly rejects both the New Critical assumption of artistic autonomy and the postmodernist assumption of the unreliability of language. "Bliss is the indispensable goal," he insists (80). Because the poem exists in relation to the world, structure is essential. "Structure is intelligibility" (82), Berry asserts, though the form of a poem should be unobtrusive, if not invisible. Most important, poetry should be rooted in a particular place. By its very nature, it is local and regional, inhabiting a particular physical landscape rather than a universal landscape of the mind. As Berry remarks: "I am endlessly in need of the work of poets who have been concerned with living in place, the life of a place, long-term attention and devotion to a settled home and its natural household, and hence to the relation between imagination and language and a place" (88).

Berry is a poet of deep personal conviction. Like Thoreau, he has felt a need to reestablish himself from the ground up by articulating the ecological and economic convictions by which he would live and by trying to live and write in accordance with those principles. He has striven to achieve clarity and directness in his work by reworking the same basic themes and insights: the proper place of human life in the larger natural cycle of life, death, and renewal; the dignity of work, labor, and vocation; the central importance of the human and natural history of his native region; and precise, lyrical descriptions of the native flora and fauna, especially of the birds, trees, and wildflowers. He has written elegies to family members and friends, topical and occasional poems (especially antiwar poems expressing his strong pacifist convictions), didactic poems expressing his environmental beliefs, and a surprising number of religious poems expressing a deeply felt, if nondenominational, faith.

One finds in Berry's verse a continual effort to unify life, work, and art within a coherent philosophy or vision. Put simply, that vision includes a regional sensibility, a farming vocation, the poetic voice of the farmer-husband-countryman, and a strong commitment to a localized environmental ethic. His most notable persona is the "Mad Farmer"— passionate, exuberant, indignant, eccentric. From childhood, Berry always hoped to become a farmer, and his verse celebrates the life of the land. His vision, however, is that of the diminishment of the land, the community, and the culture, and of the need for discipline and renewal.

One senses in Berry's poetry a keen awareness of living in a fallen world that can only be redeemed, if at all, through hard work, loyalty to place, fidelity to one's obligations, disciplined self-knowledge, and a gradual healing of the land. Though he is predominantly a lyric poet, his lyrics often declaim rather than sing: his muse is Delphic rather than Orphic, prophetic instead of lyrical. His discursive, sometimes didactic verse is quiet and often understated, literal rather than metaphoric. The Berry persona can be passionate and exuberant but is more often meditative and reflective. His lyrics span a wide range of categories, including elegiac, discursive, historical, occasional, pastoral, seasonal, personal, philosophical, religious, and meditative/reflective.

Berry's poems are noted for their quiet attentiveness to the surroundings, almost as though the speaker tried to make himself part of his habitat. His farmer persona is a keen naturalist, carefully observing the seasonal behavior of birds and animals and meticulously noting the botanical descriptions of trees and flowers. His speaker is especially attuned to birdsong, and the variety of birds mentioned in his poems is notable—kingfishers, song sparrows, phoebes, herons, wild geese, finches, wrens, chickadees, cardinals, titmice, and warblers. Taken together, his poems comprise a veritable natural history of his region of Kentucky. Implicit in these nature poems is a sense of the grace and renewal, the pleasure and contentment available through the natural world.

Berry first published many of his poems in literary journals and small magazines or through specialty presses, so that original editions of his work are often hard to find. His individual poetry volumes were first published with Harcourt Brace (*The Broken Ground* [1964], *Openings* [1968], *Farming: A Hand Book* [1970], *The Country of Marriage* [1973], and *Clearing* [1977]), later with North Point Press (*A Part* [1980], *The Wheel* [1982], *Collected Poems* [1985], and *Sabbaths* [1987]), and most recently with Pantheon (*Entries* [1994]). *Collected Poems* is not inclusive: the poems were selected from each previous volume. Berry also added some important poems to the collected edition, such as the contents of the volume *Findings* (1969), which was originally published by a small specialty press and had been out of print.[1]

Though Berry had been publishing poems in literary magazines and journals since the mid-1950s, his first critical recognition came in 1964 with the appearance of *The Broken Ground*, his first poetry volume, and "November Twenty Six Nineteen Sixty Three," his elegy that has been called the most successful commemoration of John F. Kennedy's death. Berry's 11-stanza elegy makes use of repetition and refrain and incorporates the traditional elegiac cycle of shock, grief, mourning, the funeral procession, the interment, and the apotheosis of the subject's memory. Berry's interest in the elegy form is also apparent in "Elegy," the opening poem in *The Broken Ground*, written in memory of his grandfather. Other elegiac works include "Three Elegiac Poems" (*Findings*), "In Memory: Stuart Egnal" (*Openings*), and "Requiem" and "Elegy" (*The Wheel*). Death is often present in Berry's work, presented naturalistically without a compensating theme of either carpe diem or renewal, except in the natural cycles of life.

The Broken Ground

The Broken Ground (1964) is a collection of 31 lyrics with a distinctly regional flavor; 20 of them later appeared in *Collected Poems*.[2] Many of these poems first appeared in *Stylus*, *Poetry*, *The Nation*, and *Prairie Schooner*. This early collection introduces the Berry voice and some of his major themes: the cycle of life and death, responsiveness to place, pastoral subject matter, and recurring images of the Kentucky River and the hill farms of north-central Kentucky. His language is relaxed, expansive, and colloquial, drawing upon the domesticated, pastoral images of farming rather than those of natural wilderness. The stylistic influence of William Carlos Williams and the Orientalism of Kenneth Rexroth are apparent in some of these early poems. Berry's domesticated nature images contrast with the wilderness imagery of his friend and fellow poet Gary Snyder. Yet for all of their domestication, some of Berry's poems seem curiously detached and impersonal. He makes few specific allusions, aside from the historical evocation of the early Kentucky pioneer in "Boone." Berry draws his language from farming life and presents himself as a working farmer whose poetry is redeemed from abstraction by his love of farming and the rhythms of his labor—its purposefulness, its physicality, and its tangible rewards.

To a large degree, the poems in *The Broken Ground* are preoccupied with death. The collection opens with "Elegy," written as a memorial to Berry's paternal grandfather, Pryor Thomas Berry. The imagery is cold, stark, and somber, befitting a winter burial. Five irregular stanzas present a series of disjointed, loosely associative images of winter bleakness that convey a mood of numbness in grief and loss. The snowfall, clouds, hidden sun, and silence convey a sense of the family's anguish in confronting their loss: the weather serves as a metaphor for their grief. His grandfather's interment is accompanied by rain, suggesting erosion, entropy, dissolution, darkness, decay. Death is final. The only consolation comes through time and seasonal change, with the return of spring and life to the hillside grave and the body's rebirth in the tree, birds, wind, and rain.

Two other meditations on death, "A Fit of Winter" and "Canticle," proclaim death's finality. "A Fit of Winter" imagines the body, "exhumed

from sleep," staring open-eyed but sightless, unable to communicate
what it has seen and heard. "Canticle" explicitly rejects any possibility of
religious consolation through belief in a spiritual life after death:

> What death means is not this—
> the spirit, triumphant in the body's fall,
> praising its absence, feeding on music.
> If life can't justify and explain itself,
> death can't justify and explain it.
> A creed and a grave never did equal the life
> of anything (38).

The theme of death is conveyed in the paradoxical metaphor of the
title poem, "The Broken Ground," suggesting both furrow and grave,
planting and harvesting, procreation and death. Berry's imagery alludes
to the complex metaphysical associations of death in Elizabethan poetry,
suggesting sexual climax and the spending of one's vital energy, as well
as the emergence of life from death, in a mysterious cycle of continuity:
bud, flower, fruit, seed, husk.

> The opening out and out,
> body yielding body:
> the breaking
> through which the new
> comes, perching
> above its shadow
> on the piling up
> darkened broken old
> husks of itself: (56)

We participate in a mystery beyond our comprehension, to which we
can respond only in awe and wonder. "The Apple Tree" conveys this perfection of the moment, amid the freshly cut grass, orange poppies, sunlit
leaves, and crimson finches darting through its branches. "Be Still in
Haste" further amplifies the Zen-like perfection of the present moment.

Berry's poems convey a mythic vision of a lost, primeval paradise, a
fall from grace, and a guarded hope in work, discipline, and renewal.
"Paradise might have appeared here" (33), he announces in "The
Aristocracy," but instead he finds a wealthy old dowager airing her cat.
Like Frost's pastoral world, a diminished New England landscape,
Berry's Kentucky River Valley has suffered from neglect and abuse. The

moments of grace are few—birdsongs, the return of spring, the cycle of the seasons, glimpses of the natural order—and death is always present. Like Frost, Berry has chosen to make a "strategic retreat" to a pastoral world in which the poet-farmer can take stock of his resources, but in other ways his sensibility is different from Frost's. Berry is much more committed to a specific place; Frost's loyalty is to his region. For Frost, the sense of diminishment came from the abandonment of rural New England farms after the Civil War. For Berry, the sense of loss comes from the environmental despoliation of the Cumberland Plateau, first by careless farming practices and later by timber interests and the big coal companies.

Berry's version of the "Paradise Lost" myth centers on the massive environmental destruction visited upon the Cumberland region by absentee corporate owners. He has been radicalized by Kentucky's legacy of corrupt government and indifference to environmental concerns, a legacy that has left the region virtually a Third World economy, based upon cheap, large-scale mineral extraction with little regard for the human and environmental consequences of pit and surface mining. The practice of strip-mining has been particularly devastating to watersheds. Living downstream from the despoiled hills and polluted creeks of Appalachia, Berry has seen firsthand the flooding and pollution of the Kentucky River—hence, the preoccupation with the destructiveness of erosion and floods in Berry's poetry. In "Diagon," which was not included in *Collected Poems*, the river is presented as a malevolent, destructive force, scouring the shores, extending out into the fields, and dumping brown mud. In "Observance," the river god is more tranquil and observant, "resting from his caprices," as the townspeople return to picnic or fish on his shores, but his forbearance is only temporary, for his "seasonal wraths" will return (10–11).

Openings

Berry's second poetry volume, *Openings* (1968), contains 36 poems, of which 29 were later reprinted in *Collected Poems*.[3] The first poem in *Openings*, "The Thought of Something Else," announces the speaker's desire to leave the city for country life. But first he must make his peace with the legacy of slavery; he does so in "My Great-Grandfather's Slaves." The next three poems are autumnal in tone, placing the speaker within a seasonal cycle. In "The Snake," he comes across a small reptile hidden in the leaves, preparing for hibernation. The "living cold" of the

snake parallels the winter solitude of the speaker in "The Cold." The
starkly descriptive lyric "Winter Rain" leads to "March Snow" and "April
Woods: Morning," which resemble haiku in their delicate imagery. In
"Porch on the River," the speaker establishes himself in his riverside
writer's cabin, like the classical Chinese poet Tu Fu. The longest and
most abstract piece, "Window Poems," comprises 27 sections that reflect
the speaker's changing moods as he watches the shifting patterns of the
river scenery from his study window. "Grace" and "Discipline" reflect the
strength that the speaker draws from nature, allowing him to withstand
the destructiveness of his society, in which people are at war with the
environment, one another, and themselves.

Many of these discursive and lyric poems are closely related to essays
that express the same ideas. "My Great-Grandfather's Slaves" repeats the
theme of residual guilt over slavery that Berry develops in *The Hidden
Wound*. "The Return" expresses once again Berry's dream of returning the
land to wilderness and undoing the environmental damage of human settlement. Berry later revised "The Return" and used two of the stanzas as
separate poems in *Collected Poems*. Stanza 3 became "The Dream," in which
he imagines the surrounding countryside restored to its pristine beauty,
unspoiled by greed and acquisitiveness. Stanza 7 became "The Sycamore,"
in which Berry admires as a symbol of natural resiliency a venerable speci-
men whose gnarled trunk has been scarred by lightning. "East Kentucky,
1967" bitterly protests the damage caused by strip-mining.

Some of the most memorable poems in this volume are personal or
descriptive lyrics, such as "The Change," which uses a change in the
weather as a metaphor for the speaker's depression. "The Quiet" evokes
the peacefulness of a fisherman on the river. "The Migrants" describes
those who leave the land, having failed at farming. "The Dead Calf" and
"The Burial of the Dead" return to a familiar Berry theme, treated starkly
and naturalistically. "In Memory: Stuart Egnal" eulogizes an artist friend
by recalling the high wooded hills and valley farms outside of Florence
that Egnal sketched one April afternoon the friends spent together.

Farming: A Hand Book

Berry's next poetry volume, *Farming: A Hand Book* (1970), includes 55
selections, of which 47 were reprinted in *Collected Poems*.[4] These poems
are less solitary in mood. As the collection's title implies, the poems celebrate the pleasures of the agrarian life. The first poem, "The Man Born
to Farming," links the speaker with the cycles of organic growth and

decay, as a kind of vegetative deity who "enters into death / yearly, and comes back rejoicing" (3). The volume introduces the colorful persona of the Mad Farmer, an exuberant, Bunyanesque fertility figure who flaunts social conventions in "The Mad Farmer's Revolution" and "The Contrariness of the Mad Farmer"; dances in the streets in "The Mad Farmer in the City"; offers wry, homespun comments in "Prayers and Sayings of the Mad Farmer"; and celebrates the abundance of his farm in "The Satisfactions of the Mad Farmer."

"The Birth," a dramatic dialogue, marks an interesting departure from Berry's customary lyrical verse. A retelling of the nativity story on a Port William farm one cold winter night during lambing season, the story is about three local farmers—Billy, Raymond, and Uncle Stanley—who come across a husband, wife, and newborn child resting on the straw in one of their lambing barns. They stay to make the family comfortable, leave them some money, and depart. Later the three men express their wonder at the strange event, heralded by a low singing in the wind. Raymond, the one who has "a talent for unreasonable belief," asserts that they have seen more than they will understand (53). He recognizes the birth as an incarnation:

> "It's the old ground trying it again.
> Solstice, seeding and birth—it never
> gets enough. It wants the birth of a man
> to bring together sky and earth, like a stalk
> of corn. It's not death that makes the dead
> rise out of the ground, but something alive
> straining up, rooted in darkness, like a vine." (53–54)

Many of the poems suggest making a "strategic retreat" into the countryside to escape from the political and social chaos of the late 1960s. There is a sense of impending catastrophe, both natural and social, conveyed by images of flood and war. The occasional poem "March 22, 1968" contrasts the spring rise on the river, full of floating debris, with the speaker lying awake at night, his mind heavy "with official meaningless deaths" (18). "The Morning's News" dramatizes the agony of the Vietnam War, and "A Wet Time" describes the height of the spring flood, which both buries and nourishes the croplands. "Enriching the Earth" employs the imagery of cover crops and composting to suggest how death serves life. "The Silence" asks the prescient question, "What must a man do to be at home in the world?" (23). Two evocative

lyrics, "In This World" and "On the Hill Late at Night," describe the
solace the speaker finds in his hilltop meadows. "The Wish to Be
Generous" expresses his desire to serve the natural processes of death and
regeneration. "A Standing Ground" indicates his need for a perspective
that allows him to withdraw from public debate to the healing comfort
of his land. In "The Current," the speaker identifies himself with the wisdom of the original dwellers, the Native Americans who dug with sticks
to plant their corn, squash, and beans in forest openings: "He is made
their descendent, what they left / in the earth rising into him like a seasonal juice" (41). The verse-play "The Bringer of Water" recounts the
courtship of Nathan and Hannah Coulter. The collection ends with a
lovely fantasy poem inspired by Berry's daughter, "To the Unseeable
Animal," which invokes the invisible presence of the spirit of the woods.

The Country of Marriage

The Country of Marriage, Berry's fourth poetry volume published by
Harcourt Brace Jovanovich, contains 35 poems, 29 of which later
appeared in *Collected Poems*.[5] These poems celebrate Berry's central
metaphor of marriage—to one's spouse, family, home, vocation, farm,
and region. Berry's relationships with his wife and children have been
central to his task of renewal as a pastoral poet. An accomplished love
poet, he has written many poems to his wife Tanya, on the anniversaries
of their marriage and to express his gratitude for their common life
together. For his children, too, Berry has written poems, on their births,
their coming of age, their marriages, and the births of his grandchildren.
In "The Gathering," he realizes that he holds his son in his arms the
same way his father held him, and that his son will someday hold his
own future child. In the long title poem, "The Country of Marriage,"
farming and marriage serve as complementary and inseparable extensions of each other. Husbandry and marriage to the land are recurring
tropes in Berry's poetry, illustrated in clearing fields, sowing crops,
planting gardens, tending livestock, mowing hay, and taking in the harvest. His poems celebrate farming as a labor of love, a work of regeneration and fecundity that is at once vital and procreative.

The opening poem in the collection, "The Old Elm Tree by the
River," presents the theme of transience and imperceptible change in the
natural world, even in what appears to be the most durable of living
forms on the speaker's farm, a great old elm that nevertheless is slowly
dying. Entropy and dissolution take place alongside growth and renewal,

apparent in the crash of a great limb from the dying elm, awakening the speaker from his sleep. "Breaking," "Zero," and "The Silence" are three poems that reflect Berry's interest in Zen and the Oriental tradition of nature poetry. Each shows an awareness of the paradoxical logic of Zen and mirrors those same paradoxical qualities in nature and language. In "Breaking," light and dark mingle in the mind like river water rising over broken ice. "Zero" evokes the frozen motion of the river in winter, water flowing beneath the ice, the bitter cold holding all life in suspended animation, the metaphoric "zero" of winter, "the elemental poverty / of all that was ever born" (10–11). "The Silence" probes the inadequacy of language to express the ineffable, fleeting pleasures of the moment; the speaker places his hope in "the silence" of a nonverbal world that "lives in the death of speech / and sings there" (25).

Two poems about death, "At a Country Funeral" and "Testament," question the artificiality of modern funeral customs. "At a Country Funeral" echoes William Carlos Williams's "Tract" in its plea for a simplicity and dignity that do not attempt to mask the reality of death. Berry objects to the intrusion of strangers and the bland smoothness of the funeral home, both of which keep friends and kinsmen from "knowing the extremity they have come to" (27). "Testament," with echoes of William Butler Yeats, offers Berry's own instructions for his burial and interment. He does not want his face made up with cosmetics and wax; he asks simply to be dressed in his work clothes and laid in a plain wooden box.

Berry shows a new interest in rhyme and meter in this volume, employing a tetrameter couplet in "The Clear Days," a poem, dedicated to Allen Tate, about seeking clarity of vision, and "To William Butler Yeats," a tribute to Yeats for keeping faith with his own "native truth and place" (45). "Testament" also employs rhymed stanzas, and "Song" self-consciously announces its intention to "tell my love in rhyme" (46). The last poem in the volume, "An Anniversary," celebrates the cycles of regeneration with a delicate pattern of interlocking rhyme. This interest in more formal poetic structures has become increasingly evident in Berry's poetry, especially in *Sabbaths*.

Clearing

Clearing (1977) was the last poetry volume Berry published with Harcourt Brace Jovanovich. Of the seven poems published in the original volume, five were reprinted in *Collected Poems*.[6] The poems in *Clearing* articulate Berry's sense of region and place. "Where" is a long pastoral meditation on the history and ownership of Lane's Landing, the 50-acre farm the Berrys purchased between 1965 and 1968. The history of the farm provides a case study in attitudes toward stewardship and land use, from the earliest settlers to the Louisville developer who sold Berry the farm. The transition from wilderness to settlement to worn-out land rehearses an ecological myth of the fall from primeval abundance into reckless waste and decay. Berry presents the history of his farm as a parable of the American frontier and an indictment of the reckless habits that quickly exhausted the land's natural richness and abundance. "Where" is both a personal credo and a contemporary ecological statement of the need to change both land management practices and cultural attitudes toward the land.

"Where" exists in two forms: a long, didactic form originally published in *Clearing*, and a shorter, more lyrical, revised version that later appeared in *Collected Poems*. The two versions are so different, however, that they can almost be considered separate poems. The original version shifts between an impersonal, historical, third-person point of view and the more personal voice of the farmer-poet. The revised version retains more of the impersonal third-person perspective and lacks a clear persona, the speaker's presence being merely implied.

The original version of "Where" is a three-part historical meditation that addresses the general question, "Who owned this land before me and what was its history?" Berry traces the previous ownership of the farm back almost 200 years to the original land survey by two Scotch-Irish settlers, Thomas and Walker Daniels. At that time, the farm was part of a 1,000-acre tract on the Kentucky River. Subsequent owners successively subdivided and sold the land for profit, no one ever keeping it long or passing it on to his children.

The revised version of "Where" eliminates parts 1 and 3 of the original poem and retains only the first 140 lines of part 2, which has been shortened to 5 stanzas. All specific references to the names of previous owners are dropped, creating a more generalized lyric meditation on the land. The clear references to a specific place and the historic record are lost, and the theme of the poem—the consequences of poor husbandry—becomes more generalized.

The style of both versions of "Where" is deliberately terse and understated: images of silence, decay, and ecological degradation predominate. Images of lost primordial richness—clear creeks, tall hardwoods, and black topsoil—contrast with the washed-out gullies, eroded furrows, and scrub growth of the present. The land has been despoiled and the original settlers are gone, leaving little tangible evidence of their presence beyond their gravestones, silent "as fossils in creek ledges" (11). The poem unfolds its meaning through a series of absences and negations: too much of the land's history has transpired elsewhere, in the halls of the state capital, where its fate was brokered by the rich and powerful. The tangible, local cultural memory is gone, except for old property deeds on dusty courthouse shelves. This elegiac tone is tempered by the recognition that somewhere the agrarian dream survives, though haste, indifference, restlessness, and careless husbandry have discouraged the growth of a prosperous local rural community. The ruin of the land resulted from the wrong vision—a vision of greed and quick wealth. We do not yet understand the land well enough to create a sustainable, independent local culture. The poem offers muted hope, however, for eventual renewal through wiser, less destructive patterns of land use.

"Where" is a mythic poem about the possibility of regaining the lost Eden. Like Adam and Eve expelled from Eden, the narrator is left with the dilemma of trying to recover what has been lost; also like Adam and Eve, he is left with hard-won moral understanding. However, he may also reclaim the legacy of those few who came before him who loved the land and saw the possibility of a good life there. The oblique allusions in "Where" to the story in Genesis of man's creation and fall also reinforce the implicit judgment of environmental destruction. It is a parable of the American frontier and an indictment of the cultural mindset that heedlessly exploits and wastes the natural resources of the land. The history of Berry's farmland has been a history of neglect and abuse, yet there is some reason for hope. The narrator has chosen to return here; he has laid claim to his land; and he is in a position to benefit from the mistakes of the past. The knowledge he carries with him is cause for song, and like the clear song of the cardinal, the narrator's stubborn loyalty to his native land is reason for hope.

Elsewhere, in the long autobiographical essay "The Long-Legged House," Berry has written about how hard it is to acquire a genuine sense of place. "Where" describes the process of assimilation to a place, an important theme in Berry's work. The poem chronicles his return to the region where he was born and where both sides of his family have lived for generations. For him, buying Lane's Landing Farm meant establishing himself in the region where he could be in touch with his past. There is an almost sacramental quality to his reconsecration of himself and his life to the place of his origins.

According to Berry, one learns to belong to a particular place through the power of silence and attentive observation, or mindfulness, which allows a place quietly to reveal its life in moments of deep intimacy and beauty. This kind of attentiveness permits people to live in the world as though they were not in it—that is, doing no harm—and encourages them to view human life as only a small part of the larger harmony of life around them. A statement of our responsibility to leave the places that sustain us in better condition than we find them, "Where" offers a vision of renewal, based on the promise of wise husbandry and permanent allegiance to a particular place.

The volume's title poem, "The Clearing," is a long descriptive poem in 11 sections, dedicated to Berry's fellow poet Hayden Carruth. It is another poem about the renewal of the land, this time about reclaiming abandoned farmland. The speaker describes his extensive efforts to clear thick, second-growth scrub from neglected pasture. He contrasts his vision of healthy, productive pastureland and community neighborliness with the Louisville developer's vision of subdevelopment into country homes and with the hostility of local country folk who just want to be left alone. The speaker acknowledges the difficulty of his task, wondering:

> Then why clear
> yet again an old farm
> scarred by the lack of sight
> that scars our souls? (27)

"Work Song" also traces the transformation of the speaker's relationship to his land, from vision to passion to fulfillment through physical labor, though he wonders whether his preoccupation with work will diminish his interest in books and poetry.

A Part

A Part (1980) was the first of Berry's poetry volumes to be published by North Point Press after he left Harcourt Brace Jovanovich. Of the 54 poems included in *A Part*, 39 were later reprinted in *Collected Poems*.[7] *A Part* and *The Wheel*, Berry's next poetry volume, reflect in their titles Berry's increasingly ecological awareness.

A Part includes a selection of pastoral lyrics; some religious poems; translations of two poems by the sixteenth-century French poet Pierre de

Ronsard; "Three Kentucky Poems," a narrative triptych based in part on historical accounts of the McAfee brothers' 1773 expedition into Kentucky; and "Horses," a commemorative verse tribute to the traditional skills of working with draft horses, which Berry much prefers to the tractors and internal combustion engines that have destroyed the quiet pleasures of farming. "Stay Home," the opening poem in the volume, serves as a parody of Frost's "The Pasture," reversing the invitation to come outdoors implicit in Frost's lyric.

In "July, 1773," Berry returns to the McAfee brothers' 1773 expedition into Kentucky in a meditation on the pioneers' attitudes toward the wilderness. The poem describes their amazement at the large herds of buffalo, wolves, and bear at the natural salt licks near their Big Bear Lick and Drennon Creek campsites. The climax of the poem comes in the stampede that young Sam Adams precipitates by shooting into the great milling herd of buffalo. Berry reflects on young Adams's impetuous greed and lack of self-restraint:

> He saw an amplitude
> so far beyond his need
> he could not imagine it,
> and could not let it be. (78)

In the companion poem, "1975," Berry implies that, 200 years later, American attitudes have not changed very much. Now when the river floods, it carries the rich humus downstream from the mountains, which are scarred and denuded in the quest for timber and coal. The richness of the land has been so soon destroyed, millions of years of nature's work undone, and "the river has become the gut / of greed" (82).

The Wheel

The Wheel (1982) takes its title image from the mandala, or "wheel of life," of which Sir Albert Howard speaks in his classic study *An Agricultural Testament* (1943), an important influence on Berry's thinking about organic farming.[8] A collection of elegies of remembrance and praise, *The Wheel* celebrates the continuities of birth, growth, maturity, death, and decay. An increasing self-assurance is evident in Berry's persona, a relaxed, self-confident voice free of anxiety. Many poems employ a more traditional form and, increasingly, rhyme and regular stanzaic form, although he still seems to prefer a short line.

This collection includes three poems that serve as a pastoral elegy dedicated to Owen Flood, whom Berry honors as a teacher and friend. The first poem, "Requiem," announces Flood's passing, though his spirit remains in the fields he tended. "Elegy," one of Berry's finest poems, pays tribute to the quality of Flood's life, invoking the spirits of the dead to reaffirm the traditional values that Flood embodied: duty, loyalty, perseverance, honesty, hard work, endurance, and self-reliance. It reaffirms the continuity of the generations within a permanent, stable agricultural order. The poem's eight sections convey a sense of recycling human experience, as nature recycles organic materials back into the soil to create fertile organic humus. The poem also celebrates permanent human standards: marriage, work, friendship, love, fidelity, and death. The dominant image is of human life as a dance within the larger cycles of life, implying closure, completeness, and inclusion. "Elegy" affirms farm labor as an honorable calling, true to the biblical injunction to live by the sweat of one's brow. The opening line of the poem recalls the implicit purpose in all Berry's work: for the mind of the poet "to be at home on its native ground" (5). The poem honors the elders of the community, including Flood, who were the speaker's teachers and concludes with the affirmation that

> The best teachers teach more
> than they know. By their deaths
> they teach most. They lead us beyond
> what we know, and what they knew. (12)

The third poem in the trilogy, "Rising," dedicated to Flood's son Keith, recalls Berry's stern apprenticeship under Flood's watchful eye. He recollects an occasion when, as a young man, he wilted in the hot afternoon sun during the harvest because he had stayed out dancing too late the night before. Flood taught Berry how to work willingly and joyfully. Through the example of his character, he inspired Berry as a teenager:

> That was my awkward boyhood,
> the time of his mastery.
> He troubled me to become
> what I had not thought to be. (15)

The six sections of the poem rehearse the memory of Flood's life, a legacy Berry now holds before him, reenacting in it

                    a kinship of the fields
                    that gives to the living the breath
                    of the dead. (17)

Another important poem in this collection, "The Gift of Gravity,"
reaffirms the life-sustaining cycles of sunlight, photosynthesis, growth,
decay, and death. The poem announces its major theme, "Gravity is
grace," with the dominant image of the river of life and the return of all
life to its source (42). There is an almost mystical unity conveyed in the
opening lines:

                    All that passes descends,
                    and ascends again unseen
                    into the light. (42)

Two other poems, "The Wheel" and "The Dance," affirm the interlocking unities that knit the community together in festive celebrations of
song and dance.

Collected Poems

When his publishing contract with Harcourt Brace expired after the
publication of the Harvest/HBJ paperback edition of *Clearing* in 1977,
Berry changed publishers, moving to North Point Press in San Francisco,
California. One immediate result was the publication of his *Recollected
Essays* (1981) and his *Collected Poems: 1957–1982* (1985), which brought
back into print many of his earlier essay and poetry volumes that had
been unavailable. Not only did the publication of Berry's *Collected Poems*
permit the republishing of nearly 200 poems from his first eight poetry
volumes, but he was able to select which poems he would retain and
which he would drop from those early volumes. Since the volume reflects
Berry's revised editorial judgments about his poetry, it is certainly the
definitive volume, and one can only hope that it will remain in print.
Berry comments in his author's note: "This volume contains all of my
poems, so far published in books, that I care to have reread. That is, it is
a collection, but it is not 'complete.' I have left out some work that I
think least good. A few of the poems here, some newly titled, were published previously as parts of longer poems. Some of the longer poems
have been shortened. In some poems I have made deletions and other
changes, usually small."[9]

Among the best of Berry's early poetry is the sequence of three long poems from the short volume *Findings*, printed by a small publisher in Iowa and long unavailable.[10] The first of these poems, "The Design of a House," is about the act of establishing a household; the speaker and his family are moving into their home. It is a discursive poem in 10 parts about beginnings, dreams, plans, and intentions, and about the fabrication of a dwelling and reestablishing roots in one's native place, a goal that had previously been merely a vague dream. Establishing a household becomes the occasion for a nuptial poem, an expression of the speaker's love for his wife Tanya and his daughter Mary and a rededication of their common life together as a family. The design of their house comes to signify the design of their family relationships. Berry's son is not mentioned here, perhaps because the poem was written before his birth.

The second poem in this sequence, "The Handing Down," continues the theme of family and place, this time in terms of an old man's memories and reflections and his sense of satisfaction with the life he has led, as expressed through conversations with his grandson. The poem is divided into 14 parts, each bearing a headnote: (1) *The light*; (2) *The conversation*; (3) *The old man is older in history than in time*; (4) *He looks out the window at the town*; (5) *He has lived through another night*; (6) *The new house*; (7) *The heaviness of his wisdom*; (8) *A wilderness starts toward him*; (9) *Though he can't know death, he must study dying*; (10) *The freedom of loving*; (11) *He takes his time*; (12) *The fern*; (13) *He is in the habit of the world*; and (14) *The young man, thinking of the old*. The speaker in this poem recalls Jack Beechum, the protagonist of Berry's third novel, *The Memory of Old Jack*. Both the novel and this poem describe an old man's preparations for death, his gradual letting go of life through his memories. The last section of *Findings*, "Three Elegiac Poems," dedicated to Berry's maternal grandfather, Harry Erdman Perry, commemorates the old man's death, which the speaker hopes will occur quietly at home, away from the sterile coldness and isolation of a hospital ward and the clinical indifference of physicians. The light of life should fade slowly, Berry intimates, in its own home, surrounded by what the dying person has loved and those who have loved him.

Sabbaths

Sabbaths (1987) marks something of a departure in tone and style from Berry's earlier works. It is at once more formal, more structured, and more overtly religious in its sensibility. The 46 poems in this collection were written in the solitude of his study on Sunday mornings over a six-year period from 1979 to 1985.[11] The poems are untitled, arranged by year, and identified only by their first lines. They are quiet, restrained, almost metaphysical meditations that incorporate a number of quotations from Scripture. With their worshipful tone, they echo the pastoral Psalms. Berry makes use of a variety of traditional metrical forms, including rhymed couplets, terza rima, rhymed quatrains, longer stanzas employing interlocking rhyme, and the irregular ode. There are poems dedicated to his wife Tanya and to his children, Mary and Pryor Clifford, or "Den," and occasional poems, such as a Fourth of July poem.

These poems show a deep, nonsectarian religious sensibility, akin to the personal faith of the nineteenth-century New England poets—especially Emily Dickinson. Like Dickinson, Berry employs Christian tropes and religious pastoral imagery to describe his natural religion. The many allusions to Eden, Paradise, Garden, Creation, worship, hymns, song, grace, gift, Lord, God, Maker, Ghost, Heaven, Miracle, resurrection, darkness, and light invoke a prophetic vision of a new earth, healed and reborn—a paradise regained. Berry returns to his vision of the primal fertility and richness of the Kentucky landscape before it was destroyed by the rapacious settlers. His poems combine moral awareness of the deep wrong done to the earth by human greed and ignorance with ecological awareness of the need for the change and atonement that can come only from within. His poems offer a dualistic moral vision of nature as basically innocent, and human nature as flawed.

The overall theme of *Sabbaths* is the need for rest and renewal—both within human hearts and in the natural world. The poems themselves function as meditations, as examples of the quiet attentiveness, mindfulness, and tranquillity of spirit that elicit a close rapport with nature. Berry calls for the cultivation of a different kind of sensibility, one less inclined to impose human will on nature and more inclined to appreciate the natural world on its own terms, as a heaven on earth. Berry weaves many scriptural allusions into his poems, quoting from the Psalms, the Old Testament prophets, and the New Testament. His poems manage to convey a deep religious sensibility without making any formal religious affirmations, except by implication. The speaker comes across as a deeply thoughtful but independent spirit, reverent but unchurched. One finds in *Sabbaths* a new blend of spiritual and ecological awareness, a sense of life and earth as worthy of the deepest veneration. As poetry, these poems mark Berry's finest and most even and sustained artistic effort.

Entries

Berry's most recent poetry volume, *Entries* (1994), includes 43 new lyrics written over the past decade and arranged in four sections.[12] Many of the poems are about his family—his wife, daughter, son, father, mother, and grandmother—and others are about friends. Here as elsewhere, family, work, and place are the cornerstones of Berry's work. A number of subtle religious allusions, including epigraphs from Genesis and the Gospel of John, lend a meditative quality to what are otherwise personal lyrics. Aside from "In Extremis," a series of four poems in part 4 dedicated to his father, Berry seems to have made little formal arrangement of the poems in the other three sections. Part 1, "Some Differences," contains 15 personal lyrics; part 2 contains 11 didactic occasional poems; and part 3 contains 14 additional short lyrics, including some delicate love poems addressed to the speaker's wife.

Stylistically, Berry seems to be working toward a more subtle and informal poetic structure characterized by a regular stanzaic form but little formal rhyme scheme, the occasional use of refrain, a regular rhythmic pattern, and a preference for slant or near-rhymes. Other more didactic poems use a verse-paragraph structure and seem more like discursive verse-essays. Berry also returns to the elegy and experiments with a contemporary adaptation of the epithalamion, or marriage song, a classical and Renaissance verse form that he uses, without any mythological allusions, in "A Marriage Song," a poem dedicated to his daughter Mary. Other pieces are as short as haiku and demonstrate the Oriental cast to some of his verse. The collection also includes sonnet variants, a verse-epistle to a fellow poet, a dramatic dialogue, and a free-verse poetic manifesto by the Mad Farmer.

The 15 poems in part 1 are given the subtitle "Some Differences" because they were originally published separately as a chapbook.[13] The opening poem, "For the Explainers," rebukes the fact-based logic of cause and effect, which cannot answer the teleological question, "What curled the plume in the drake's tail / And put the white ring round his neck?" (3). Instead, the poet urges a Zen-like acceptance of what is, without explanation. "Voices Late at Night" dramatizes the poet's interior prayer, which may be likened to listening to the still, quiet voice within. In a series of five meditations, the poem contrasts our worldly aspirations with the likelihood of poverty, strife, and ruin. Another Zen-like meditative lyric, "A Difference," contrasts the noise of heavy machinery shaking the leaves of a young beech tree with the quiet tranquillity, below the road, of the ripples on the Kentucky River, which reflects the rustling leaves.

Three poets are mentioned by name in *Entries*: William Carlos Williams, Hayden Carruth, and Geoffrey Chaucer. The relationship suggested in two of the poems, "In a Motel Parking Lot, Thinking of Dr. Williams" and "To Hayden Carruth," is that of mentor and disciple. Berry had previously expressed his admiration for Williams in the essay "A Homage to Dr. Williams," in which he praises Williams's evocation of place in his poems, his exactness of description, and his sense both of the usefulness of poetry and of our culture's particular need for the voices of our American poets.[14]

"In a Motel Parking Lot, Thinking of Dr. Williams" extends this tribute in a two-part poem of 17 three-line stanzas, using Williams's characteristic accentual-syllabic line. The poem seems to echo Williams's "Elsie" in its insistence that poetry dignifies our cultural life by uplifting our minds and reminding us of what is worth preserving—our capacity to distinguish between the permanent and the ephemeral and to cherish those ordinary moments of transfiguring truth and beauty:

> one speaks of the necessities, so they may
> speak what is true, and have
> the patience for beauty: the weighted
>
> grainfield, the shady street,
> the well-laid stone and the changing tree
> whose branches spread above. (20)

Berry, like Williams, complains of the impoverishment of our general culture and our environment because of the inability of poetry to reach into and enrich the lives of ordinary Americans:

> For want of songs and stories
> they have dug away the soil,
> paved over what is left. (20)

"In a Motel Parking Lot, Thinking of Dr. Williams" serves for Berry as something of an *ars poetica*: it affirms poetry as an important expression of our common cultural memory. The poem holds the legacy of our ancestors' common experience, which could enrich and ennoble our lives and teach us to cherish our environment. For Berry, language, culture, and environment are all part of a common cultural heritage that must be cherished and preserved. Without poetry, he warns, we languish:

> The poem is important,
> as the want of it
> proves. It is the stewardship
>
> of its own possibility,
> the past remembering itself
> in the presence of
>
> the present, the power learned
> and handed down to see
> what is present (21).

In "To Hayden Carruth," Berry playfully greets the younger contemporary poet as a disciple, in language reminiscent of Emerson's letter to Walt Whitman after reading *Leaves of Grass* (1855–92). The verse-epistle praises Carruth's poems for the virtue of their necessity, for their wit, mastery, and verve. Reading Carruth's verse refreshes him, Berry affirms, as he urges Carruth to put aside thoughts of a "career" for the hard work of poetic mastery, which must be achieved time and time again.

"On a Theme of Chaucer" is a more oblique, two-quatrain poem alluding perhaps to Chaucer's retraction at the end of the *Canterbury Tales*, in which he reaffirms his orthodox religious beliefs. Berry affirms that he too has never denied scriptural teachings about heaven and hell, but he will not speculate about the hereafter.

Many of the lyrics in *Entries* are autobiographical poems in the confessional mode, with personal, abstract, or elusive meaning. Age and mortality seem to be on the poet's mind in such poems as "A Parting," Berry's elegiac tribute to Port William farmer Arthur Rowanberry. The once hardy farmer now lies in a hospital bed, far from home, surrounded by friends and family, his body ravaged by cancer, his mind mercifully detached from his suffering as he prepares for his final journey. In "One of Us," Berry protests against the indignity of empty, moralizing funeral sermons that would demean the memory of the beloved dead for the mourners. Better to cherish the memory of the dead as she was when alive—standing by a fence, holding turkey chicks in her apron, tossing the hen over the fence so that the chicks would follow—than to submit to another dull, eulogizing sermon.

Part 3 contains some subtle and beautiful love poems that show a deepening religious concern in their comparisons of eros and agape, human love and divine love. "Duality," perhaps the most interesting, is a nine-stanza confessional poem that uses an unrhymed nine-line stanza throughout. The poem opens with an epigraph from Genesis on the creation of men and women in God's own image. The poem is cast in intimate terms of "I" and "you," speaker and listener, lover and beloved, husband and wife. The speaker seems to be apologizing for the pain he has caused and to be asking for understanding. The poem explores the paradoxical nature of love: we commit ourselves to a relationship before we can possibly understand the nature of that commitment. To love is to suffer, to give and receive suffering, as husband and wife express through their eyes the pain, anger, separateness, and frailty in their relationship. Their love is a light that passes between them, a burning of their bodies as their mortality is consumed in time. Human love is a reflection of divine love, an anticipation of the joy of heaven. There are echoes in Berry's poetry of the love poetry in the Psalms, the Song of Songs, and the work of the English metaphysical poets, especially Robert Herrick, George Herbert, and Andrew Marvell.

Another religious poem, "Two Questions," recasts the parable of the wedding feast in Matthew 22, which compares the Kingdom of God to a royal wedding feast whose invited guests fail to attend, so that the king invites those on the streets, both good and bad. In Berry's two-stanza retelling of the parable, he slyly asks, would it be more offensive to have a marriage feast at which the thankless guests gobble their food without tasting it, or to have finicky guests who pick over the food, refusing to enjoy the bountiful feast? The ecological implications of Berry's version of the parable derive from his interest in what it says about human attitudes toward the earth.

"Touch-Me-Not," a pastoral lyric in this section, precisely describes the jewelweed, a native wildflower that grows in wet, shady places and blooms from July through September. Its spotted orange blossom hangs like a pendant jewel, and its ripe seedpod pops at a touch. "The Wild Rose," ostensibly another flower poem, is actually a beautiful and subtle love poem and tribute to the poet's wife, couched in terms of a conceit— an elaborate metaphorical comparison between the implicitness of their love and a wild rose

> blooming at the edge
> of thicket, grace and light
> where yesterday was only shade. (15)

The major work in part 4 is a series of 12 poems entitled "In Extremis: *Poems about My Father*," which presents an account of Berry's gradual reconciliation with his father, John M. Berry, a respected attorney. At first resenting his strong-willed, demanding father with his high standards, Berry gradually came to understand that behind the difficulty of his father's demands was his fear of losing the most precious things in life: children, home, and land. The first poem describes his quarrel with his father about the Vietnam War and their reconciliation when Berry admitted that his father was the major influence in his life. Berry writes compassionately of his father's final years, his gradual loss of health, mind, and dignity as he increasingly came to live in his memories. Evoking the continuity of the generations, Berry imagines his father, now an old man, as he might appear to his parents if they returned from the world of the dead. At other times, the old man forgets his age and infirmity and tries to go outdoors to work; when he cannot, he rages at the body that has betrayed him. His father fears the end, which is always hard, and cries out to the dead in his sleep. Finally, Berry reflects on what he has learned from his father: the difference between good work and sham, clear language and expression, honest service, and a love of good livestock and good land. In this remarkable cycle of 12 poems, Berry expresses his father's fierce independence and integrity, his love of farming, his helplessness in old age, and his imagined apotheosis in his fields, astride one of the horses he loved. "In Extremis" explicitly acknowledges the immense influence of his father in shaping Berry's vision and values. The richness and variety of the poems in *Entries* demonstrate once again that Berry is one of our necessary poetic voices.

Wendell Berry's poetry marks him—along with Gary Snyder and A. R. Ammons—as one of the most important contemporary American nature poets. His sense of the sacredness and interdependence of all life places him within the tradition of Ralph Waldo Emerson, Henry David Thoreau, and Walt Whitman. He is also one of the foremost American regional writers, insisting—like William Carlos Williams—that his poetry be firmly rooted in a sense of place. His poetry reflects the same deep concern for the natural environment and for sound conservation and farming practices that is evident in his essays and fiction. His emphasis on marriage, family, and community affirms these necessary human bonds. His poems reflect his abiding loyalty to his native region, his love of farming, his view of marriage as a sacrament, his affection for family and friends, and his deep awareness of the beauty and wonder of the natural world.

Conclusion

As an essayist, poet, and novelist, Wendell Berry has published over 30 books since 1964. As the range and versatility of his work attests, he would almost certainly have earned more extensive critical recognition had he chosen to travel the more conventional academic path of a college or university "poet-in-residence," embarking on promotional tours for his books and cultivating fashionable and influential literary circles. Instead of this kind of academic career, however, Berry has chosen the harder and more difficult road of a regional writer who not only writes but actively farms 125 acres in his native Henry County.

Berry has not isolated himself entirely from the academic world, however, teaching in the University of Kentucky English Department from 1964 through 1977, and again from 1987 to the present. He has also served as a visiting professor of creative writing at Stanford University in 1968–69; Elliston Poet at the University of Cincinnati in 1974; writer-in-residence at Centre College in 1977; visiting poet at Trinity College in 1985; and writer-in-residence at Bucknell University in 1987. In addition to being named Distinguished Professor of the Year (1971) at the University of Kentucky, he received a Guggenheim Fellowship in 1962; a Rockefeller Foundation Fellowship in 1965; a National Institute for Arts and Letters Award for writing in 1971; five honorary doctorates; the Jean Stein Award from the American Academy of Arts and Letters in 1987; the Milner Award (the Kentucky Governor's Award) in 1987; and the 1994 T. S. Eliot Award for creative writing.

Despite this recognition, Berry has held the academic world at arm's length, not hesitating to criticize the decline of the traditional liberal arts curriculum or to leave teaching for a decade, from 1977 to 1987. Essentially, Berry is a pastoral poet and writer; the greater part of his inspiration comes from his rural Kentucky heritage. In his work, he celebrates the quiet satisfactions of farming and husbandry, reasserting that oldest connection between the human imagination and the sustaining earth. Berry is primarily a discursive writer, though in his search for the continuities of self, family, work, region, and nature, his work often assumes a meditative, even elegiac quality. He cares deeply about his subjects: the renewal of the land; the dignity of physical labor; the importance of marriage, family, and community; and the continuities of history and region. One hears echoes of Thoreau, Frost, and Williams in his style and subject matter. Like Frost, he celebrates "a diminished thing," noting the passing of rural America and the self-sufficient,

independent life that farming sustained.[15] Though he regrets the loss of
the discipline of thrift, care, and conservation that farming teaches, most
of all it is the spiritual value and restorative power of living in harmony
with the land and the cycles of nature that Berry cherishes. As a farmer,
husband, and writer, Berry celebrates in his writing those moments of
continuity when he feels part of the natural cycles through which man
and nature renew themselves. A fine literary craftsman, his prose
demonstrates clarity, grace, and sureness, which grow from his deep love
and concern for language. Through his poetry, essays, and fiction, he
reminds us of the essential connections between human life and the natural order that we ignore at our peril.

Perhaps best known for his agricultural and environmental essays,
Wendell Berry is an important and versatile writer who deserves to be
more widely read and appreciated. Even now, he is increasingly recognized as one of the most prominent contemporary American regional
writers. Through his work, Berry has influenced a younger generation of
midwestern agrarian writers and agricultural reformers, such as Gene
Logsdon, Wes Jackson, and David Kline, who are determined to promote methods of sustainable agriculture and preserve the heritage of
rural American culture.

Appendix

An Interview with Wendell Berry

The following interview with Wendell Berry took place on 9 May 1991 in the book-lined living room of his farmhouse at Lane's Landing, Kentucky. I called from Lexington to arrange the interview for a weekend morning when his wife was away and he could spare some time from his farm work and writing to meet with me. The drive from Lexington took me through the hill farms and pastures of the Kentucky River Valley that provide the settings for much of Berry's writing. It was a gray, overcast day with a soft, misty rain falling. As I walked up the steep hillside to Berry's white frame house, I was struck by the tranquillity of the area: the only sounds were the tinkling of bells and the bleating of a small flock of sheep grazing on the hillside pasture above his home.

Berry met me cordially at the door, joked about the rain setting him back in his farm work, and invited me in. I thanked him for setting aside some time for our interview and we settled down to talk. What follows is an excerpt from our two-hour conversation, which ranged over topics as diverse as the history and economics of farming in Berry's region of Kentucky, the loss of rural farming communities, the need for an environmental ethic, the publication history of Berry's work, his childhood and education, and his development as a writer.

I am very much interested in the whole question of farming economy in America, and I want to begin by asking you about the economy. You've written so much about farming economy. And your work is concerned with linguistic, moral, social, and cultural issues based on your understanding of traditional agriculture.

Any concerns that you have will eventually come back to economy.

Yes.

To the issue of how you live.

And though I appreciate very much what you're saying morally and aesthetically, there's a hardheaded pragmatist in me that wants to say, "Yes, but can we make a go of this economically as well as morally?" Are your views of American agriculture practical as well as moral?

Obviously [not] if we accept the present economy and the present economic assumptions as our condition. But the present economy is not our condition. And it's not a true description of our condition.

It's not a permanent condition?

No. Our permanent condition is a condition of dependence on the land and on each other. And, of course, there is nothing easy in that condition. It means no shortcuts. It means that we live from care. Not from quantities. The quantities are ephemeral. If we were a successful society, we would have given care the same status that we now give to quantities. Care can be more or less permanent. At least, it can last longer than any quantity of food. And so what we're doing is exploiting quantities without any concern for care—for maintenance.

I wonder if this is a by-product of the industrial revolution—the industrial mentality?

It certainly has gone along with the industrial revolution. Whether there is an industrial mentality or whether the industrial means have just empowered the worst qualities in human character, I'm not able to say. You can speak of the industrial mind, but that simply is a greedy mind and a lazy one empowered by the means of modern industry.

Part of me wants to view business and growth as a modern problem, but then part of me looks at the history of agriculture in the West alone. I think there's a wonderful book by René Dubos, A God Within, *where he points out the devastation along the Mediterranean area caused by overgrazing and poor farming practices.*

I don't know that book.

And he argues that Northern Europe and Central Europe have struck some kind of balance between utter devastation and harmony. Of course, he points towards French farming practice as creating a kind of humanized landscape.

My argument would depend, as does his, on the existence of examples of caring use, of loving use. Those examples exist, and they can be found. You can't argue that destructiveness began with the industrial revolution. You can ruin land with a digging stick. You can ruin it with livestock, you can ruin it with teams of horses and mules and oxen. You can destroy on a large scale with primitive means. What the industrial revolution has done has [been to make] it possible to do the destruction on an unprecedented scale and in a quicker time with fewer people.

With fewer people?

That's right. Industrial technology has made it possible to reduce the number of workers, and in a sense it has made it possible to control the number of beneficiaries more strictly than ever.

I was going ask you about these caring examples. This is something I've thought about also. It seems to me there are too few of them in our culture. And I know the ones you mentioned—I share your admiration for the Amish, for those communities. But one simply doesn't move in and join those communities.

No.

I wonder what alternatives the rest of us have. Those are communities based solely on religion, on discipline. Many of their people are very traditional. They are wonderful farmers. But what we lack are the European examples of entire communities with intact agricultural traditions.

And we are destroying our communities at a great rate. I was just reading an article from the *Wall Street Journal* about what the article called the "youth flight"—a horrible phrase. But the young people are leaving.

Rural areas?

That's right. Towns are dying all over rural America. And you can understand why. I mean, I have two children, both of them in farming. And the penalties that they have to pay for being in farming are considerable. If they didn't love to farm, they would be very poorly compensated indeed.

I wonder if farming can be made a full-time occupation? It certainly can be an avocation, but can it be a full-time vocation as well?

Well, if people who use the land are using it under part-time constraints, they're going to damage it. I mean, you can't farm well if you farm after hours and on weekends. Farming is a discipline of time. And good farming requires you to have the margins of time and the correctness of scale that permit you to do your work at the right time. Everything depends on that. If you don't do it at the right time, you will damage the land. If you don't do it at the right time, you damage your soul—your peace of mind. You're under constraints of emergency and frenzy and frustration all the time. And that's the wrong way to do it. It's a question of what the requirements of the discipline are. What are the requirements for maintaining land in use? And these are not up to a government or a society to establish. Nature sets those requirements. What is the nature of this climate here? What is the nature of this particular piece of ground? What will these natural conditions permit me to do here without harm? And if those questions aren't asked and properly answered, then you get the Dust Bowl or an equivalent disaster. So the terms are not terms that humans set. The further practical question—the pragmatic question that you want to get to—is: Can we live without successfully meeting those terms?

For how long?

Well, the answer is, we can live as long as there is something to exploit. Or by meeting those terms—successfully answering those questions— we can go on indefinitely. And that's the choice that people are making. Those are the two possibilities. You can either live by using up the possibility of living, or you can live in a caring, loving, knowledgeable, skillful way that preserves the means of life. Those are the only two choices. If the economy at every point at which it touches the earth does not prescribe appropriate care, then you've got a failed economy.

Doesn't it require an ethical imperative?

Of course it does. And we have people who are presumably susceptible to religious and ethical imperatives. There's some little movement toward a sense of ecological responsibility in some of the religious denominations, but by and large the churches have bought into the present economy lock, stock, and barrel. They think it's the human condition, as do most of the institutions. And how you appeal to these people, I don't know. A lot of us have tried. And the hearing we've received has been appreciable. But it's an appreciable hearing among a kind of helter-skelter bunch of private people. You can't get a hearing—you can't get a real hearing—in a college or university. You can't get a real hearing in the church organizations. You can't get a real hearing in the government. So, to me, it's quite imaginable that we could go right on the way we're going until we're ruined. And this is not a possibility that can be ignored, because people before us have gone on the way they were going until they were ruined.

But is that possible?

Rome did it. The people in the Fertile Crescent did it. The people in the Dust Bowl did it.

I think about what the ecologist Garrett Hardin calls the "tragedy of the commons." Any ecological resource that is overgrazed or overused eventually crashes, and yet people will continue to exploit it because there are more short-term benefits in exploiting it than in conserving it.

There's some competent argument that the tragedy of the commons is not invariably or inescapably a tragedy. And I think that the controlling concern is that of community. If you're talking about a commonwealth that is common to people who understand that it belongs to them, that they belong to it and to each other—in other words, if the commonwealth belongs to a community, a real community—then you're going to see what we call exploitation go down and some kind of responsible care go up.

Doesn't that involve somehow getting people to stay in one place long enough to establish roots and develop a sense of community?

Sure it does.

And establish a sense of roots, an ethical and moral restraint, and an environmental consciousness?

There's a lot of popular talk right now about roots, but people assume that this means knowing your family tree or your family history. But it means knowing your place. You can learn your place, but the learning is long and hard, and the industrial culture obscures or denies it by a bunch of really shallow metaphors. The metaphor of the explosion is always right there. You want quick results.

As in making war?

In war you want to divide people into "us" and "them," and you want to believe that we're good and they're evil and that whatever you do to them is justified. And so you want to get it over as quickly as possible. We just had an illustration. We know that it's not that simple. When you came, I was reading a letter from Ron Kroese, who's the head of the Land Stewardship Project in Minnesota. Ron is studying the carryover from the world wars into agriculture. Well, of course, it's there. Sir Albert Howard tells how after World War I they converted the gunpowder factories to fertilizer factories.

Nitrates?

Nitrates. Ammonium nitrate is an explosive.

I didn't realize that.

Yes. Anyway, if you look at the advertisements and names of agricultural chemicals, many of them are based on war metaphors. Ron said that he saw an ad that shows a weed with a hand grenade underneath it. Well, farming is more complicated than that. It's slower. It's more difficult. It requires much more art—art in the broader sense of how to do things. The proper metaphor is the metaphor of community, not warfare.

And nurturing?

Nurturing, you see, comes out of the community idea. We know that if we're going to prosper in this world, we have to get along. And this means that you don't deal with everything by killing it. It means that you deal with any creature by asking first of all what it has to contribute. What part it plays.

I was up last night thinking about all of this. It occurred to me that you write a great deal about pre–World War II self-supporting rural communities and the effect that World War II had on the American worldview. You could almost trace the dislocating effect back to World War II.

That's where the explosion went off. Right there. Well, you see, my mind was formed by that other world.

Yes. Also, it occurs to me that you enjoyed the great benefits of the nurturing education from that older way of life.

That's right. That world stayed intact here, you see, through the Depression and the war. Adversity maintained it. I grew up around people who were still farming with horses and mules and whose lives had been formed by that old discipline and that ethic that was based on animal power—my grandfather, really my father as well. And so it came to me in a big way, and I really liked it. I remember when it just kind of came to me what a wonderful way it was that we had been empowered by animals and a few simple tools. I remember when it hit me. It was a kind of falling in love. In that way, I made common cause with my people, my forebears. So I know what were the informing passions in the best people of my grandfather's generation and in him.

He was your father's father?

Yes. He was a horseman. He was a mule man. He was a tobacco farmer. You know, maybe I should go over for you what I understand to be the traditional agriculture here. It was pretty good. It was a livestock-based agriculture. Grass-based. People were grazing cattle and sheep. They were using their pastures and their little fields for power.

Sun power, right.

That's right. The farms were almost entirely solar-powered, except the power that went into manufactured goods. But the people and the horses and mules were converting solar energy. So they were growing grass, and they were growing mostly grass. A farm of a large acreage would probably not be plowing more than 5 to 10 percent.

Now what were the cash crops?

Tobacco mainly. Some corn, but mostly the corn was fed. And tobacco and corn, the row crops, would have been followed by small grain. It wouldn't have been unusual for a 300-acre farm to plow 10 or 15 acres. And maybe that would have been 3, 4, or 5 acres in tobacco and the rest in corn. The corn would have been used to feed livestock and, of course, the dooryard flock.

Yes, that's still the practice in Central Europe. When I traveled in Hungary last year in the plains region, I was so impressed with the vitality of Hungarian traditional village agriculture, even after 40 years of communism.

First of all, these people were feeding themselves. They were feeding their meat hogs and their chickens and their milk cows. And so we're talking about an economy centered on the household—the kitchen economy. So they ate what they grew, and they sold what they didn't eat, even in that kitchen economy! They ate eggs, and they sold eggs. They ate chickens, and they sold chickens. They ate pigs, and they sold pigs.

At the local market?

There was a local market for all the small by-products. Then, after the row crops, would come small grains.

Now what were those small grains? Were they grains for bread?

Mostly wheat and barley. And the wheat could be fed to the hogs. Some barley was ground and fed, but those small grains were also sold. So you would have a little money crop. The cover crops would be undersown with clover and grass. And for a while you'd have hay off those fields.

That was the typical crop rotation?

Yes. You'd have high-quality hay being raised. Then you'd have grass hay raised wherever you could scratch it up off the pastures. And then those fields, after yielding a row crop, a small grain crop, hay crops for a year or two, would go back to pasture. The rotations were typically long. And so it was a pretty benign form of agriculture. If practiced by somebody with good judgment, it was a superb way of farming.

And sustainable?

And sustainable. At its best, it could have lasted forever.

At what point did it begin to change?

After World War II the young farmers came back from the war, and they were under the influence of the machine, as you can imagine. They had been using machines to fight for four years, and I remember them coming back talking about tractors. And so, between the end of the war and the early fifties, the conversion from horse to tractor was nearly complete. By, let's see, sometime in the early sixties the sheep began to fade away.

Why did farmers abandon sheep raising?

When the sheep went, you see, that was indicative of something else. That was the relinquishment of a skill, and it also indicated probably that the population was getting older and help was getting harder to find.

Are the sheep coming back now?

They're drifting back in little flocks, but I don't expect they'll fully return anytime soon. You've got to have the people. When you're talking about all these things, you're going to be coming back always to the question of where you're going to get the people. The help. Through my childhood and on up until fairly recent years, you could depend on getting local boys to help you. You can't do that anymore. I don't know where they've gone, but they're not working at farming.

And what happens when one of these farmers becomes sick or injured?

Well, things that would stop an industrial worker don't stop a farmer because he can't stop. Never has been able to. You have to smile when you hear about things that people in offices and factories get off work for. The farmer can't do that. If he gets really incapacitated, then he fails. We've laughed about it a good deal around here: farmers get something wrong with them and go to a city doctor, and he says don't do anything for a week or take three weeks' rest. You can't do that. It isn't possible. It's like saying go to heaven for three weeks. But you see, these people are living in what I call our condition. The doctor is operating in the economy, which is another proposition altogether.

I know you're definitely opposed to specialization, but I wonder if there aren't some specialized uses of the land that could be made to pay for agriculture—Christmas tree farming, herbs, landscape shrubs, trees?

I'm not against specialization per se. I'm against too much specialization. If you go among the Amish, who I think live pretty well, you'll find people who are specialists. But they don't, by their specialty, separate themselves from the generality of their community. They don't quit taking part in the economic life of the community and the social life and so on. I've written about this somewhere; a certain amount of specialization is desirable. If you want good houses, you're going to have to have people who are good carpenters. And you can't get to be a good carpenter by being an amateur. You can be a pretty good amateur carpenter. But if you want a fine building, you're going to have people who carpenter a lot. If you want good stone walls, you've got to have people who devote themselves to stone masonry. If you're going to have good poetry, you have got to have people who devote themselves to poetry. But the idea of becoming a poet or a mason and ceasing to be anything else at all is preposterous. That damages the disciplines, in my opinion. And you don't have a right to live that way. Even if you make a lot of money by it. The idea of being only a metallurgist or an economist is a preposterous thing. So the issue is balance. Exactly how does a specialist take part in the community, not just by doing his or her kind of work but by being a member?

Aren't these questions of scale also?

Absolutely! They are.

Isn't there an optimal scale or community size for the kind of skills that you describe? Not too big and not too small?

If a good mason takes on too much work and tries to do too much, the work deteriorates. And so what you get at the extremes of specialization is a poor specialist.

I sometimes think that {an} optimal balance of skills can be found in stable agricultural communities. The question is, how does one sustain those skills and discourage the wrong kind of growth?

Well, you have got to make up your mind [about] what's valuable. You know, if you let the economy determine what you do with your time, you're sunk. The only sanity there is in my life is that I refuse to value my time the way the economy does. If I value my time according to my salary as a teacher, I couldn't afford to do almost any of the other things that I like to do.

You manage to have a marvelous balance.

It's a marvelous strain, that's what it is. It isn't a balance. As a balancer, I'm like the guy who's about ready to fall.

Notes and References

Chapter One

1. For Wendell Berry's discussion of his Irish ancestry, see *The Long-Legged House* (New York: Harcourt, Brace & World, 1969), 172, hereinafter cited in the text; and "Irish Journal," *Home Economics* (San Francisco: North Point Press, 1987), 24–25.

2. "John Berry, Sr.: Plain-Speaking Man," *Louisville Courier-Journal*, 26 March 1978.

3. See Wendell Berry, *The Hidden Wound* (Boston: Houghton Mifflin, 1970), 4–7, the 1970 edition hereinafter cited in this chapter.

4. "John M. Berry, Sr."

5. "Formation of Henry County," *Henry County Historical Society* (April 1979): 1.

6. Phil Norman, "The Berry Family: Straight Talk and Strong Traditions," *Louisville Courier-Journal*, 26 March 1978.

7. Berry describes the self-sufficient rural economy in Henry County in *The Unsettling of America: Culture and Agriculture* (San Francisco: Sierra Club Books, 1977), 39–42.

8. "The Berry Family."

9. Carol Polsgrove and Scott Sanders, "Wendell Berry" [interview], *Progressive* 54 (May 1990): 36.

10. For a fuller account of the Kentucky "Tobacco Wars," see Harry H. Kroll, *Riders in the Night* (Philadelphia: University of Pennsylvania Press, 1965), and Robert Penn Warren, *Night Rider* (New York: Random House, 1939).

11. Information supplied in a 25 April 1991 note to the author from Amy Rankin, secretary of the Burley Tobacco Growers Cooperative Association, Inc.

12. "John M. Berry, Sr."

13. Phil Norman, "Wendell Berry: A Simpler Life," *Louisville Courier-Journal*, 26 March 1978.

14. "John M. Berry, Sr."

15. Wendell Berry, "Writer and Region," *What Are People For?* (San Francisco: North Point Press, 1990), 71–72, hereinafter cited in the text.

16. "The Berry Family."

17. Wendell Berry, "A Reading in Honor of Dr. Stroup," given at the University of Kentucky, 8 March 1973, University of Kentucky Archives, 2.

18. Ibid., 1, 3.

19. Ibid., 4

20. *The Green Pen* 3 (May 1953): 27–30.

21. Berry published a poem, "Spring," and a short story, "Summer Crop," in *Stylus* 2, no. 2 (Spring 1954): 14, 32–35; a short story, "The Brothers" (part 1), in *Stylus* 3, no. 1 (Fall 1954): 5–6; a short story, "Generations of Men," in *Stylus* 3, no. 2 (Spring 1955): 13–18; a short story, "The Chestnut Stud," and a poem, "A Question," in *Stylus* 4, no. 1 (Fall 1955): 15–21, 38; a short story, "The Brothers" (part 2), and a poem, "Rain Crow," in *Stylus* 4, no. 2 (Spring 1956): 13–18, 34–35; a long narrative poem, "Boone," in *Stylus* 5, no. 1 (Fall 1956): 33–38; a poem, "Elegy," and a short story, "The Skull Tree," in *Stylus* 5, no. 2 (Spring 1957): 19–21, 46–52; and a poem, "Two Excerpts from Diagon," in *Stylus* 6, no. 1 (Fall 1957): 27–28.

22. The first part, which was initially published as "The Brothers" in the Fall 1954 issue of *Stylus*, was later retitled "The Crow," and the second part became "The Brothers." The Dantzler Prize was apparently awarded for "The Crow."

23. *Carolina Quarterly* 8, no. 3 (Summer 1956): 5–11.

24. *Coraddi: Arts Forum* 1957, 8:20–21; 9:21–22.

25. Bennett H. Wall, letter to the author, 30 January 1990.

26. Ibid.

27. Ralph L. Curry, letter to the author, 24 April 1991.

28. Cf. "Wallace Stegner and the Great Community," *What Are People For?*, 48–49.

29. Wendell Berry, interview with the author, 9 May 1991.

30. Ibid.

Chapter Two

1. Berry alludes to Stegner's essay "The Book and the Great Community" in his tribute to Stegner, "Wallace Stegner and the Great Community," in *What Are People For?*, 48–57. Stegner's essay is found in *The Sound of Mountain Water* (Garden City, N.Y.: Doubleday, 1969), 276–86.

2. Wallace Stegner, "A Letter to Wendell Berry," *Wendell Berry*, ed. Paul Merchant, American Authors Series (Lewiston, Idaho: Confluence Press, 1991), 48.

3. Berry published the poem "Boone" in *Contact* 3 (1959): 94–96; the poems "Envoy" and "How It Will Be" in *Sequoia* 5, no. 2 (Winter 1960): 36–37; the poem "Song" in *Sequoia* 5, no. 3 (Spring 1960): 32; and the short story "Harvest" in *Stanford Short Stories 1960*, ed. Wallace Stegner and Richard Scowcroft (Stanford, Calif.: Stanford University Press, 1960), 1–26.

4. "Ripe" was first published in *Symbolism and Modern Literature: Studies in Honor of Wallace Fowlie*, ed. Marcel Tetel (Durham, N.C.: Duke University Press, 1978), 158. It later appeared as "Fall" in *A Part* (San Francisco, Calif.: North Point Press, 1980), 35. The information above came from Wallace Fowlie, interview with the author, 29 April 1991.

5. "Irish Journal," in *Home Economics*, 24–28.

6. Craig Wylie, letter to Prof. Walker Gibson, 13 September 1961.

7.   Margaret Bridwell, "The Tobacco Country Harvests a Novel," *Louisville Courier-Journal*, 24 April 1960.

8.   Ibid.

9.   Two other episodes were published as "Whippoorwills" and "Apples" in *Coraddi: Art Forum 1957* (8:20; 9:21–22) but never found their way into the novel.

10.   Oscar Cargill, letter to Wendell Berry, 10 October 1961.

11.   Wendell Berry, "The Country Town in Early Summer Morning," "Be Still in Haste," "The Aristocracy," "The Apple Tree," and "The Habit of Waking," *Poetry* (September 1962): 351–58.

12.   *Nation* 197 (21 December 1963): 437.

13.   Ben Shahn, preface, *November Twenty Six Nineteen Hundred Sixty Three* (New York: George Braziller, 1964), [np].

14.   Wendell Berry, "A Native Hill," *Recollected Essays 1965–1980* (San Francisco: North Point Press, 1981), 76–77, hereinafter cited in the text. Prof. Joseph A. Byrnes, in a 8 May 1991 letter to the author, commented that "one of my superiors" whom Berry alludes to sounds remarkably like Oscar Cargill.

15.   Craig Wylie, letter to Prof. Walker Gibson, 13 September 1961.

16.   Wendell Berry, preface, *A Place on Earth*, rev. ed. (San Francisco: North Point Press, 1983), [np].

17.   Berry interview.

18.   Wendell Berry, *A Place on Earth* (New York: Harcourt, Brace & World, 1967), 544.

19.   Wendell Berry, "The Bringer of Water," *Farming: A Hand Book* (New York: Harcourt Brace Jovanovich, 1970), 66–97.

20.   Wendell Berry, *The Memory of Old Jack* (New York: Harcourt Brace Jovanovich, 1974), 117.

21.   "William Faulkner," Interview with Jean Stein. *Writers at Work: The Paris Review Interviews,* ed. Malcolm Cowley (New York: Viking, 1958), 141.

22.   Wendell Berry, "Uncle Trav Wilson and the Dog," *Blue-Tail Fly* 1, no. 3 (December 1969): 13.

Chapter Three

1.   See Mindy Weinreb's "A Question a Day: A Written Conversation with Wendell Berry," in Merchant, *Wendell Berry*, 33.

2.   Thomas Jefferson, *Notes on Virginia*, in *The Life and Selected Writings of Thomas Jefferson*, ed. Adrienne Koch and William Peden (New York: Modern Library, 1944), 280.

3.   Ibid., 377.

4.   See *I'll Take My Stand: The South and the Agrarian Tradition*, ed. Louis D. Rubin, Jr. (Baton Rouge: Louisiana State University Press, 1977), and David E. Shi, *The Simple Life: Plain Living and High Thinking in American Culture* (New York: Oxford University Press, 1985).

5. See especially "Some Thoughts on Citizenship and Conscience in Honor of Don Pratt," *Long-Legged House*, 78–93.

6. See Aldo Leopold's discussion of the "conservation esthetic" and "the land ethic" in *A Sand County Almanac* (New York: Oxford University Press, 1949), 165–77, 201–26.

7. See David E. Shi's discussion in *The Simple Life*, esp. chaps. 8–9.

8. Wendell Berry, *The Rise* (Lexington: University of Kentucky Library Press, 1968). The limited edition of 100 copies was published as the result of a unique three-week seminar in calligraphy and bookmaking held during the summer of 1968 at the Margaret I. King Library of the University of Kentucky. Cf. "Wendell Berry Writes about a Canoe Trip," *Lexington Herald-Leader*, 10 November 1968.

9. Henry David Thoreau, *A Week on the Concord and Merrimack Rivers* (New York: Thomas Y. Crowell, 1961).

10. Wendell Berry, "Diagon," *Poetry* 93 (February 1959): 313–19; reprinted in *The Broken Ground* (New York: Harcourt, Brace & World, 1964), 4–8.

11. From Lewis Collins's *History of Kentucky* (1874), as quoted in *Long-Legged House*, 180–81.

12. Wendell Berry, *The Hidden Wound*, with a new afterword (1970; San Francisco: North Point Press, 1989), 109; the 1989 edition is hereinafter cited in the text.

13. See especially Richard Wright, *The Outsider* (New York: Harper & Row, 1953); Ralph Ellison, *Invisible Man* (New York: Random House, 1952); James Baldwin, *Notes of a Native Son* (Boston: Beacon Press, 1956); Martin Luther King, Jr., *Why We Can't Wait* (New York: Harper & Row, 1964); and Malcolm X with Alex Haley, *The Autobiography of Malcolm X* (New York: Grove Press, 1965).

14. Berry explores the theme of racial differences in "The Long Night," an uncollected dramatic dialogue between a white and a black woman set in Kentucky during the Civil War. See "The Long Night," *Southern Review* 14 (October 1978): 726–35.

15. Wendell Berry, foreword, *The Unforeseen Wilderness: An Essay on Kentucky's Red River Gorge*, with photographs by Eugene Meatyard (Lexington: University Press of Kentucky, 1971; San Francisco: North Point Press, 1991), x, the 1991 edition hereinafter cited in the text.

16. Howard Fineman, "Opponents of Red River Gorge Dam Stage a Rally at Kentucky Capital," *Louisville Courier-Journal*, 27 April 1975.

Chapter Four

1. Wendell Berry, "Discipline and Hope," *A Continuous Harmony: Essays Cultural and Agricultural* (New York: Harcourt Brace Jovanovich, 1972), 86–168, hereinafter cited in the text.

2. Lynn White, Jr., "The Historical Roots of Our Ecologic Crisis," *Science* 155, no. 3767 (10 March 1967): 1203–7.

3. Cf. White, "Historical Roots," 1205; and Berry, *Continuous Harmony*, 6. Berry also indicates his disagreements with White's arguments in the title essay "The Gift of Good Land," in *The Gift of Good Land: Further Essays Cultural and Agricultural* (San Francisco: North Point Press, 1981), 268–69, hereinafter cited in the text.

4. Berry alludes to Merton in *Continuous Harmony*, 16.

5. White, "Historical Roots," 1207.

6. William Carlos Williams, *Selected Poems* (New York: New Directions, 1968), 150–51.

7. "Think Little" actually appeared in *The Whole Earth Catalogue—Supplement* (Menlo Park, Calif.: Portola Institute, September 1970): 3–5, and in *The Last Whole Earth Catalogue* (Menlo Park, Calif.: Portola Institute, 1971), 24–25.

8. F. H. King, *Farmers of Forty Centuries; or, Permanent Agriculture in China, Korea, and Japan* (1911; Emmaus, Penn.: Rodale Press, 1973).

9. E. F. Schumacher, *Small Is Beautiful: Economics as If People Mattered* (New York: Harper & Row, 1973).

10. Albert Howard, *An Agricultural Testament* (New York: Oxford University Press, 1943; reprint, Emmaus, Penn.: Rodale Press, 1972).

11. Wendell Berry, *The Unsettling of America: Culture and Agriculture* (San Francisco: Sierra Club Books, 1977; paperback reprint, New York: Avon Books, 1978), the 1978 edition hereinafter cited in the text.

12. Berry actually debated Earl Butz on agricultural policy issues in a taped debate. See "Earl Butz Versus Wendell Berry," *Co-Evolution Quarterly* 17 (Spring 1978): 50-59.

13. Telleen returned the favor that same year by reprinting Berry's poem "Horses" in the preface to his book *The Draft Horse Primer: A Guide to the Care and Use of Work Horses and Mules* (Emmaus, Penn.: Rodale Press, 1977), viii–ix.

14. See Rachel Carson, *Silent Spring* (Boston: Houghton Mifflin, 1962), esp. chap. 3, "Elixirs of Death."

15. Thomas S. Kuhn, *The Structure of Scientific Revolutions,* 2d ed., enlarged (Chicago: University of Chicago Press, 1970).

16. Wendell Berry, "The Reactor and the Garden," in *Gift of Good Land*, 161. See also Scott Payton, "Marble Hill Protest Ends in Jail for 89," *Lexington Herald*, 4 June 1979.

17. Cf. William Morris, "Useful Work versus Useless Toil," in *William Morris*, ed. G. D. H. Cole (New York: Random House, 1948), 603–23.

18. Wendell Berry, "The Making of a Marginal Farm," originally entitled "Abundant Reward of Reclaiming a 'Marginal' Farm," *Smithsonian* (August 1980): 76–82.

Chapter Five

    1.   Berry had previously published the poem "To Gary Snyder" in *A Part* (San Francisco: North Point Press, 1980), 4. Snyder returned the compliment in the poem "Berry Territory," published in *Axe Handles* (San Francisco: North Point Press, 1983), 12–13.

    2.   Wendell Berry, *Standing by Words* (San Francisco: North Point Press, 1983), hereinafter cited in the text. The essays in *Standing by Words* were originally published in *Hudson Review* ("The Specialization of Poetry" and "Standing by Words"); *Lindisfarne* ("Standing by Words"); *Resurgence* ("People, Land, and Community"); *Sierra Club Bulletin* ("People, Land, and Community"); and *Co-Evolution Quarterly* ("Poetry and Marriage").

    3.   For a thorough discussion of this idea, see Arthur O. Lovejoy, *The Great Chain of Being: A Study of the History of an Idea* (New York: Harper & Row, 1936). Berry's arguments seem at least indirectly indebted to those of Lovejoy in many respects. See also E. M. W. Tillyard, *The Elizabethan World Picture* (New York: Vintage Books, 1959).

    4.   George Orwell, "Politics and the English Language," *A Collection of Essays by George Orwell* (New York: Doubleday, 1954), 162–77.

    5.   Berry takes issue with Shelley's separation of imagination from reason, in "A Defense of Poetry," and his giving poetry entirely to imagination. See "Poetry and Place," *Standing by Words*, 153–55.

    6.   T. S. Eliot, "Tradition and the Individual Talent," *Selected Essays*, new ed. (New York: Harcourt, Brace & World, 1950).

    7.   Berry specifically rebukes Shelley for his rebellion against the conventions of marriage, which Shelley believed to be a tyrannical and degrading institution. Shelley's beliefs, of course, had disastrous consequences in his personal life, leading to the suicide of Harriet Westbrook and to Shelley's loss of custody of their two children after he eloped with Mary Wollstonecraft Godwin. See "Poetry and Marriage: The Use of Old Forms," *Standing by Words*, 204–7; and "Poetry and Place," 152–62.

    8.   Cf. Jim White, "Author Berry Balances Teaching, Writing, Farming," *Lexington Herald-Leader*, 18 September 1987; and Sean Anderson, "Prize-Winning Poet/Writer Wendell Berry Returns from Farm Life to Teach at UK," *Kentucky Kernel*, 15 September 1987.

    9.   Wendell Berry, *Home Economics* (San Francisco: North Point Press, 1987), hereinafter cited in the text. The essays in this collection first appeared in *Country Journal*, *Orion Nature Quarterly*, *Katellagate*, *Review and Expositor*, *Whole Earth Review*, *Tri Quarterly*, *Draft Horse Journal*, *Land Stewardship Newsletter*, *Resurgence*, *Los Angeles Times Magazine*, and *Wilderness*.

    10. See Herman E. Daly and John B. Cobb, Jr., "From Chrematistics to Oikonomia," *For the Common Good: Redirecting the Economy toward Community, the Environment, and a Sustainable Future*, 2d ed. (Boston: Beacon Press, 1994),

138–58. Many of Daly and Cobb's arguments parallel those of Berry, and they quote from him extensively in their chapter on agriculture.

11. Wes Jackson, Berry, and Bruce Colman had edited *Meeting the Expectations of the Land: Essays in Sustainable Agriculture and Stewardship* (San Francisco: North Point Press, 1984), which reflects many of Berry's arguments.

12. Lester Brown et al., *State of the World 1994* (New York: Norton, 1994), 8.

13. Berry's analysis of the economic dislocations of the 1980s parallels that of Donald L. Bartlett and James B. Steele, *America: What Went Wrong?* (Kansas City: Andrews and McMeel, 1992).

14. See Raymond Williams, "Enclosures, Commons, and Communities," in *The Country and the City* (New York: Oxford University Press, 1973), 96–107.

15. Alfred North Whitehead, *Science and the Modern World* (New York: Macmillan, 1925): 51.

16. Daly and Cobb, *For the Common Good*, 35.

17. Wendell Berry, "Whose Head Is the Farmer Using? Whose Head Is Using the Farmer?" in Jackson, Berry, and Colman, *Meeting the Expectations*, 19–30.

18. North Point Press did publish *The Unforeseen Wilderness* in 1991, but that edition was a reissue of a title first published by the University Press of Kentucky in 1971.

19. "North Point Press to Stop Publishing New Books," *Publishers Weekly* (14 December 1990): 16. See also "North Point Press up for Sale," *Publishers Weekly* (5 January 1990): 17; and F. Peter Model, "True North," *Wilson Library Bulletin* 65, no. 4 (December 1990): 65–66, 190. In 1995, Farrar, Straus & Giroux announced it would "reissue some of [North Point's] classics and release new frontlist titles under the imprint." "North Point to Publish New Titles at FSG," *Publishers Weekly* (27 February 1995): 19.

20. The essays, poems, and reviews in *What Are People For?* were originally published in *American Poetry Review*, *Antaeus*, *The Nation*, *Yale Review*, *Whole Earth Review*, *South Dakota Review*, *Seneca Review*, the American Authors Series (Confluence Press), *Firmament*, *Land Report*, *Chicago Tribune*, *Biocycle*, *Journal of Gastronomy*, *Harper's*, *Utne Reader*, and *Hudson Review*.

21. Stegner returned the tribute with his warm appraisal of Berry's career in "A Letter to Wendell Berry," in Merchant, *Wendell Berry*, 47–52.

22. For another perspective on the value of arboriculture, see Jean Giono, *The Man Who Planted Trees* (Post Mills, Vt.: Chelsea Green Publishers, 1985).

23. For a further discussion of this topic, see Josef Pieper, *Leisure: The Basis of Culture* (New York: Pantheon, 1952).

24. Wendell Berry, *Sex, Economy, Freedom and Community: Eight Essays*

(New York: Pantheon, 1993), hereinafter cited in the text. The essays in this collection first appeared in *Louisville Courier-Journal*, *Atlantic Monthly*, *Progressive*, *Journal of the Soil and Water Conservation Society*, *Wild Earth*, *Amicus Journal*, *Land Report*, *Appalachia*, and *Northern Forest Forum*, as well as in a pamphlet published by the Louisville Community Foundation.

25. Twain's "The War Prayer" was occasioned by his opposition to American intervention in the Philippines during the Spanish-American War; it remained unpublished during his lifetime.

26. "Sex, Economy, Freedom, and Community" was first delivered as the "Victory of Spirit" Ethics Award Lecture in Louisville on 8 April 1992.

Chapter Six

1. Wendell Berry, *The Wild Birds: Six Stories of the Port William Membership* (San Francisco: North Point Press, 1986), hereinafter cited in the text. "Thicker Than Liquor" and "The Wild Birds" first appeared in *Mother Jones*.

2. Wendell Berry, *Remembering* (San Francisco: North Point Press, 1988), hereinafter cited in the text.

3. Carl D. Esbjorson notes the allusions to Dante in "*Remembering* and Home Defense," in Merchant, *Wendell Berry*, 155–70.

4. Wendell Berry, "The Discovery of Kentucky" (Frankfort, Ky.: Gnomon Press, 1991).

5. Wendell Berry, *Fidelity* (New York: Pantheon, 1992), hereinafter cited in the text. "Pray without Ceasing" first appeared in *Southern Review* (Fall 1992); "A Jonquil for Mary Penn" in the *Atlantic* (February 1992); "Making It Home" (as "Homecoming") in *Sewanee Review* (Winter 1992); "Fidelity" in *Orion* (Summer 1992); and "Are You All Right?" in Merchant, *Wendell Berry*.

6. Many of the details in "Fidelity" closely resemble those in an elegy Berry wrote for his kinsman Harry Erdman Perry (1881–1965), first published in *Findings* (1969); see "Three Elegiac Poems," in Wendell Berry, *Collected Poems: 1957–1982* (San Francisco: North Point Press, 1985), 49–51.

7. The Blazer Lecture Series was endowed in 1948 at the University of Kentucky by Paul G. Blazer, Sr., to bring outstanding scholars in the humanities and social sciences to the university.

8. The University Press of Kentucky and Gnomon Press have reprinted all of Hubbard's work: *Shantyboat: A River Way of Life* (1953; Lexington: University Press of Kentucky, 1977); *Payne Hollow: Life on the Fringe of Society* (1974; Frankfort, Ky.: Gnomon Press, 1985); *Harlan Hubbard Journals, 1929–1944*, ed. Vincent Kohler and David F. Ward (Lexington: University Press of Kentucky, 1987); and *Shantyboat on the Bayous* (Lexington: University Press of Kentucky, 1990).

9. Wendell Berry, *Harlan Hubbard: Life and Work* (Lexington: University Press of Kentucky, 1990); paperback reprint, New York: Pantheon, 1990), the paperback edition hereinafter cited in the text.

10.   Berry cites a study by Don Wallis (*Harlan Hubbard and the River* [Yellow Springs, Ohio: OYO Press, 1989]) in the footnotes to his biography of Hubbard.

11.   Martin Lings, *Ancient Beliefs and Modern Superstitions* (Cambridge: Quinta Essentia, 1980), 12.

12.   Wendell Berry, *Watch with Me: And Six Other Stories of the Yet-Remembered Ptolemy Proudfoot and His Wife, Miss Minnie, Née Quinch* (New York: Pantheon, 1994), hereinafter cited in the text. All of the stories except "Wait with Me" first appeared in the *Draft Horse Journal*. "A Consent" was also published as a chapbook by (Monterey, Ky.: Larkspur Press, 1993).

13.   For a fuller discussion of southern humor, see Walter Blair's *Native American Humor* (Scranton, Penn.: Chandler Publishing, 1960); Constance Rourke, *American Humor: A Study of the National Character* (New York: Harcourt Brace, 1931); and Kenneth S. Lynn, *The Comic Tradition in America* (New York: Norton, 1958).

Chapter Seven

1.   Wendell Berry, *Findings* (Iowa City: Prairie Press, 1969).

2.   Wendell Berry, *The Broken Ground* (New York: Harcourt, Brace & World, 1964), hereinafter cited in the text. The poems that Berry later chose not to reprint in *Collected Poems* were "Diagon," "The River Voyagers," "Be Still in Haste," "Nine Verses of the Same Song," "The Apple Tree," "The Country Town in Early Summer Morning," "A Fit of Winter," "The Morning Blue," "An Old Woman Feeding the Birds," "On the Front Porch," and "Ascent."

3.   Wendell Berry, *Openings* (New York: Harcourt Brace Jovanovich, 1968), hereinafter cited in the text. The poems not reprinted in *Collected Poems* are "The Change," "The Quiet," "White-Throated Sparrow," "The Fearfulness of Hands That Have Learned Killing," "The Migrants," "The Return," "The Dead Calf," "The Burial of the Old," and "East Kentucky, 1967." One of these poems, "The Return," was divided; stanza 3 appeared in *Collected Poems* as "The Dream," and stanza 7 as "The Sycamore."

4.   Wendell Berry, *Farming: A Hand Book* (New York: Harcourt Brace Jovanovich, 1970), hereinafter cited in the text. Not reprinted in *Collected Poems* were "Water," "The Barn," "The Buildings," "A Letter," "A Failure," "The Illumination of the Kentucky Mountain Craftsman," "The Wages of History," and the verse-play "The Bringer of Water."

5.   Wendell Berry, *The Country of Marriage* (New York: Harcourt Brace Jovanovich, 1973), hereinafter cited in the text. Not reprinted in *Collected Poems* were "Zero," "The Strangers," "The Cruel Plumage," "To William Butler Yeats," "The Asparagus Bed," and "Inland Passages." Part 1 of "Inland Passages," entitled "The Long Hunter," was published as a separate poem in *Collected Poems*.

6. Wendell Berry, *Clearing* (New York: Harcourt Brace Jovanovich, 1977), hereinafter cited in the text. Not reprinted in *Collected Poems* were "The Bed" and "Reverdure." Another poem, "Where," was revised and shortened.

7. Wendell Berry, *A Part* (San Francisco: North Point Press, 1980), hereinafter cited in the text. Not reprinted in *Collected Poems* were "The Watchers," "In Place of Happiness," "A Grace," "No Thanks," "Walnut St., Oak St., Sycamore St., etc.," "Now," "The Mad Farmer's March," "Confession," "The Necessity of Flight," "Eight Below," "An Encore Maybe," "Ronsard's Lament for the Cutting of the Forest of Gastine," "The Salad," "Watching the Mid-Autumn Moon," and "1975."

8. Wendell Berry, *The Wheel* (San Francisco: North Point Press, 1982), hereinafter cited in the text. All of the poems in *The Wheel* were reprinted in *Collected Poems*.

9. Wendell Berry, author's note, *Collected Poems*.

10. All quotes from *Findings* are from *Collected Poems*, since *Findings* was originally printed in a small run and is difficult to find, even among used-book dealers.

11. Wendell Berry, *Sabbaths* (San Francisco: North Point Press, 1987), hereinafter cited in the text.

12. Wendell Berry, *Entries* (New York: Pantheon, 1994), hereinafter cited in the text.

13. Wendell Berry, *Some Differences* (Lewiston, Idaho: Confluence Press, 1987).

14. Wendell Berry, "A Homage to Dr. Williams," *A Continuous Harmony*, 56–62.

15. Robert Forst, "The Oven Bird," *The Poetry of Robert Frost* (New York: Holt, Rinehart and Winston, 1969), 120.

Selected Bibliography

Primary Sources

Fiction

The Discovery of Kentucky. Frankfort, KY: Gnomon Press, 1991.
Fidelity: Five Stories. New York: Pantheon, 1992.
The Memory of Old Jack. New York: Harcourt Brace Jovanovich, 1974.
Nathan Coulter. Boston: Houghton Mifflin, 1960. Revised edition, San Francisco: North Point Press, 1985.
A Place on Earth. New York: Harcourt Brace, 1967. Revised edition, San Francisco: North Point Press, 1983.
Remembering. San Francisco: North Point Press, 1988.
Watch with Me: And Six Other Stories of the Yet-Remembered Ptolemy Proudfoot and His Wife, Miss Minnie, Née Quinch. New York: Pantheon, 1994.
The Wild Birds: Six Stories of the Port William Membership. San Francisco: North Point Press, 1986.

Nonfiction

The Agriculture Crisis: A Crisis of Culture. Proceedings No. 33. New York: Myrin Institute, 1977.
A Continuous Harmony: Essays Cultural and Agricultural. New York: Harcourt Brace Jovanovich, 1972.
The Gift of Good Land: Further Essays Cultural and Agricultural. San Francisco: North Point Press, 1981.
Harlan Hubbard: Life and Work. Lexington: University Press of Kentucky, 1990; paperback, New York: Pantheon, 1990.
The Hidden Wound. Boston: Houghton Mifflin, 1970. Reprint, with a new afterword, San Francisco: North Point Press, 1989.
Home Economics. San Francisco: North Point Press, 1987.
The Long-Legged House. New York: Harcourt Brace & World, 1969.
Recollected Essays: 1965–1980. San Francisco: North Point Press, 1981.
The Rise. Lexington, Ky.: University of Kentucky Library Press, 1968.
Sex, Economy, Freedom and Community: Eight Essays. New York: Pantheon, 1993.
Standing by Words. San Francisco: North Point Press, 1983.
The Unforeseen Wilderness: An Essay on Kentucky's Red River Gorge. With Photographs by Eugene Meatyard. Lexington: University Press of Kentucky, 1971; San Francisco: North Point Press, 1991.

The Unsettling of America: Culture and Agriculture. San Francisco: Sierra Club
    Books, 1977; paperback, New York: Avon Books, 1978.
What Are People For? San Francisco: North Point Press, 1990.

Poetry

The Broken Ground. New York: Harcourt Brace & World, 1964.
Clearing. New York: Harcourt Brace Jovanovich, 1977.
Collected Poems: 1957–1982. San Francisco: North Point Press, 1985.
The Country of Marriage. New York: Harcourt Brace Jovanovich, 1973.
An Eastward Look. Berkeley, Calif.: Sand Dollar Press, 1974.
Entries. New York: Pantheon, 1994.
Falling Asleep. Austin, Tex.: Cold Mountain Press, 1974.
Farming: A Hand Book. New York: Harcourt Brace Jovanovich, 1970.
Findings. Iowa City: Prairie Press, 1969.
The Gift of Gravity. Deerfield, Mass.: Deerfield Press, 1979.
Horses. Monterey, Ky.: Larkspur Press, 1975.
The Kentucky River: Two Poems. Monterey, Ky.: Larkspur Press, 1976.
The Nativity. Great Barrington, Mass.: Penamen Press, 1981.
November Twenty Six Nineteen Hundred Sixty Three. New York: George Braziller,
    1964.
Openings. New York: Harcourt Brace Jovanovich, 1968.
A Part. San Francisco: North Point Press, 1980.
Sabbaths. San Francisco: North Point Press, 1987; Frankfort, Ky.: Gnomon
    Press, 1992.
The Salad. San Francisco: North Point Press, 1980.
Sayings and Doings. Frankfort, Ky.: Gnomon Press, 1975.
"Sayings and Doings" and "An Eastward Look." Frankfort, Ky.: Gnomon Press, 1990.
Some Differences. Lewiston, Idaho: Confluence Press, 1987.
There Is Singing around Me. Austin, Tex.: Cold Mountain Press, 1976.
Three Memorial Poems. Berkeley, Calif.: Sand Dollar Press, 1977.
To What Listens. Crete, Nebraska: Best Cellar Press, 1975.
The Wheel. San Francisco: North Point Press, 1982.

Collections

*"Higher Education and Home Defense." From the Heartlands: Photos and Essays from
    the Midwest*. Midwest Writers Series No. 1. Introduced and edited by
    Larry Smith. Huron, Ohio: Bottom Dog Press, 1988.
The Landscape of Harmony: Two Essays on Wildness and Community. Introduction by
    Michael Hamburger. Hereford, Eng.: Five Seasons Press, 1987.
*Meeting the Expectations of the Land: Essays in Sustainable Agriculture and
    Stewardship*. Edited by Wes Jackson, Wendell Berry, and Bruce Colman.
    San Francisco: North Point Press, 1984.

Uncollected Prose: Fiction

"Apples." *Coraddi: Arts Forum 1957*, 9:21–22.

"The Brothers" (part 1, also titled "The Crow"). *Stylus* [University of Kentucky]
    3, no. 1 (Fall 1954): 5–6.

"The Brothers" (part 2). *Stylus* 4, no. 2 (Spring 1956): 13–18.

"The Chestnut Stud." *Stylus* 4, no. 1 (Fall 1955): 15–21.

"Generations of Men." *Stylus* 3, no. 2 (Spring 1955): 13–18.

"Harvest." In *Stanford Short Stories, 1960*, edited by Wallace Stegner and
    Richard Scowcroft (Palo Alto, Calif.: Stanford University Press, 1960),
    1–26.

"The Skull Tree." *Stylus* 5, no. 2 (Spring 1957): 46–52.

"Summer Crop." *Stylus* 2, no. 2 (Spring 1954): 32–35.

"Whippoorwills." *Coraddi: Arts Forum 1957*, 8:20–21.

"The Wings of the Future." *Green Pen* [annual anthology of freshman writing at
    the University of Kentucky] 3 (May 1953): 27–30.

Uncollected Prose: Nonfiction

"American Pox." *Nation* 207 (4 November 1968): 457.

"Antennae to Knowledge." *Nation* 198 (23 March 1964): 304–6.

"Boatmen's Paradox: Consumers of the River." *Nation* 203 (14 October 1966):
    381–85.

"Composting Privy." *Organic Farming and Gardening* 20 (December 1973):
    88–97.

"Farming with Horses." *Organic Farming and Gardening* 21 (March 1974): 72–77.

Foreword to David Kline, *Great Possessions: An Amish Farmer's Journal*. San
    Francisco: North Point Press, 1990.

Foreword to Gene Logsdon, *At Nature's Pace: Farming and the American Dream*.
    New York: Pantheon, 1994.

Foreword to Gary Paul Nabhan, *Enduring Seeds*. San Francisco: North Point
    Press, 1989.

"Hill Land Farming: How the Experts View Its Future." *Organic Farming and
    Gardening* 24 (April 1977): 68–71.

Introduction to J. Russell Smith, *Tree Crops*. Washington, D.C.: Island Press
    Books, 1987.

Introduction to T. Stanwell-Fletcher, *Driftwood Valley*. New York: Penguin
    Nature Library, 1989.

"In True Unity There Is Profound Strength." *New York Times*, 8 October 1977.

"James Dickey's New Book." *Poetry* 105 (November 1964): 130–31.

"Life on and off Schedule." *Organic Farming and Gardening* 24 (August 1977):
    44–48.

Preface to Masanobu Fukuoka, *The One-Straw Revolution*. Emmaus, Penn.:
    Rodale Press, 1978; New York: Bantam Books, 1985.

"Response to a War." *Nation* 204 (24 April 1967): 527–28.
"Sanitation Laws Squeeze out Small Producers." *Organic Farming and Gardening* 24 (October 1977): 43–46.
"Some Difficulties to Think about before Buying a Farm." *Organic Farming and Gardening* 24 (July 1977): 59–61."The Specialization of Poetry." *Hudson Review* 28 (Summer 1976): 11–27.
"Strip-Mining Morality: Landscaping of Hell." *Nation* 202 (24 January 1966): 96–100.
"The Tyranny of Charity." *Nation* 201 (27 September 1965): 161–64.

Uncollected Poems

"Anniverse." *Harper's* 225 (September 1977): 65.
"The Apple Tree." *Poetry* 100 (September 1962):353–54.
"Architecture." *Nation* 193 (21 October 1961): 274.
"The Aristocracy." *Poetry* 100 (September 1962): 352–53.
"Be Still in Haste." *Poetry* 100 (September 1962): 352.
"Boone." *Stylus* 5, no. 1 (Fall 1956): 33–38. Also in *Contact* 3 (1959): 94–96.
"Buckeye." *Nation* 193 (14 October 1961): 255.
"Converse." *Harper's* 255 (September 1977): 65.
"The Country Town in Early Summer Morning." *Poetry* 100 (September 1962): 351.
"The Current." *Hudson Review* 22 (Autumn 1969): 453.
"The Dance." *Sewanee Review* 84 (Summer 1976): 395.
"Desolation." *Hudson Review* 30 (Spring 1977): 46.
"Dogs." *Hudson Review* 25 (Summer 1972): 262.
"Early Morning Dark." *Hudson Review* 30 (Spring 1977): 50–51.
"Elegy." *Stylus* 5, no. 2 (Spring 1957): 19–21.
"Envoy." *Sequoia* [Stanford University] 5, no. 2 (Winter 1960): 36.
"Fear of Darkness." *Nation* 198 (27 January 1964): 102.
"The Fearfulness of Hands That Have Learned Killing." *Arts and Sciences* [New York University] (Spring 1965): 13.
"The First." *Harper's* 255 (September 1977): 65.
"A Fit of Winter." *Epoch* 14 (Fall 1964): 58.
"For Two Friends Fallen in Love." *Mademoiselle* 72 (January 1971): 102.
"From the Distance." *Hudson Review* 30 (Spring 1977): 51.
"Going." *Poetry* 108 (July 1966): 237.
"Green and White." *Prairie Schooner* 34 (Winter 1961–62): 335.
"Guest." *Nation* 198 (10 February 1964): 156.
"The Habit of Waking." *Poetry* 100 (September 1962): 354–58.
"The Hidden Singer." *Harper's* 255 (September 1977): 65.
"How It Will Be." *Sequoia* 5, no. 2 (Winter 1960): 37.
"The Law That Marries All Things." *Hudson Review* 30 (Spring 1977): 49.
"Let Him Escape Hospital and Doctor." *Arts and Sciences* (Spring 1965): 13.

"The Long Night." *Southern Review.* 14 (October 1978): 726–35.
"A Meeting." *Harper's* 255 (September 1977): 65.
"The Morning Blue." *Epoch* 13 (Spring 1964): 269.
"A Music." *Chelsea* 16 (March 1965): 94–95.
"My Children, Coming of Age." *Sewanee Review* 84 (Summer 1976): 396.
"A Natural Grace." *Perstare* (1964): 46.
"November 26, 1963." *Nation* 197 (21 December 1963): 437.
"Now." *Harper's* 255 (September 1977): 65.
"On the Front Porch." *Nation* 197 (7 December 1963): 396.
"Owl." *Prairie Schooner* 31 (Spring 1957): 45.
"A Question." *Stylus* 4, no. 1 (Fall 1955): 38.
"Rain Crow." *Poetry* 89 (February 1957): 291–92. Also in *Stylus* 4, no. 2 (Spring
    1956): 34–35.
"Return." *Chelsea* 17 (August 1965): 66–67.
"The Return." *Hudson Review* 20 (Autumn 1967): 385–88.
"The Room." *Epoch* 15 (Fall 1965): 36.
"September 2." *Poetry* 116 (May 1970): 77.
"Serenade in Black." *Poetry* 91 (March 1958): 359–60.
"Setting Out." *Hudson Review* 30 (Spring 1977): 50.
"The Slopes of Waban." *Hudson Review* 22 (Autumn 1969): 455–56.
"Some of the Parts." *Hudson Review* 24 (Summer 1971): 263.
"Song." *Sequoia* 5, no. 3 (Spring 1960): 32.
"Song in a Year of Catastrophe." *Hudson Review* 22 (Autumn 1969): 452.
"Spring." *Stylus* 2, no. 2 (Spring 1954): 14.
"A Standing Ground." *Hudson Review* 22 (Autumn 1969): 454.
"The Start." *Hudson Review* 30 (Spring 1977): 46–47.
"Summits." *Hudson Review* 25 (Summer 1972): 262.
"The Thief." *Nation* 198 (4 May 1964): 468.
"A Turn of the Head." *Arts and Sciences* (Spring 1965): 12.
"Two Elegiac Poems." *Nation* 201 (20 September 1965): 220.
"Two Excerpts from Diagon." *Stylus* 6, no. 1 (Fall 1957): 27–28.
"Walking and Thinking." *Chelsea* 17 (August 1965): 65.
"Washington Square." *Perstare* (1964): 46.
"The Watchers." *Harper's* 255 (September 1977): 65.
"White-Throated Sparrow." *Arts and Sciences* (Spring 1965): 13.
"The Wind, Too." *Harper's* 255 (September 1977): 65.

Secondary Sources

Bibliographies

Freedman, Russell. "A Bibliography of the Works of Wendell Berry." Fourth
    version. Lanesborough, Mass.: Second Life Books, 1985. An annotated

bibliography that includes a complete publishing history of all of Berry's work through 1985.

Hicks, Jack. "A Wendell Berry Checklist." *Bulletin of Bibliography* 37, no. 3 (July-September 1980): 127–31. A complete bibliographic checklist of Berry's published work through 1978.

Book

Merchant, Paul, ed. *Wendell Berry*. American Authors Series. Lewiston, Idaho: Confluence Press, 1991. A collection of critical essays and appreciations of Berry's work, along with a short story, poem, and interview by Berry. Includes a selected bibliography of Berry's primary work and secondary sources through 1991.

Articles

Altherr, Thomas L. "The Country We Have Married: Wendell Berry and the Georgian Tradition of Agriculture." *Southern Studies* 1, no. 2 (Summer 1990): 105–15. An examination of the influence of Virgil's *Georgics* on Berry's treatment of agriculture.

Askins, Justin. "A Necessary Darkness." *Parnassus* 15 (1989): 317–30. An examination of Berry's use of the theme and metaphor of darkness in his poetry.

Basney, Lionel. "Wendell Berry: The Grace That Keeps the World." *The Other Side* 23, no. 1 (January-February 1987): 46–48. A discussion of the concept of grace in Berry's writing.

———. "Having Your Meaning at Hand: Work in Snyder and Berry." In *World, Self, Poem: Essays on Contemporary Poetry from the "Jubilation of Poets,"* edited by Leonard Trawick (Kent, Ohio: Kent State University Press, 1990): 130–43. An examination of the meaning of work in the poems of Snyder and Berry.

———. "Five Notes on the Didactic Tradition, in Praise of Wendell Berry." In *Wendell Berry*, edited by Paul Merchant (Lewiston, Idaho: Confluence Press, 1991), 174–83. Defends Berry's use of didacticism in his poetry.

Bauer, Douglas. "We Saved Our Land." *Today's Health* 52 (October 1974): 30–34. A discussion of Berry's influence on good land use practices.

Carruth, Hayden. "Human Authenticity in the Face of Massive Multiplying Error." *Parnassus* (Spring-Summer 1986): 140–43. Discusses Berry's treatment of choice in his writings.

———. "Essays for Wendell." In *Wendell Berry*, edited by Paul Merchant (Lewiston, Idaho: Confluence Press, 1991), 71–78. A series of discursive poems addressed to Berry by a friend and fellow poet.

Collins, Robert. "A More Mingled Music: Wendell Berry's Ambivalent View of Language." *Modern Poetry Studies* 11 (1982): 35–56. Examines Berry's sometimes ambivalent attitudes toward language.

Connelly, Joseph F. "*Sabbaths*: Wendell Berry's Songs of Praise." *Kentucky Philological Review* 3 (Autumn 1988): 14–18. A useful discussion of Berry's use of the Psalms and other religious allusions in *Sabbaths*.

Cornell, Daniel. "*The Country of Marriage*: Wendell Berry's Personal Political Vision." *Southern Literary Journal* 16, no. 1 (Fall 1983): 59–70. A thoughtful examination of Berry's pastoral metaphors that places him in an agrarian populist tradition.

———. "A Vision of Stewardship: Wendell Berry's Ecological Ethic." *Literature and Belief* 12 (1992): 13–25. An examination of Berry's ideas about environmental stewardship as presented in his writings.

Creech, Jeremiah. "The Power of Global Thinking." *Utne Reader* 56 (March-April 1993): 22–26. Discusses Berry's opposition to global thinking and the concept of "planetary consciousness."

Decker, William. "'Practice Resurrection': The Poesis of Wendell Berry." *North Dakota Quarterly* 55, no. 4 (Fall 1987): 170–84. An examination of the resurrection theme in Berry's poetry.

Dietrich, Mary. "Our Commitment to the Land." *Bluegrass Literary Review* 2, no. 1 (Fall-Winter 1980): 39–44. An examination of Berry's attitudes toward the land in his writings.

Ditsky, John. "Wendell Berry: Homage to the Apple Tree." *Modern Poetry Studies* 2 (1971): 7–15. A study of the pastoral themes and imagery in Berry's first two novels and his early poetry volumes.

Ehrlich, A. W. "*Publishers Weekly* Interviews Wendell Berry." *Publisher's Weekly* 212, no. 5 (September 1977): 10–11. A short interview with Berry about forthcoming books.

Engell, John. "*The Wild Birds*: A Review." *Chattahoochee Review* 11, no. 1 (Fall 1990): 73–76. Examines Berry's treatment of organicism and cultural decline.

Esbjornson, Carl D. "*Remembering* and Home Defense." In *Wendell Berry*, edited by Paul Merchant (Lewiston, Idaho: Confluence Press, 1991), 155–70. Traces the themes in *Remembering* back to Berry's agricultural essays and discusses the allusions to Dante.

Feld, Ross. "The Where, How, Who and the What in Wendell Berry's Writing." In *Wendell Berry*, edited by Paul Merchant (Lewiston, Idaho: Confluence Press, 1991), 152–54. Examines Berry's attitudes toward and treatment of land in his work.

Fields, Kenneth. "The Hunter's Trail: Poems by Wendell Berry." *Iowa Review* 1 (Winter 1970): 90–100. A poetry review and appreciation of Berry's poems.

Freyfogle, Eric T. "The Dilemma of Wendell Berry." *University of Illinois Law Review* 2 (1994): 363–85. A detailed study of the moral implications of Berry's cultural criticism, especially in his fictional works.

Gamble, David E. "Wendell Berry: The Mad Farmer and Wilderness." *Kentucky Review* 8, no. 2 (Summer 1988): 40–52. A study of the attitudes toward wilderness found in Berry's "Mad Farmer" poems.

Hall, Donald. "His Dailyness." In *Wendell Berry*, edited by Paul Merchant (Lewiston, Idaho: Confluence Press, 1991), 171–73. A brief appreciation of Berry's verse by a friend and fellow poet.

Hamburger, Michael. "The Writings of Wendell Berry: An Introduction." Introduction to Wendell Berry, *The Landscape of Harmony: Two Essays on Wildness and Community*. Hereford, Eng.: Five Seasons Press, 1987. Reprinted in *Wendell Berry*, edited by Paul Merchant (Lewiston, Idaho: Confluence Press, 1991), 81–89. Examines Berry's treatment of rural society in his work.

Hass, Robert. "Wendell Berry: Finding the Land." *Modern Poetry Studies* 2 (1971): 16–38. Discusses Berry's attitudes toward the land in his poetry.

Heinzelman, Kurt. "Indigenous Art: The Poetry of Wendell Berry." *Cencrastus* 2 (1980): 34–37. Examines Berry's localism and sense of place in his poetry.

Helge, Per. "En Amerikansk Moralist." *Studiekamraten* [Lund, Sweden] 67, no. 6 (1985): 3–7. Compares Berry's attitudes toward religion and his relationship to nature with those of Thoreau.

Hicks, Jack. "Wendell Berry's Husband to the World: *A Place on Earth*." *American Literature* 51 (May 1979): 238–54. Reprinted in *Wendell Berry*, edited by Paul Merchant (Lewiston, Idaho: Confluence Press, 1991), 118–34. One of the best critical discussions of Berry's work. Examines the farmer-husband-countryman theme in Berry's fiction and the need for atonement.

Hiers, John T. "Wendell Berry: Love Poet." *University of Mississippi Studies in English* 5 (1984–87): 100–109. Examines Berry's treatment of love and its relationship to agrarianism.

Jackson, Wes. "On Cultural Capacity." In *Wendell Berry*, edited by Paul Merchant (Lewiston, Idaho: Confluence Press, 1991), 68–70. A brief appreciation of Berry's environmental thought by a friend and fellow environmentalist.

Johnson, William C. "Tangible Mystery in the Poetry of Wendell Berry." In *Wendell Berry*, edited by Paul Merchant (Lewiston, Idaho: Confluence Press, 1991), 184–90. Examines Berry's attitudes toward treatment of the earth and its spiritual implications in his poetry.

Kusma, Greg. "Wendell Berry's Natural Piety." *Pebble* 8 (1972): 1. A brief discussion of Berry's attitude of reverence for nature.

Lang, John. "'Close Mystery': Wendell Berry's Poetry of Incarnation." *Renascence* 35, no. 4 (Summer 1983): 258–68. A valuable study of the development of Berry's nature imagery and the incarnational theology in his poetry.

Logsdon, Gene. "Back to the Land." *Farm Journal* 96 (March 1972): 30–32. A discussion of Berry's traditional farming practices by a friend and fellow farmer.

Manning, Richard. "Wendell Berry and His Fight against the Red River Dam." *Louisville Courier-Journal and Times*, 12 May 1975. A feature article about Berry's opposition to the Red River Dam in *The Unforeseen Wilderness*.

McNamee, Gregory. "Wendell Berry and the Politics of Agriculture." In *Wendell Berry*, edited by Paul Merchant (Lewiston, Idado: Confluence Press, 1991), 90–102. An examination of Berry's support of family farming in the context of Jeffersonian and southern Agrarian ideals.

Morgan, Speer. "Wendell Berry: A Fatal Singing." *Southern Review* 10, no. 4 (Fall 1974): 865–77. Places Berry's work within a larger tradition of romantic-transcendentalist nature writing. Focuses on the central theme of death and decay in Berry's work.

Murphy, Patrick D. "Two Different Paths in the Quest for Place: Gary Snyder and Wendell Berry." *American Poetry* 2, no. 1 (Fall 1984): 60–68. A useful comparison of the treatment of wilderness and place in the poems of Snyder and Berry.

———. "Penance or Perception: Spirituality and Land in the Poetry of Gary Snyder and Wendell Berry." *Agetrieb* 5, no. 2 (Fall 1986): 61–72. A study of the contrasting religious and spiritual views of Snyder and Berry.

Nibbelink, Herman. "Thoreau and Wendell Berry: Bachelor and Husband of Nature." *South Atlantic Quarterly* 84 (1985): 127–40. Reprinted in *Wendell Berry*, edited by Paul Merchant (Lewiston, Idaho: Confluence Press, 1991), 135–51. Another important study of the farmer-husbandry theme in Berry's work. Contrasts Thoreau's love of wildness with Berry's preference for cultivated land.

Payne, Warren E. "Wendell Berry and the Natural." *Resonance* 1, no. 2 (1969): 5–16. A discussion of Berry's views of the natural in his writings.

Pevear, Richard. "On the Prose of Wendell Berry." *Hudson Review* 35, no. 2 (Summer 1982): 341–47. A perceptive review of Berry's prose and a critique of his religious view of nature from an orthodox Christian perspective.

Reader, Willie. "A Correspondence with Wendell Berry." *Poets in the South* 1 (1977–78): 27–31. Summary of a literary correspondence with Berry.

Rodale, Robert. "The Landscape of Poetry." *Organic Gardening and Farming* 23 (April 1976): 46–52. A brief appreciation of Berry's writing by the editor of *Organic Gardening*.

Serebnick, Judith. "New Creative Writers." *Library Journal* 85 (1 February 1968): 632. A brief mention of Berry's forthcoming work.

Shadle, Mark. "Traveling at Home: Wandering and Return in Wendell Berry." In *Wendell Berry*, edited by Paul Merchant (Lewiston, Idaho: Confluence Press, 1991), 103–17. A discussion of Berry's treatment of land and the attitudes toward home in his writing.

Snyder, Gary. "Berry Territory." In *Axe Handles* (San Francisco: North Point
    Press, 1983), 12–13. Reprinted in *Wendell Berry*, edited by Paul Merchant
    (Lewiston, Idaho: Confluence Press, 1991), 59–60. An occasional poem
    dedicated to Berry as a friend and fellow environmentalist.
Stegner, Wallace. "A Letter to Wendell Berry." In *Wendell Berry*, edited by Paul
    Merchant (Lewiston, Idaho: Confluence Press, 1991), 47–52. An appre-
    ciative essay written by Berry's former creative writing teacher and men-
    tor at Stanford.
Tarbet, Donald W. "Contemporary American Pastoral: A Poetic Faith." *English
    Record* 23 (Winter 1972): 72–83. A discussion of Berry's adaptation of
    the literary pastoral form in his poetry.
Triggs, Jeffrey Alan. "Moving the Dark to Wholeness: The Elegies of Wendell
    Berry." *Literary Review* 31, no. 3 (Spring 1988): 279–92. A perceptive
    discussion of the religious imagery in Berry's elegies, his fondness for the
    elegiac form, and his treatment of death.
———. "A Kinship of the Fields: Farming in the Poetry of R. S. Thomas and
    Wendell Berry." *North Dakota Quarterly* 57. no. 2 (Spring 1989): 92–102.
    A comparison of pastoral and farming themes in the poetry of Berry and
    R. S. Thomas, a contemporary Welsh poet.
———. "Farm as Form: Wendell Berry's *Sabbaths*." In *Wendell Berry*, edited by
    Paul Merchant (Lewiston, Idaho: Confluence Press, 1991), 191–203. An
    examination of the cyclical structure and use of poetic form in Berry's
    Sabbaths.
Waage, Frederick O. "Wendell Berry's History." *Contemporary Poetry* 3, no. 3
    (1978): 21–46. A discussion of Berry's use of regional history in his poetry.
Weiland, Steven. "Wendell Berry: Culture and Fidelity." *Iowa Review* 10
    (Winter 1979): 99–104. An examination of the political implications of
    Berry's personal and domestic values.
Weissman, Judith. "An Open Letter." In *Wendell Berry*, edited by Paul
    Merchant (Lewiston, Idaho: Confluence Press, 1991), 53–58. A personal
    appreciation of Wendell Berry.
"Wendell Berry." *Contemporary Literary Criticism* 4 (Detroit: Gale Research,
    1976), 59–60. An introduction and overview of Berry's work.
Williams, Terry Tempest. "A Full Moon in May." In *Wendell Berry*, edited by
    Paul Merchant (Lewiston, Idaho: Confluence Press, 1991), 61–67. A rec-
    ollection of the writer's trip west with Berry to attend the memorial ser-
    vice for Edward Abbey.
Woolley, Bryan. "Wendell Berry." *Louisville Courier-Journal and Times*, 4 August
    1974. A feature article on Wendell Berry.

Interviews

"Earl Butz versus Wendell Berry." *Co-Evolution Quarterly* (Spring 1978): 50–59.
Fisher-Smith, J. "Field Observations." *Orion* 12 (Autumn 1993): 50–59.

McNamee, Gregory, and James R. Hepworth. "The Art of Living Right."
    Bloomsbury Review (June-August 1983): 23–33. Reprinted in *Living in
    Words: Interviews from the "Bloomsbury Review," 1981–1988*, edited by
    Gregory McNamee (Portland, Oregon: Breitenbush Books, 1988).
Snell, Marilyn B. ed. "The Art of Place." *New Perspectives Quarterly* 9, no. 2
    (Spring 1992): 29–34.
Weinreb, Mindy. "A Question a Day: A Written Conversation with Wendell
    Berry." In *Our Other Voices*, edited by John Wheatcroft (Bucknell, Penn.:
    Bucknell University Press, 1991). Reprinted in *Wendell Berry*, edited by
    Paul Merchant (Lewiston, Idaho: Confluence Press, 1991). A brief inter-
    view using the question-a-day format.
Williamson, Bruce. "The Plowboy Interview: Wendell Berry." *Mother Earth
    News* 20 (March 1973): 6–12.
Woolley, Bryan. "An Interview with Wendell Berry." *Louisville Courier-Journal
    and Times Magazine*, 4 August 1974, 8–10.

Dissertations

Collins, Robert Joseph. "A Secular Pilgrimage: Nature, Place and Morality in
    the Poetry of Wendell Berry." Ph.D. dissertation, Ohio State University,
    1978.
Cornell, Daniel T. "Practicing Resurrection: Wendell Berry's Georgic Poetry,
    an Ecological Critique of American Culture." Ph.D. dissertation,
    Washington State University, 1986.
Taft, Edward Donley. "The Land and Moral Responsibility in the Work of
    Wendell Berry." *Dissertation Abstracts International* 52, no. 11 (May 1992),
    3931A. Ph.D. dissertation, University of Rhode Island, 1992.
Tolliver, Gary. "Beyond Pastoral: Wendell Berry and a Literature of
    Commitment." Ph.D. dissertation, Ohio University, 1978.
Triggs, Jeffrey Alan. "At Home with Generalizations: A Study of the Poetry
    and Prose of Wendell Berry." *Dissertation Abstracts International* 47, no. 11
    (May 1987), 4091A–92A. Ph.D. dissertation, Rutgers, 1986.

Index

The Author

Andrew J. Angyal has long been interested in American environmental writers, particularly those with a strong loyalty to a particular place. He became an early admirer of Wendell Berry after discovering his writings about alternative farming and agriculture. He initiated a correspondence with Berry, who encouraged his interest in small-scale organic gardening. He has twice visited Berry at Lane's Landing Farm in Port Royal, Kentucky.

The author of Twayne biographies of Loren Eiseley and Lewis Thomas, Angyal has also published a number of book reviews and articles about environmental and natural history writers and about American poets. He is currently a professor of English at Elon College in North Carolina, where he has taught for the past 19 years. His degrees include a B.A. in English from Queens College of the City University of New York, an M.A.R. from Yale Divinity School, and a Ph.D. in English from Duke University. A Fulbright lecturer in American literature at Louis Kossuth University in Debrecen, Hungary, he has also taught during several summers in Poland, Czechoslovakia, and China. He has served as a Piedmont Independent College Association visiting instructor at Guilford College and has recently taken part in a National Endowment for the Humanities faculty seminar on environmental studies.

The Editor

Frank Day is a professor of English and head of the English Department at Clemson University. He is the author of *Sir William Empson: An Annotated Bibliography* (1984) and *Arthur Koestler: A Guide to Research* (1985). He was a Fulbright lecturer in American literature in Romania (1980–81) and in Bangladesh (1986–87).